Democracy Under Fire

Democracy Under Fire

Memoirs of a European Socialist   ADOLF STURMTHAL

Edited by Suzanne Sturmthal Russin

Duke University Press   Durham and London 1989

Contents

Preface and Acknowledgments

Our father worked on his memoirs for the last several years of his life, until his death in June of 1986. During his stay in Vienna in 1981 and later at the Berlin Historical Commission he did research for this work, which is a record of the first of his two lives. We were part of his second life, after he left Europe and became a professor in America. For us, these memoirs are a chance to get to know better the father who took an active part in the political and economic maelstrom of Europe between the two world wars. Now we can appreciate what he left behind when he came to the United States at the age of thirty-five. He was on a first-name basis with many of the major figures on the European stage, and was known throughout Europe because of his byline as editor of a socialist periodical. If not for the rise of Nazism and the subsequent upheaval, his life would have been very different.

He was forced to leave Europe and start over again in a strange country, but he never abandoned his interest in the proposition that society could organize itself to provide a better life for the common man. The passion of his political beliefs gave energy to his intellectual study of the changes in postwar labor and economics in Europe, yet he maintained a clear eye and a sense of objectivity in his thinking and research. He integrated himself into the American academic community while keeping current on what was happening in Europe. Although he wrote many books, this is the only one in which he took a more personal view, and we are grateful that he did.

This book would not have been published without the help of many of our father's colleagues and friends. First we must thank Walt Franke, Melvin Rothbaum, Martin Wagner, and Milton Derber of the Institute of

Labor and Industrial Relations at the University of Illinois in Urbana. George Rosen of the University of Illinois Chicago Circle, a friend and colleague for as long as we remember, encouraged us to have this manuscript published and offered good advice on the ins and outs of "how to publish." Gerard Braunthal of the University of Massachusetts at Amherst was a supportive reader of this work. His guidance made the manuscript's publication possible. He also introduced us to Leonard Shanks, who verified innumerable details and made major editorial revisions. William M. Johnston of the University of Massachusetts at Amherst also provided much needed guidance. Thanks also to John Windmuller of Cornell; Fritz Heine of Bad Münstereifel, West Germany; Henry Fleischer of Silver Spring, Maryland; and finally to Karen Obermeier and Michelle Blair, typists; and Susanne Kord, translator. Special thanks to Suzie's husband, Lincoln Russin.

Preparing this book for Duke University Press is one more step on a long road of understanding and appreciating our father. The book has permitted us a glimpse into our father's early life and given us a chance to continue our contacts with the men and women to whom our father introduced us as we grew up. It has been a wonderfully rewarding experience.

Suzanne Sturmthal Russin
Anne Sturmthal Bergman
Joan Sturmthal

The Writings of Adolf Sturmthal

Adolf Sturmthal was an internationally known scholar of the Western European trade union and socialist movements. His death in 1986 meant the loss of a distinguished member of the American émigré community, which had been formed from those forced to flee the Nazi tentacles. This volume is a testimony to his role as a perceptive observer and friend of many European socialist leaders whom he met during his years as a university student in Vienna, as an editor of a weekly news service on labor, as a staff member of the Labor and Socialist International in Zürich, and as a professor in the United States. The reader soon becomes aware that on many occasions the author played an active political role on the socialist stage during his many trips crisscrossing Western Europe.

Woven into these fascinating accounts are his assessments of key political developments in Central Europe, especially during the interwar and immediate post-1945 years. The reminiscences add new information to the history of this turbulent and tragic period.

The memoirs end soon after Sturmthal began a distinguished academic career. As a professor of economics who taught for several decades at Bard College (Annandale-on-Hudson, New York), Roosevelt University (Chicago), and the University of Illinois (Urbana-Champaign), he specialized in labor economics and industrial relations. As a scholar, he focused on the international democratic trade union movement, especially on European socialist unions and their relations to the socialist parties. His scholarly output was prodigious. He wrote or edited many books, some appearing in foreign translation, and numerous articles in professional journals.

Sturmthal's publications, including this volume, are invariably objective and elegantly written; they reflect the impressive breadth of knowledge at his command. In the United States, he became well known as the author of *The Tragedy of European Labor, 1918–1939*, first published in 1943. The volume provides detailed historical and political information on the decline and fall of the European trade unions and the socialist and communist parties in the face of the fascist onslaught; it thus serves as a useful companion to the present volume. Sturmthal rightly insists that the European movements were the backbone of democratic forces; their destruction as independent organizations helped seal the fate of shaky democratic states. Contributing to the crisis within each country was the lack of integration among warring social forces and among competing trade union movements divided along ideological, political, or religious lines. Those divisions had historical antecedents going back to feudal times and the emergence of hierarchical societies based on strict class separations and stratified social structures. In addition, the unions failed to become more than mere pressure groups; hence their lack of political punch.

In his later publications Sturmthal helped to fill a lacuna in the American literature on the development of foreign labor movements. His attention remained focused on Western Europe where socialists and communists vied for control of trade union federations in the post–World War II era. In *Unity and Diversity in European Labor* (1955), he emphasizes the variety of economic, social, and political conditions in various countries necessitating solutions to problems that are unique to each country. He concentrates on types of collective bargaining under conditions of full employment, on nationalized enterprises, on government planning, and on the rise of social democratic governments. He notes a high degree of state intervention in the economies on the continent, but little in Britain. Yet, differences aside, there is a measure of unity among West European and other unions, a concern for independence in free societies which eventually led to the formation of the International Confederation of Free Trade Unions in Brussels, in order to rival the communist-dominated World Federation of Trade Unions.

In his writings, addressed as much to American labor leaders as to general readers, Sturmthal notes that nonpartisan, business unionism would not work in Western Europe. There, "political unionism," in which unions are linked to political parties or are involved in politics, remains a tradition. Even in instances where unitary labor federations eschew partisan activities, their leaders often hold cabinet or parliamentary posts.

In his later books, Sturmthal repeatedly advances the thesis that there is much to be learned from studying foreign and international labor movements. Thus in his edited book, *Contemporary Collective Bargaining in Seven Countries* (1957), he notes the similarities and differences between collective bargaining in the United States and Britain, Norway, the Netherlands, France, West Germany, and Italy. The increased American involvement in foreign economics through trade and investments necessitates knowing more about industrial relations practices in other states.

Sturmthal continued his mission to educate American labor leaders and the scholarly community in *Workers' Councils: A Study of Workplace Organization on Both Sides of the Iron Curtain* (1964). His pioneering study of workers' councils in West Germany and France, contrasted with those in Poland and Yugoslavia, helped to spark a growing interest in developments at the plant level. It also marked the author's interest in studying labor relations in Eastern Europe in order to compare labor practices in communist and non-communist states. He contends that at various historical stages of industrial development, unions will shift their focus from broad national issues, such as universal suffrage, to narrow local problems, such as grievance settlements in factories. One of the central issues of an industrial relations system is the admission of unions into the factory, partly through the establishment of councils.

Sturmthal edited *White-Collar Trade Unions: Contemporary Developments in Industrialized Societies* (1966), in which the authors focus on a still-current topic—the shift from blue-collar to white-collar in the labor forces of Australia, Austria, France, Germany, Japan, Sweden, the United Kingdom, and the United States. They seek to answer questions about the social, cultural, and political effects of the shift to a white-collar force, particularly its effects on industrial relations and the labor movements. Sturmthal concludes that even though white-collar workers are more difficult to organize than blue-collar workers, their large-scale organization in many advanced industrial states is likely.

Sturmthal's interest in labor movements in the Third World began to be reflected, though not at length, in two books published in the 1970s:

Comparative Labor Movements: Ideological Roots and Institutional De-velopment (1972) and *The International Labor Movement in Transition: Essays on Africa, Asia, Europe, and South America* (1973), coedited with James G. Scoville. In the former book, Sturmthal contends that labor movements in the Third World will most likely not evolve in the same manner as their counterparts in the industrialized world. The adverse economic and social circumstances, compounded by government inter-vention in wages policy, pose major problems for the growth of unions in underdeveloped countries. In the latter book, the editors argue that if in former Western colonies minimum levels of democracy and public educa-tion are not met, the unions will have to first concentrate on workers' rights, the elimination of social discrimination against workers, and the acquisition of education before they can engage in free collective bargain-ing or push for income redistribution.

Sturmthal returned to his original area of interest—Europe—in *Left of Center: European Labor Since World War II* (1983), characterizing the book as a sequel to *The Tragedy of European Labor, 1918–1939*. He traces the development of the noncommunist unions in Britain, Germany, France, and Italy and explores the evolution of industrial relations by examining nationalization, codetermination, income policies, and other national and transnational policies. In a major shift from the pre-1945 era, the integration of the European working class into the existing social order meant that collective bargaining became a process by which agreements were reached with management, now considered a "social partner" rather than a class enemy. Similarly, left political parties shed their Marxist ideologies and became parties of the people, accepting the existence of mixed economies.

Sturmthal must have regarded some of these developments away from socialism with skepticism. In my conversations with him, I had the impression that as a realist he knew that to cling to socialist dreams of a classless society was a utopia that had little chance of becoming an actuality. Yet his contacts with leading socialists during the interwar years and since, reported so colorfully in these memoirs, gave him hope that at least these men and women, when in power, would try to realize a part of the dream—to make the world a better place for all, not just a few.

This volume is but one legacy of the major literary contribution Adolf

Sturmthal made to an understanding of European socialist and labor movements. He received international recognition; he was a guest lecturer at leading universities in the United States, Canada, Europe, and Asia; he received numerous grants, awards, and honors (including a prestigious Austrian one in 1975); and he was a consultant to U.S. government agencies and business and labor organizations.

I extend warm thanks to Professor Sturmthal's daughters for ensuring the publication of the manuscript that he finished shortly before his death, to Leonard Shanks for able editorial assistance, and to the staffs of Duke University Press and the Verlag Hermann Böhlaus in Vienna for letting readers share Adolf Sturmthal's vivid memories of a once-vibrant European socialist subculture that never took root in the United States.

Gerard Braunthal
University of Massachusetts at Amherst

Foreword

Only in a limited sense can this book be described as an autobiography. It lacks almost all the very personal stuff, the kind of things that children and grandchildren may ask about: "Grandpa, how did you go to school when you were a child? When did you start watching television? Who was your first date?" All that is of no interest to the outside reader of a book of recollections by a person of no outstanding historic distinction.

The purpose of the pages that follow is a far more modest one. Fate and accident, profession and inclination brought me into the company of people of distinction, many of whom are known by contemporaries only from specialized literature and history books. I was fortunate in being able to observe them while they were outside of the spotlight. My recollections of these encounters may have some interest for this generation and perhaps one or two more. This is the justification for writing this book.

One additional fact: I am impressed by the rapidity and thoroughness of the changes that occurred in my lifetime. When I was a child the United States had just emerged onto the world stage, Europe was dominated by three or four great powers, and it in turn dominated most of the rest of the world. Telephones rarely existed; horse-drawn car services ran through the streets of Vienna. And Vienna itself was a significant center of human culture in the most diverse ways, from medicine and technology to art, music, and the social sciences. The change since the 1920s is shocking, all in the life span of one man.

This, in essence, is the justification for this book. It is up to the reader to decide whether this is enough.

My thanks go first of all to Anice Birge, the incomparably competent secretary, or rather more than a secretary. Not only can she decipher my impossible handwriting and make sense of my marginal notations; she is also a first rate editor, who many times drew attention to repetitions in my text, often widely separated but still clear in her mind. If it were not for her, this would be a much worse book. I owe her a sincere debt of gratitude.

My thanks also go to Mrs. Wesemaun-Wittgenstein, who interviewed me at length for Austrian Television. She must have found the interview sufficiently interesting to draw the attention of Dr. Georg Hauptfeld of the Böhlaus Verlag to the possibility of developing the material into a book. In a sense, she has to accept part of the responsibility for its existence, for better or worse.

Dr. Hauptfeld's enthusiasm was infectious, and I finished the draft of the book much faster than I would have without his praise and encouragement. Even veteran writers are susceptible to both.

Finally, the librarian, Margaret Chaplan, and the staff of the Institute of Labor and Industrial Relations at the University of Illinois in Urbana-Champaign deserve my sincere thanks and praise. Their competence and willingness to assist far beyond the ordinary requirements of their jobs have helped the author tremendously. Walter Franke, director of the Institute, deserves special mention for his tolerance of my use of Institute facilities while my status has for some time been that of professor emeritus.

Adolf Sturmthal

Friedrich Adler

It was Saturday, October 21, 1916. In the dining room of the elegant Hotel Meissl und Schadn in Vienna, on the second floor of the hotel, luncheon was being served. Among the guests, as usual, at a re-served table, sat the prime minister of the Austro-Hungarian empire, Count Karl Stürgkh.

Shortly after one o'clock, a tall, rather thin, intelligent, and distinguished-looking man of early middle age appeared at the hotel. He looked for Count Stürgkh, first on the ground floor of the hotel, then on the floor above. He deposited his hat and coat in an anteroom, then entered the dining room. The first man he saw was the prime minister, eating his meal. The two tables next to the prime minister were occupied. The gentleman sat down at the third table away from the prime minister and ordered a meal and mineral water. He was biding his time.

Never having met Count Stürgkh in person, he was not quite sure that the man he looked at was indeed the powerful head of the Austrian government. A waiter confirmed his tentative identification. An hour and a quarter passed. A lady was sitting at a table right behind the prime minister, and the thought of harming her restrained the gentleman. He waited. In the meantime, two men joined the prime minister: the governor of Tyrol, Count Friedrich Toggenburg, and Captain Franz Baron von Aehrenthal. At long last, at half past three, the wait ended. The woman at the table behind Count Stürgkh and his associates left. No waiter was anywhere in sight. The propitious moment had arrived.

The man rose from his chair. In his right coat pocket he held a revolver, nothing else. The safety catch had been removed during the luncheon. Rapidly he crossed the short distance to the prime minister's table. Taking a hurried last step, he stretched out his right hand so that the revolver was barely five or six inches from the Count's head. In rapid succession he fired four shots at the prime minister. Three of the shots hit his head, killing him instantly; the fourth scraped his shoulder.

The state's attorney described the next few moments as follows in presenting his case: "in order to escape from the lynching he expected, Friedrich Adler—the defendant—sought to get to the exit. He was pursued and stopped in the outside hall. While the revolver was being wrested from his hand, it was discharged and wounded one of the pursuers, Captain Baron von Aehrenthal. Friedrich Adler was arrested."

The event (even more so the defendant's speech before the court) was a turning point in the history of Europe. This may be impossible to prove since other even more dramatic events occurred shortly after Count Stürgkh's death: the Russian Revolution of 1917 and the entry of the United States into World War I. Still, no one can deny the powerful impact of Friedrich Adler's deed and words upon the history of the Hapsburg empire, then the second largest empire in Europe in both territory and population. Adler became the hero of hundreds of thousands of Austrian workers, youths, and intellectuals. His name was on everyone's lips in revolutionary Russia and throughout the world. He changed the course of many lives. He certainly changed mine.

In 1914 the Austrian government, by declaring war upon Serbia, had unleashed World War I. Whatever the merits of the Austrian case against Serbia (and historians agree that Austria deliberately took advantage of the assassination of Archduke Franz Ferdinand in Sarajevo to crush Serbia once and for all), one outstanding aspect of the situation was the authoritarian manner in which the Austrian government proceeded. A world that has experienced the Bolshevik and the Nazi dictatorships may not be quite as shocked by the dictatorial features of the Austrian regime in 1914 as were its subjects in those bygone days. Thus even before the war broke out, an imperial decree in open violation of the constitution transferred jurisdiction of all political crimes from civilian juries to military courts. War was declared without convening Parliament. Indeed, Parliament had not been allowed to meet for two years prior to the day of Count Stürgkh's assassination. The Imperial government ruled by decree. And since it was Parliament alone that could invoke the constitution and impeach the government before the Supreme Court, the absence of a functioning parliament deprived the nation of any legal recourse against violations of the constitution. Violence was the only weapon left to the citizens against such an authoritarian system.

Even Imperial Germany, the Germany of Wilhelm II, was more liberal during World War I than was the Hapsburg empire. War credits were passed by the Reichstag in a constitutional fashion on August 4, 1914, and the parliamentary regime continued to function throughout the war. Next to czarist Russia, Austria-Hungary had the most authoritarian government of the warring nations, perhaps because it felt especially insecure in the presence of centrifugal forces threatening to tear the country apart. Paragraph 14 of the Austrian constitution, which enabled the government to rule by decree in an emergency rather than by the normal process of legislation, was misused by the prime minister in order to set aside the constitution itself. Trial by jury was abolished, censorship of the press prevailed, and Parliament was prevented from operating. When the state's attorney pointed out that in an orderly state, murder should not be used as a political weapon, the defendant could give an irrefutable answer: "I quite agree. We would have first to examine, however, whether we live in an orderly state."

A reader of the verbatim record of the trial today—after the experience of Communist and Nazi terror, World War II, and the war in Vietnam—may find Adler's justification for his action somewhat thin. But in light of the advancing liberal and democratic ideas at the beginning of this century, his complaints may be understandable. Thus he referred to the fact that the Prague socialist daily, *Pravo Lidu,* had been threatened with permanent suspension if it again printed a military command on its second page, and that the same newspaper was compelled to print editorials prepared by the police under the paper's own name. (Prague was then part of the Hapsburg empire.) Adler found even more revolting the deliberate efforts of the prime minister to prevent Parliament from meeting. When the president of Parliament called a conference of the chairmen of the various parliamentary groups for October 23, 1914, to discuss preparations for a regular session of the legislature, Count Stürgkh announced by way of communiqué that he did not recognize the existence of such a conference and refused to attend it.

Still more significant than the deed itself was Adler's speech before the court. The word "defense" does not apply, for Adler accepted not only full responsibility for the assassination, but protested against all attempts to describe it as the act of an unbalanced mind. These efforts originated not only with his attorney, who regarded it as his duty to attempt to save the life of his client. It was also, and perhaps even more so, the leadership of Adler's own party, the Social Democratic Party of Austria, which endeavored in this way to dissociate itself from the defendant in an effort to escape the possible repressive reaction of the government. In many ways Adler's deed was a protest against the party leadership and, to use Adler's own terms, its "patriotic excesses."

Thus Adler's speech—some one hundred and fifty printed pages—was directed not only against the Austrian government, but also against the leadership of the party to which he had devoted his life. The issue was the attitude of the party toward the war. Since this question has been widely misunderstood or misrepresented, it may be worth describing in some detail the conflict in which Friedrich Adler and a small group of his associates confronted the most influential leaders of the Austrian Social Democrats. This conflict was closely related to the internal cleavages of the Russian socialist movement, which provided the fertile soil for the rise of the Bolsheviks to power. Finally, Adler's deed cannot be fully understood without reference to the war issue: his protest was directed not only against the immediate victim, but also against the policies of the leaders of his own party, whom he accused of betraying the internationalist faith— one of the fundamental tenets of socialism.

In the absence of any generally accepted socialist policy toward a threatening war, the socialist parties and to a large extent the trade union movements of the warring countries divided into three main groupings. During World War I the great majority not only supported their respective governments and governmental war policies once hostilities had started, but a substantial number of working-class leaders adopted programs of military victory leading to territorial aggrandizement and the imposition of financial tributes upon the enemy countries. This majority group was labeled "social patriots" or even "social imperialists" by its enemies. At the other extreme were Lenin and his Bolshevik followers. Lenin advocated policies and actions that would lead, or at least contribute, to the defeat of one's own country. A government weakened by military defeat, deprived of its armed support, would more easily fall prey to a resolute minority embarking upon a revolutionary attack. This very small minority within the socialist movement was labeled the "revolutionary defeatists." They would turn an imperialist war into a civil war.

Between these two extremes—one large, the other very small in number, though destined to play an important role in world history—were the "socialist internationalists." Their program was essentially a refusal to identify with either of the warring groups. "Neither annexations nor tributes" was their battle cry. In principle, this was the only program upon which an international organization, which included members of both sides of a bloody conflict, could be based. This group, though far stronger than the "revolutionary defeatists," was, at the time of Count Stürgkh's violent death, a small minority in the international socialist movement.

As the war continued and the death toll and misery increased and ever greater sacrifices were imposed upon the population, the "socialist internationalists" advanced at the expense of the "social patriots" and here and there became the dominant faction. Friedrich Adler belonged to this group. From the beginning of the war, along with a small group of associates, he defended his views against the official leadership of his own party. There was Karl Renner, later chancellor of Austria, who, in Adler's view, became the main spokesman of loyalty to the Hapsburg Empire within the party. There was Karl Leuthner, one of the editors of the party daily and a member of Parliament, who held pan-German views. And, to top it all, there was, trying to keep the divergent factions together, the undisputed leader of the party, its founder, and later the first foreign minister of the Austrian Republic: Viktor Adler, Friedrich Adler's father. The unity of the party which he had established was for him the key to its past and future successes. This attitude brought him into the company of the "social patriots" who represented the great majority of the party and who forced him to side with Renner and Leuthner against his son. Thus the political disagreements separating the younger Adler from the official party leaders also became a father-son conflict. A good deal of the bitterness in Friedrich Adler expressed a son's disappointment with the father whom he worshipped.

Not that there was not enough about the "social patriots" to criticize from the point of view of an internationalist. Even in the relatively restrained speech of Friedrich Adler, enough emerged to make the blood of an inveterate supporter of socialist internationalism boil. Thus Karl Leuthner, spokesman of an aggressive German nationalism both within the party and in its leading daily, the highly respected *Arbeiter-Zeitung,* managed to avoid military service by having himself declared "indispensable" to the newspaper. It is possible, said Adler, that Leuthner was indeed indispensable to the *Arbeiter-Zeitung,* but what made the paper indispensable to the government? Was it the fact that on August 5, 1914, the main Austrian socialist paper published an editorial titled "The Day of the German Nation," praising the German Social Democratic deputies in the Berlin Reichstag for voting on August 4 for war credits? "An article," Adler said, "which without reservation places itself on the side of war, not only that, on the side of the idea of nationalism and—perhaps not consciously—which breaks with the principles of internationalism."

The majority of the party soon changed its goal from a position of avoiding its country's defeat to aiming at victory. That position was not only logically inconsistent with the tenets of the Socialist International, which spanned both sides of the trenches; it was also morally incompatible with the principles of internationalism to which the party had paid ardent lip service throughout its entire history. Indeed, the editorial of August 5, 1914, had already spoken of "the burning desire . . . that the outcome be victory for the holy cause of the German people." Those who continued to defend the internationalist tradition within the party found themselves not only in a small minority but also the subject of irony and contempt on the part of the party leaders. Karl Renner, then one of the most talented of the younger party spokesmen, regarded the war-imposed organization of the economy as a forerunner of socialist planning.

Adler's deed was thus as much a protest against his own party as against the dictatorial government of Austria-Hungary. To a large extent, Adler also rebelled against his father.

Friedrich Adler was the scion of a royal family of socialism, if this contradiction in terms be permitted. His father, Viktor, the son of a wealthy financier, became a medical doctor in order to devote his life to the care of the poor. This work led him into a circle of radical working class clubs trying to combat the social, political, and cultural impediments which the workers of the nineteenth-century Hapsburg empire faced. Entering this milieu as an outsider, well-educated and financially secure, the doctor succeeded where everyone else had failed: he united the feuding groups into an effective political party, the Social Democratic Worker's Party of Austria. Under his undisputed leadership, the party embarked upon a successful campaign of organizing, setting up trade unions, and obtaining the right to vote—although a highly unequal vote—for the workers. Together with the German Social Democrats, Adler's party became one of the main pillars of the Socialist International. The galaxy of young intellectuals and working-class leaders whom Adler recruited and assembled contributed major political talent to both the Austrian and the German parties. Closely allied with Karl Kautsky, the great popularizer and interpreter of Karl Marx, with August Bebel, the leader of the German party, the avant-garde of the Socialist International, with Friedrich Engels, Marx's collaborator, and with many other great figures of socialism at the end of the nineteenth century and the first decade of the twentieth century, Viktor Adler was one of the outstanding men and leaders of men in this time.

Viktor Adler's wife, Emma, came from a distinguished family of social scientists and politicians. One of her brothers, Adolf Braun, was the author of a pioneering study of German trade unionism, member of the German Reichstag, and editor of a German socialist daily. Heinrich Braun, her older brother, founded the first social science periodical in Germany, which for many years was published as the *Archiv für soziale Gesetzgebung* [legislation] *und Statistik*. His wife, Lily, was a descendant of Napoleon's youngest brother, Jérôme, king of Westphalia. Heinrich Braun, the leftist, won her away from a Prussian general. She wrote an enduring socialist classic on women and socialism. Heinrich and Lily's son Otto was a child prodigy, comparable to John Stuart Mill. Otto wrote a study of Greek philosophy before reaching high school age and mastered several languages while still a teenager. He volunteered for the German army and died on the battlefield in 1918.

Emma Braun was a student of Goethe's works all her life and brought her knowledge of art and literature to the family. Her husband introduced his sons to a world of politics which was dedicated to improving the life of the poor. However, as Viktor Adler testified before the court, this family also contributed toward the formation of psychological problems for Friedrich Adler. His father deliberately steered him away from a life devoted to political action, for this life would expose Friedrich to strains beyond the capacity of his nervous system. Friedrich Adler thus became a student of physics in Zürich, then one of the centers of advanced research in that branch of science. He met some of the most promising young physicists of Europe, including Albert Einstein, who worked in the patent office in Bern. It was in Zürich that he met his wife, Kathia, a fellow student.

In the end, however, politics won out over physics and an academic career, and Friedrich Adler—his friends called him Fritz—returned to Vienna where he became a full-time party official and editor of the famous theoretical monthly of the party, *Der Kampf* (*The Struggle*). As party secretary, one of his tasks was preparing the International Socialist Congress called for in Vienna in the summer of 1914, the same congress which was to debate the "Keir Hardie-Vaillant amendment" on the nature of the socialist action against war, a congress which was never to meet. Indeed, the International as it existed prior to 1914 never emerged again. War broke out a few weeks before the congress was scheduled to begin.

Marx and Engels had not been pacifists. In fact, almost any war that would weaken the czarist regime, main oppressor in Europe and a mortal danger to all democratic movements, was welcome. Hence the praise, in Marx's 1864 inaugural address to the First International, of the proud mountain people of the Caucasus—some of whom were in fact backward, primitive tribes—because they were resisting czarist domination. The attitude of the nineteenth-century masters of socialist thought toward war depended on whether or not a particular war would further the cause of socialism. They clearly hailed wars of national liberation and regarded wars of defense as justified. The crucial issue in each war was thus to determine whose victory would strengthen the party of democracy, favor the interests of the workers, and further the advance of socialism. Sometimes this required rapid changes of attitude and policy. Thus, at the beginning of the Franco-Prussian war in 1870, Marx and Engels and the (First) Socialist International sided with Prussia against Napoleon III, with the cause of German unification against tyrannical rule of the French emperor. Once Napoleon was ousted and democracy emerged in France, the socialist leaders changed sides and favored the victory of the French Republic over the king of Prussia and emperor of Germany.

Friedrich Engels's last article was a forerunner of change, or perhaps of refinement, in socialist policy. It was devoted to the question of disarmament, which had been put on the agenda of European politics by a czarist initiative. One of the key points in Engels's article was a proposition that the evolution of military technology had changed the nature of violence. Numbers no longer counted so much in revolutionary movements. Small, well-organized and well-equipped military detachments with modern weapons (such as the machine gun) would prove superior to large, poorly equipped masses. Violence now had become the weapon of the reactionaries; democratic constitutional government was to be the tool of the oppressed.

From this thesis on the changing character of violence, a further step led to a new policy towards war. While wars of national liberation might still occur and deserve socialist support, most future international conflagrations would be conflicts among imperialist powers for the control of markets and sources of raw materials. Socialist duty was, first of all, to make a maximum effort to prevent the outbreak of an imperialist war. The proposed details of this effort became the subject of a long, drawn-out, and inconclusive debate among socialists.

This debate started toward the end of the nineteenth century, when the idea of a universal general strike to avert a war was advanced by Domela Nieuwenhuis on behalf of the Dutch socialists. Most socialists felt far too weak to take such a proposal seriously. They took refuge in the belief that with the end of capitalism the danger of war would disappear. The Russian Social Democrat Georgii Plekhanov added that a universal general strike would be of some effect in the advanced industrial nations, but without impact on the military preparations of a country like Russia where socialist movements barely existed. The call for a general strike would thus "disarm the cultured nations and offer Western Europe as a prize to the Russian Cossacks." The Dutch proposal, so revolutionary in appearance, in effect turned into a weapon of reaction. An overwhelming majority of the International Socialist Congress followed this reasoning and rejected the Dutch proposal.

At the 1907 Stuttgart International Socialist Congress the leaders of the radical wing of the Second International (Vladimir Lenin, Julius Martov, and Rosa Luxemburg) proposed a resolution which was to have historic consequences. At the end of a long compromise declaration, their resolution added that it was the duty of the socialists to try to prevent the outbreak of war with all means that appeared effective to the different parties, thus avoiding setting down the general strike as universally applicable. Their last paragraph, crucial for later events, said:

> In case war should break out anyway, it is their duty to intervene in favor of its speedy termination, and with all their powers to use the economic and political crisis created by the war to rouse the masses and thereby to hasten the downfall of capitalist class rule.[1]

This remained the official party policy of the Socialist International. The inconclusive dispute over the recommended use of the general strike as a means of preventing the outbreak of a war did not affect the resolution, which, together with the entire compromise declaration, was unanimously adopted by the Stuttgart Congress.

The ideas expressed in the Stuttgart resolution seemed so impressive and persuasive to the Socialist International that, a few years later, it reminded the European governments of the revolutionary potential of wars. Yet the problem still remained of coordinating the action of the parties at an international level. At the Copenhagen Congress of 1910, Keir Hardie of Great Britain and his French colleague Edouard Vaillant again proposed the general strike, this time as a way to implement the Stuttgart resolution. This proposal was tabled for Vienna in 1913. In November 1912 an extraordinary congress was held in Basel, Switzerland, at a time when conflicts in the Balkans threatened to involve the great powers of Europe. A solemn manifesto was addressed to the governments:

> Let them remember that the Franco-German War was followed by the revolutionary outbreak of the Commune; that the Russo-Japanese War set in motion the revolutionary energies of the peoples of the Russian Empire; that the military and naval arms race gave the class conflicts in England and on the Continent an unheard-of sharpness and unleashed an enormous wave of strikes. It would be insanity for

1. Julius Braunthal, *History of the International, 1854–1914* (New York: Praeger, 1967), p. 337.

the governments not to realize that the very idea of a monstrous world war must inevitably call forth the indignation and the revolt of the working class.[2]

At the Basel Congress in 1912 the Vienna Congress was rescheduled for late summer 1914. The Keir Hardie-Vaillant amendment was to have been debated. The leading theorist of the Austrian Social Democrats, Otto Bauer, was to have given the major address on the issue.

Essentially, Bauer was to have summarized Plekhanov's arguments, which in the light of the social and political progress made in Austria-Hungary and in Germany (except perhaps Prussia) were even more impressive than when the Russian socialist leader had first advanced them in 1893. Bauer's arguments were twofold. On the theoretical level, he pointed out that the period just preceding the outbreak of hostilities was also a time of tremendous nationalist propaganda, with patriotic feelings running exceptionally high. The appeal of patriotic slogans was almost irresistible in this situation. The fatherland was in danger, and anyone who opposed defending one's country against its enemies was their conscious or unconscious agent. A call for a strike in this situation was unlikely to be sufficiently effective to prevent the start of hostilities. If it was not possible to stop the development of the crisis at an earlier stage, the outbreak of war could not be prevented at the last moment by working-class action. On the practical level, the opponents of the general strike argued that working-class action would be of unequal effectiveness in different countries. Where trade unions and socialist movements were strong and well-disciplined, their call for a general strike, though unlikely to be fully successful, might be effective enough to delay the mobilization of troops and to delay, at least for a time, the deployment of armed forces. In countries with weak labor movements the strike order would remain on paper with little effect on the activities of the military in these countries. As a result, organized labor, against its intentions and its vital interests, would assist the most reactionary countries against those with the most powerful labor movements. In the world that existed prior to 1914, this reasoning translated into what would now be called a scenario in which organized labor

2. John Riddell, ed., *Lenin's Struggle for a Revolutionary International* (New York: Monad Press, 1984), p. 89.

helped czarist Russia against the relatively less oppressive countries of Central Europe, Germany, and Austria-Hungary and their large labor organizations.

This reasoning and the document which embodied it were never discussed or voted on because the outbreak of the war caused the cancellation of the international socialist congress. No settled international socialist policy existed in 1914 except the generally accepted opposition to imperialist wars; in practice, "imperialist wars" meant conflicts among the great powers of the time. The tragic failure of international socialism thus did not lie in its inability to prevent the outbreak of war. Rather, it was the policies pursued by different socialist movements in support of the war effort of their own country, once war had broken out, which constituted the downfall of socialist internationalism.

When war broke out in 1914 the great majority of socialists and trade unionists on both sides, after calling for peace, rallied to their respective national causes. Despite the opposition of a small minority led by Karl Liebknecht and Hugo Haase, the German Social Democrats voted for the appropriations required for war. (Rosa Luxemburg, who opposed the war, was not a member of the Reichstag.) The German socialists felt threatened by czarist tyranny, and thus entitled to defend themselves and their organizations against the oppressive power in the East. The French socialists had the same fear of German militarism and the absolutism of the Hohenzollern Empire. They issued a manifesto in terms reminiscent of the struggle for the defense of the French Revolution, calling upon the French people to fight for France on behalf of freedom and civilization. The socialist daily in Vienna spoke of "The Day of the German Nation."

Still, by lining up behind their governments the socialists on both sides of the trenches incapacitated the Socialist International. Step by step, the majority of socialists, pushed on by the nationalist fervor created by the war, spoke not simply of defense, but of victory. Socialists who wanted to defeat each other by military means could not meet for peaceful and cooperative discussion. The International ceased to function as a universal organization.

Student Days

Although I was too young at the time of the death of Count Stürgkh and the trial of Fritz Adler to understand more than the barest outlines of what happened, it was clear to me and to thousands of youngsters of my age group that we were living through historic events. It was less the assassination of the prime minister which impressed us than the spectacle of a man openly assuming, nay eagerly assuming, responsibility for what he had done. It was the contrast between the scientist and his deed, the idealist and the cruel world in which he lived, the picture of a defendant who became accuser, a man willing to die for his cause, that filled an entire generation with enthusiasm and a resolve to dedicate itself to a noble cause. The courses of many lives were changed by the example of this man. Mine was one of them.

I was a high school student in 1917, still in one of the lower grades. I was preparing to enter the university in due course, probably as a law student. As with many of my fellow students, Adler's speech in court turned all my attention toward public affairs and, in particular, to the cause of peace and socialism. One of the few expressions I found for my new dedication was a refusal to subscribe to a war loan for the imperial government, even for the small amount of money that was expected from me as a scholarship student. When the roll call of students occurred for the purpose of determining their contribution, I proudly proclaimed my refusal to contribute money to provide the tools of death to be inflicted upon people who had never done me the slightest harm. My words aroused considerable commotion, and a teachers' conference was called to decide what to do about or with me. I still do not know by what miracle I avoided punishment. I suspect that secretly some of the teachers were sympathetic toward my pacifism and appreciated the fact that I dared to express it publicly. In any case, as I continued my studies, I remained outspoken about my intense interest in politics.

By the time of Adler's trial in May 1917 the political situation in Austria, and in all of Europe, had greatly changed. What role the assassination played in this change is difficult to establish. True, Count Stürgkh's successor was far less authoritarian and sought to reconvene Parliament in order to establish better relations between the government and the people. However, a far more important event than Adler's deed had occurred in the meantime: The first Russian Revolution, that of March 1917, had brought the Russian Social Democrats and a socialist peasant party, the Socialist Revolutionaries, to the fore. One member of the latter party, Alexander Kerensky, had become prime minister of Russia, and the Central Powers were anxious to establish contact with the new men of power. As Adler put it in his speech—which, like he himself, I refuse to call his "defense"—"no one seeks more eagerly communications with those 'revolutionaries' who have been my friends than Count Czernin, the new Austrian minister of foreign affairs." In any case, the change of political climate was such that Adler, though sentenced to death by the tribunal, was transferred to a prison in Stein-on-the-Danube on October 12, 1917, and his sentence was commuted to eighteen years of hard labor. In the face of the rising revolutionary sentiment of the workers, even this sentence would not long be maintained. While Adler refused to submit a request for amnesty to the emperor, and forbade his lawyer to do so, the government itself submitted such a request to the emperor, who signed the corresponding decree immediately. On November 2, 1918, ten days before the end of the empire and the proclamation of the Austrian Republic, Friedrich Adler left prison and resumed political activity in the emerging Austrian revolution.

He was, then and for some years to come, the single most powerful individual in Austrian politics. The defeat of Austria-Hungary appeared to justify his actions. His associates acquired control of the Social Democratic Party. His father, appointed foreign minister, died shortly after the proclamation of the Republic; his statue stands next to Parliament on one of the most beautiful spots of the Ringstrasse, the grand boulevard encircling the inner city of Vienna where once the walls protected the old town against invaders. Otto Bauer, Fritz's closest associate, took Viktor Adler's place in the government and in the party leadership. Karl Renner was the first chancellor of the Austrian Republic. Fritz himself was elected chairman of the Workers' and Soldiers' Council of Austria—the main instrument of power in the country during the revolutionary period. When the emperor, who had abdicated, returned secretly to Austria hoping to reconquer his throne, it was Fritz Adler alone who could protect his life from the hatred of his former subjects. When the victorious allies—France, Italy, and England—threatened to cut off indispensable food supplies to Austria unless the former emperor was protected against violence and permitted to leave the country, Adler, recognizing the need for submission to the Allies' command, attempted to save the ex-emperor. Representatives of the Workers' and Soldiers' Council manned the train carrying the former emperor back into exile. They stood on the steps of the railway wagons holding in their hands copies of an appeal by Adler, asking the workers, who in their fury surrounded the train at each stop, to let the former emperor pass in the interests of the Republic itself. Only Adler's undisputed authority saved Charles of Hapsburg from a lynching at the hands of the Austrian workers, and saved Austria from starvation.

There followed a comedy of errors between the Soviet regime and Adler. The Communists, supported in Austria at the end of World War I by only an insignificant number of people and without any outstanding leaders, set all their hopes upon Adler's joining their ranks. He, more than anyone else, could have given their budding party the prestige and moral authority that could have provided mass support. Thus the Soviet government showered him with honors. The square in front of the Kremlin was named Fritz Adler Square. He was appointed honorary commander-in-chief of the Red Army and honorary chairman of the Central Soviet. All to no avail. Fritz Adler was no communist; he was and remained a social democrat, loyal to both the internationalist and the democratic principles of his party. Indeed, he turned the Austrian Workers' and Soldiers' Council—the very instrument which the Bolsheviks had used in Russia to obtain power—into an anti-Communist weapon. When a Soviet Republic was proclaimed in Hungary and a rather utopian left-wing revolution broke out in Bavaria in the spring of 1919, Austria found itself encircled by communist movements on two sides. The Austrian Communist Party tried to take advantage of this favorable situation to attempt a revolutionary takeover in Vienna. A Communist mass meeting was organized for June 15, 1919. On the eve of that fateful day, Adler called a meeting of the Workers' and Soldiers' Council and upon his urging the Council passed a resolution hostile to the Communist plan. Some blood was shed, but the putsch failed. The profoundly disappointed Russians withdrew, one after another, the honors they had bestowed upon Adler. He responded in an open letter to Leon Trotsky, published in the distinguished Austrian socialist monthly *Der Kampf;* its main theme was: "You did not understand me when you honored me; you don't understand my thinking any better now." Undoubtedly Fritz Adler's attitude kept thousands of young men and women out of the communist movement, which remains to this day a small sect with little if any influence upon the Austrian labor movement.

Little did I then suspect that I was to see my hero in person some years later when I had completed my university studies and was looking for my place in the world.

I entered the University of Vienna as a student of law and at the same time set out on a long and frustrating search for a job. It had to be a part-time job, since, beginning with the third semester of my studies, attendance at some university seminars was required and unfortunately they were held during daytime working hours. I soon discovered that such jobs were in exceedingly short supply. Indeed, jobs in general, in the truncated Austria created by the peace treaty following World War I, were hard to find. The structural changes in public administration and private enterprise, made inevitable by the reduction of the Hapsburg empire, from a country of fifty-six million people—Hungary included—to a republic of six million inhabitants, were slow in coming and extremely painful. Civil servants, who had governed the empire on behalf of the central administration located in Vienna, were returning to the newly created successor states (Czechoslovakia, Yugoslavia, Poland) or to the countries that absorbed parts of the former empire: Rumania, which had swallowed the eastern part of Hungary, or Italy, which took southern Tyrol. Many banks and industrial firms established new headquarters outside of Austria and staffed them with nationals of the new states, dismissing former personnel—mainly those of Austrian origin. Following the runaway inflation in the wake of the war, a long depression set in. In short, there were no jobs.

What was worse, there were no jobs for students in particular. The Austrian university student was traditionally the scion of a well-to-do family; studying plus the happy life of the student absorbed all his time. Indeed, the amount of pleasure was quite considerable since, for instance in the case of the law student, the first examination occurred after the third semester. One semester's assiduous work was sufficient preparation for the examination; the first two semesters could be devoted to fun or to studying other subjects—Austrian lawyers frequently exhibited an impressive general education, with literature, history, and philosophy enjoying the greatest popularity.

Until 1914 very few sons, and even fewer daughters, of working-class or poor families managed to enter institutions of higher learning. Not only was such ambition beyond the imagination of parents and children alike; very few working-class families could dispense with the earnings of their children once the children had passed the eight years of compulsory education. World War I and the postwar inflation produced some changes in this situation. Formerly well-off families found themselves in dire straits, but persisted, often by almost unbelievable sacrifices, in sending their sons through the long schooling process that led to higher professions. At the other extreme, a small number of sons—almost never daughters—of working-class families entered the higher engineering schools and the universities. However, few if any arrangements existed to provide them with part-time jobs that would have allowed them to combine work and study. The Austrian Chamber of Labor, an official trade-union-dominated institution, provided some modest stipends for a few working-class students, but the main problem of how to compensate families for the loss of their children's earnings was not solved.

What concerned me most was the total absence of part-time jobs for students. How could I support myself and continue my law studies? During the first two semesters, the problem was somewhat simpler: I could accept a full-time job, because my presence at the university—apart from the payment of the very low fees—was not required. The signature of the professor on the attendance records could be obtained, with the payment of another low fee, by way of the *Pedell*, a kind of glorified janitor. He put record blanks by the hundreds on the desk of the respective professors, who signed them automatically without ever inspecting them or checking

names. Thus for the first academic year the university created no problems.

Finding a job in post-World War I Austria, however, was a task that
challenged even the most dedicated and talented. The most sought-after
jobs were in banking, partly because inflation and currency fluctuations
encouraged speculation, from which the banks derived substantial benefits
by way of commissions as well as through speculations of their own.
Another reason for the rush into banking jobs was their high social prestige. Jobs in banking, more than any other office jobs, attracted the sons of
the upper-class families who, when the empire still existed, would have
joined the government bureaucracy—now reduced to a tiny fraction of its
former size.

Nevertheless, by some miracle I managed to get a job in one of the
larger banks. I seriously doubt that I owed this major achievement to my
talents as a banker. At the ripe old age of eighteen I barely knew what a
bank was supposed to do. The representative of the personnel department,
who interviewed me, inquired into my qualifications. I proudly presented
my diploma, admitting me to the university, and asserted in as firm a voice
as I could manage: "This document indicates what I can do." Shorthand? I
was asked. Not that, I had to admit. Typing? Not really, was my answer.
My self-confidence greatly impaired, I hardly expected a favorable reply.
Yet I was lucky—my mother had worked for the bank until her death and it
was the memory of her, rather than my dubious achievements, that now
proved to be decisive.

Being a full-time employee of a bank only postponed my dilemma for
one year. The problem still remained: how could I pursue my studies and
earn a living at the same time? I finally chose a solution which was to
influence my entire life. I abandoned the study of jurisprudence in favor of
economics, where required seminars were held during the evening hours.
All I had to do was to arrange my heavy overtime schedule at the bank so
as to have one or two evenings a week free for the seminars at the
university. The study of economics, combined with my political interests,
introduced me to a group of friends and finally into a world different from
the one in which I had grown up.

Since the trial of Friedrich Adler, I had followed the exciting political
events that surrounded the end of the Hapsburg empire and the birth of the

Austrian Republic. I had joined a socialist group of high school students, who asked—without too much knowledge of detail—for a thorough reform of the authoritarian school system inherited from the days of the monarchy. I had even managed to be elected deputy chairman of the school council, representing the upper grades of the high school which I had attended. But my serious participation in political activities did not begin until I joined the socialist university association.

Traditionally, Austrian students came from upper- and upper-middle-class homes and were conservative or reactionary. The great majority of them were German nationalists (or pan-Germans, as the expression went) or followed the Christian Social Party. The pan-Germans favored Anschluss with Germany, i.e., the absorption of the Danube republic by a Germany dedicated to a policy of power and aggression. The Christian Social Party, in spite of its progressive-sounding name, was, apart from a weak working-class segment, the party of the upper classes. Included in its dominant group were spokesmen of business as well as some of landed property, both dreaming of a return to a Hapsburg Empire including as large a part of the former Austro-Hungarian monarchy as circumstances would permit. Both groups—the pan-Germans and the Catholic Christian Socials—consisted of the sons of privileged families (female students were still rare) or of those who, by their studies, hoped to be able to join the privileged group.

In contrast, if we disregard a few exceptions, socialist students came in two varieties. They were either sons of working class families who, by a combination of talent, persistence, and luck, had fought their way through the maze of material and psychological handicaps that excluded most of their peers from higher education; or they came from Jewish families who traditionally, in Austria as elsewhere, regarded higher education as the best and surest road to social and economic advancement for their children. The Jews probably formed a large part of the socialist organization, and it is likely that some of the antipathy among the groups competing for the leadership of the socialist student organization was a barely camouflaged expression of the age-old Austrian conflict between the Jews and "Aryans." While it represented a small minority of the students at the University of Vienna—the great majority were either pan-German or Conservative Catholic—the socialist organization still managed to develop factions that fought bitterly for control. I find it almost impossible today to reconstruct the issues which divided the three main groups.

One group consisted mainly of students of working-class origin. They were in control and carried the label of the street in which a home for working-class students had been established by the Social Democratic Party: the d'Orsay Street turned them into d'Orsists. For them, the primary (or perhaps only) purpose of the socialist student association was to recruit members for the party. The second group, to which I belonged, was asked to make a major intellectual contribution to the labor movement. Because the largest single bloc within this group consisted of students in the social sciences, their involvement in the main activities of the party was often intimately related to their academic studies and interests. Economists, political scientists, and sociologists felt competent and called upon to spread the good word, recruit new party members, and, most important, to develop the philosophy of the party. "We are not only to read *Der Kampf* (the theoretical monthly of the party), said one spokesman for this group, "but also to write for it."

The third group was led by Paul Lazarsfeld, later a distinguished sociology professor at Columbia University, and Ludwig Wagner, an inspiring speaker and Lazarsfeld's faithful ally. They stressed the need for a diversified psychological appeal to the students. Lazarsfeld, originally a mathematician, soon turned most of his attention to high school students, upon whom he exerted an almost fascinating influence. He also performed a good deal of brilliant work in a new scientific discipline whose growth owed a large debt to his initiative and creative imagination: empirical sociology. Together with Marie Jahoda and Hans Zeisel, both later distinguished academicians, he organized and published the first empirical study of the life of the long-term unemployed.

I owe Lazarsfeld a personal debt of gratitude. Much later, in the United States, I visited him at his vacation home in New England. There I met Robert Lynd, professor at Columbia University and the pioneer of empirical sociology in the United States. Apparently I made a favorable impression upon Lynd, because he recommended me to the dean of Bard College—then a part of Columbia University. His recommendation surely was the main reason I was hired, and thus I entered the academic profession in the United States with some prospect of permanency.

In post-World War I Austria the conflicts between the student factions created dangerous tensions within the Social Democratic Party, to such an extent that its most august body, the Executive, felt compelled to intervene. And thus a group of youngsters, the spokesmen of the three main groups in the socialist student organization, were invited to meet with some of the celebrated socialist leaders of Austria, whose renown made them outstanding figures in the international labor movement as well. Among them were Otto Bauer, foreign minister of the Austrian Republic shortly after it was proclaimed in 1918 and leader and theorist of the party during the interwar period, and Karl Renner, president of the second Austrian Republic following the liberation of the country from the Nazi occupation. Bauer was to play a decisive role in my later career.

At the time of the meeting, of course, none of the student participants was known to either the party leaders or the public, with the possible exception of Lazarsfeld, whose family was acquainted with some party leaders. Our conflicts took place within the organization and were not discussed in the press, and the student leaders ranked rather low in the hierarchy of the movement. The main concern of party leaders was to heal the split in the student group. Under their pressure the conflict was settled by some structural changes in the socialist student organization. One of the new subgroups that emerged from this change was a special section of socialist social scientists, and one of its first activities was the organization of a weekly seminar on economic theory. Helene Bauer, wife of Otto Bauer, was invited to take charge of the seminar, and she accepted.

Helene Bauer was born Helene Gumplowicz in Cracow—then part of the Austro-Hungarian Empire, now in Poland. A niece of the famous sociologist Ludwig Gumplowicz, she grew up in a highly intellectual milieu and was greatly attracted to intellectual ability. After an unsuccessful first marriage, she met Otto Bauer. The rapidly rising star of the Austrian socialist movement fascinated her, and in spite of a considerable difference in age—she was several years older than he—they married. It was a happy marriage—based on love as much as on intellectual affinity—until the last years of Bauer's life, when he became involved with another woman. While Helene's publications were not numerous or voluminous, they were competent interpretations of Marxian economics and were highly respected as such.

I well remember attending the first session of the seminar. Helene Bauer was one of those emancipated women of Polish-Jewish origin who had gone against the traditions of her milieu and her time in order to pursue university studies. Rosa Luxemburg, the great foe of Lenin within the leadership of the socialist movement's left wing, was another member of this select group of brilliant women, as was Kathia Adler, the wife of Friedrich Adler. Outstanding in her own right, Helene Bauer also basked in the reflected glory of being Otto Bauer's wife. Her husband was then at the height of his power and prestige, especially among the younger intelligentsia. Thus, all who were present at that first session of the seminar listened respectfully—and silently. I too kept my mouth shut, even though—or perhaps because—I disagreed with a good deal of her presentation.

Helene Bauer was a Marxist: her view of economic theory was firmly based on the labor theory of value. I had just become a convert to neoclassicism and the marginal utility value theory. Later, acquired wisdom taught me that the two theoretical approaches were not as mutually exclusive as I then thought, and in fact dealt with different problems. Back in my student days, however, I felt differently. Marx was, according to my recently acquired wisdom, a great philosopher and a first-rate analyst of society and its evolution, but I questioned his economic theories. Still, I thought it good manners not to contradict our distinguished guest speaker.

The aftermath was rather surprising. The seminar chairman, Hans Adler (no relative of Friedrich Adler), told me a few days later that Helene Bauer had been disappointed, even shocked, by the absence of any student response to her presentation. "Are these really social science students?" she had asked. "Have they nothing to say or to discuss? Intelligent students ought to be articulate, critical, and active participants in a seminar." Taking his report of Helene Bauer's criticism at full value, I resolved to be less polite and more expressive. I not only participated in the discussion at the next seminar session, but expressed my disagreements rather clearly and without reservation. I must have gone pretty far in my new role as critic, for Hans Adler told me in no uncertain terms at the end of the session: "Now you have gone to the other extreme. You can't talk to Otto Bauer's wife the way you did. If you had any plans for a political career in Austria, you might as well forget them."

I confess I was not too disturbed by my friend's warning. I had never seriously considered a career in politics and in my youthful dedication to the newly found truth of neoclassical economics would not have permitted selfish designs to stand in the way of proclaiming the truth. Still, I was pleasantly surprised to get, a few days later, a message from Helene Bauer asking me to telephone her at the Bauer apartment in Vienna's sixth district. I expected a cold dressing-down for my impertinence. Instead, Helene asked me to have luncheon with Otto Bauer and herself the following day.

Otto and Helene Bauer

I was startled by the invitation even though I did not know, of course, that it was only the first link in a chain of surprising events. No greater honor could be conceived of by a budding intellectual with progressive ideas in the 1920s in Vienna, than an invitation to the home of the most brilliant among the many shining lights of the intellectual elite in a city full of first-class intellects. Otto Bauer's home was the meeting place for most of the distinguished men and women who lived in the former capital of the Austro-Hungarian empire. Vienna in the 1920s still retained some of the glory of its past when it had attracted—just like its western counterpart, Paris—all of the talent of a far-flung empire. It was said that after World War I Austria's main export items were intellectuals, artists, and soccer players. The supply of brain power that had once served a country of close to sixty million people vastly exceeded the needs and possibilities of the six million Austrians living in the Alpine republic—all that was left of Austria in 1918. Berlin was soon to attract a sizable number of these surplus intellectuals.

Those who remained behind found themselves confronted with the strongest competition. To survive demonstrated high merit. To excel was evidence of talent bordering on genius. During the 1920s the triumvirate of Otto Bauer, former foreign minister, Karl Renner, former chancellor, and Professor Max Adler, the philosopher of the Austrian brand of Marxism and a lawyer by profession, dominated the political scene of Austrian progressivism. Renner came from the "provinces" of the former empire, from the German sector of Moravia in what is now Czechoslovakia. Both Otto Bauer and Max Adler were of Viennese origin. And Helene Bauer, as noted, was a personality in her own right, not merely as Otto Bauer's wife.

Next to Friedrich Adler, with whom I was to be in daily contact for more than a decade, the two most important intellectual influences to whom I was exposed were Otto and Helene Bauer. The son of a well-to-do businessman from Bohemia, then a part of the Austro-Hungarian empire and later the heart of Czechoslovakia, Otto Bauer studied law and economics at the University of Vienna.

Early in his life he came under the influence of one of the truly great men of his time: Viktor Adler, whose genius was not that of a theoretician or journalist, but that of a born leader of men. He presided over the reconciliation of the warring factions, which made possible the founding of the party. He also sought out promising young men and women, who formed the center of that intellectual group that is referred to as the Austro-Marxists. Among them were Karl Renner; Rudolf Hilferding, an Austrian-born physician, who became minister of finance of the German Weimar Republic only to end miserably at the hands of the Nazis; Max Adler, no relative of Viktor; and the most brilliant of them all—Otto Bauer.

Bauer was very young when he came under the influence of Viktor Adler, who quickly became aware of his disciple's unusual gifts. Bauer was a powerful orator, the leading journalist of his time, party chief, and a first-rate interpreter and developer of Marxian ideas, all powered by a deep sense of humanism and a devotion to the fate of the poor and oppressed. His early theoretical works dealt with the basic problem of the Austro-Hungarian empire, the "nationalities" question. How could the seven major language groups that were intertwined in the second largest empire of Europe live together without trying to dominate each other? Both he and Renner devoted much of their early intellectual efforts to a solution of this fundamental problem of Austria-Hungary.

As Viktor Adler's assistant, and increasingly in his own right, Bauer began to make his influence felt in the Socialist International as well. As will be remembered, a Congress of the International had been called for the summer of 1914 and was to be held in Vienna. The main issue to be settled there was one of long standing in the deliberations of the Socialist International: what to do about the increasing danger of a large-scale war. It was one of Bauer's assignments to prepare a paper setting out the attitude of the Austrian party on this vital question.

The congress for which Bauer prepared his policy paper never took place; Otto Bauer was drafted into the army when war broke out and was taken prisoner by the Russians. The story is that he worked so hard, learning Russian and writing in the prisoner-of-war camp, that a doctor urged him to engage in some physical activity, such as walking, in order to preserve his health. However, this took up too much of the time which he wished to devote to his intellectual pursuits. So he ended up running rather than walking the prescribed distance in order to economize on the time absorbed by what he regarded as a useless pursuit.

The situation changed radically for Bauer when the first Russian Revolution in the spring of 1917 brought a new regime into office. Political and personal friends played a large and increasingly influential role in the revolution. They saw to it that Bauer was released from the prisoner-of-war camp and brought to St. Petersburg, then the capital, in order to advise them. However, since Austria-Hungary and Russia were still at war, Bauer had to protect himself against the possible accusation, upon his return to Vienna, that he had willingly assisted "the enemy." Accordingly, the prisoner-of-war camp commander was given an official order by the new government to "deliver" the prisoner of war, Otto Bauer, to St. Petersburg.

In due course an exchange of prisoners was arranged between the Russian and Austrian governments and Bauer returned to Vienna and Austrian politics. With Fritz Adler in jail, the leadership of the left wing of the party fell automatically into Bauer's hands. He carried forward the opposition to Renner, spokesman of the pro-Austro-Hungarian wing of the party, which saw in the multinational monarch a forerunner of future supranational developments. The other pro-war wing of the party was animated by German nationalist feelings, which their representatives embroidered with progressive ideas by pointing out how far ahead in social legislation Imperial Germany was when compared to Russia. The Russian Revolution deprived this group of its intellectual argument, and the misery caused by the war strengthened the antigovernment left wing led by Bauer.

In contrast to Germany, no split occurred in the Austrian party, but the leadership shifted more and more to the left. Even though Viktor Adler's moral authority remained undisputed and served to hold the party together, Otto Bauer emerged as the leading spokesman of the party.

In November 1918 the monarchy collapsed and a republican government was created to "rule"—insofar as the victorious Western powers permitted it—over what was at first called "German-Austria." Viktor Adler was the first foreign minister, but upon his death in the midst of the birthpangs of the new republic, Otto Bauer became his successor. From then until the fall of the republic in 1934 Bauer was the unquestioned leader of the party. His career as foreign minister came to a rapid end; he resigned in 1919 when the victorious powers prohibited the Anschluss. Bauer did not regard Austria, the leftover of the Hapsburg empire, as a viable entity, and thus the merger of Austria with Germany was, in his view, indispensable for the survival of the Austrian people.

After 1920 Bauer became the leader of the opposition in the Austrian Parliament. He was a most effective speaker, but also a highly provocative one, whose caustic remarks, ruthless criticism, and open contempt aroused helpless hatred among those he criticized: they felt hopelessly inferior to his eloquence and intellectual brilliance. Indeed, the question could be asked whether such ruthless opposition was compatible with a well-functioning democratic system. In fairness, it must be added that the Christian Social government, especially Chancellor Ignaz Seipel, pursued Bauer and his party with equal hatred and fervor.

It was during this period that Bauer, continuing in Viktor Adler's footsteps, became the magnet attracting large numbers of young intellectuals to the party. While Renner, his defeated rival for party leadership, became the symbol of compromise and accommodation, Bauer appeared as the representative of pure ideas untainted by the adjustments imposed by the realities of political life.

It was thus with trepidation that I visited the Bauer home for the first time; even though my visits became more frequent as time went on, I never got over this feeling of reverence and astonishment that such an honor should come my way. The explanation was probably rather simple: Viktor Adler had been on the lookout for promising young members of the intelligentsia who could be recruited into the party. Bauer, Julius Deutsch (later minister of war in the First Austrian Republic), Rudolf Hilferding, and others were his protégés. Bauer, though far less interested in individuals than Viktor Adler, followed Adler's example on a more modest scale. Helene acted occasionally as his scout. I was one of those she found worthy of closer examination.

A minor incident during one of my visits added to their impact upon my life. Somehow—I do not remember anymore how—Helene discovered that I spoke French rather fluently. A Polish friend of hers came to Vienna for a visit; she belonged to the Polish branch of the Curie family, the great French physicists. Since she spoke French, and I could at least communicate simple ideas and carry on a conversation in that language, Helene asked me whether I could serve as a guide for her friend. She was due to stay in Vienna a few days and Helene did not feel like devoting full time to the task of tour guide. It seems that I discharged my task with some measure of success, for Helene retained from this fortuitous incident an exaggerated recollection of my competence in foreign languages. This became a major factor in shaping the course of my life.

Actually, my knowledge of foreign languages was limited to French—apart from classical Latin. The latter was a major subject in my eight years of high school education and may have been indirectly helpful in my ability to learn modern languages. But until the last year of my studies at the university, French was the only modern language which I could more or less claim to have mastered.

My knowledge of English, which later proved to be of great value, was acquired as a result of economic necessity during my student days. This story may be worth telling. While working in the foreign exchange department of a bank, I was elected a member of the Workers' Council: a kind of shop steward whose status was regulated by law. One of the guarantees which the law, enacted after the revolution of 1918, provided for the councillors was protection against dismissal. Under the law, my election was of a somewhat shaky nature: I was not yet of age—a legal requirement for council members. No one objected, however, except for one of my colleagues, a pan-German carrying the colors of the old German empire—black, white, and red—on a ribbon hanging from the pocket watch he carried in his waistcoat. As was the case with many of the German nationalists in Austria, he was of Czech or Slovak extraction; his name, which I remember because he was the first of his kind whom I met in person, was Krcal.

To cut a long story short: Banking business declined rapidly in 1925 because of the stabilization of the Austrian currency and the end of the French franc crisis. The bank in which I worked proceeded with a wholesale reduction in force. Several of my colleagues were affected, including one middle-aged woman who was the sole supporter of her aged mother. In my capacity as member of the Workers' Council, I took up her case with the personnel department. No success. The number of people to be discharged in my department was fixed and not subject to negotiations. In an obviously exaggerated belief in my usefulness to the bank, I offered to resign and to serve as a substitute for my colleague. After some attempts to dissuade me, the bank accepted my offer, and I found myself joining the rather crowded ranks of the unemployed. As solace, I received a fairly large sum of money as severance pay. It was the summer of 1925. I used most of the windfall to finance a highly enjoyable vacation in Tyrol and the Bavarian Alps. Mountain-climbing and the company of pretty girls made this a most pleasant experience.

When the university semester opened in the fall of 1925, I returned to Vienna for the last year of my studies. Obviously, I had to find new sources of support since very little was left of my severance pay. I went to see my professors and asked for their assistance in finding some employment of a kind that would permit me to complete my own studies, including the dissertation in economic theory on which I had started work. The first opportunity soon came my way. One of my professors suggested that I assist a fellow student in the preparation of his thesis. Unfortunately, he had already chosen his topic and started work on it. I say "unfortunately" because his thesis dealt with British electoral reforms from 1885 to 1918. This meant that the main source material was in English. I could not afford to reject the opportunity of accepting an assignment, which in every other respect—including the financial aspect—corresponded to my requirements. Thus, I had to work my way through considerable amounts of English-language material. I decided that my knowledge of German and French would make the task bearable, bought a small English-German dictionary, borrowed a stack of essential English literature on the subject of the thesis from the university library, and disappeared into the countryside.

So that I could concentrate fully on my assignment, I had chosen a small village near Vienna that would offer no temptations. With tremendous persistence, and the help of my dictionary, I worked my way through the first of the English volumes. It was a difficult task and took a full week.

However, the second book proved far less exacting. Since the topic was the same as that of the first book, the vocabulary was the same. The necessity of looking up words in the dictionary diminished as I progressed from book to book, and after a month of this top-speed training, I managed quite nicely in English—as long as the subject was electoral systems. This kind of knowledge was of course limited to reading and to a somewhat narrow subject matter.

The difficulty one encounters when passing from written to spoken English was brought home to me on my first trip to London a few years later. It was a hot summer afternoon when I crossed the English Channel on a boat and took the train from Dover to London. As was then the custom on British trains, tea was served in the passenger cars and soon everyone around me was enjoying the beverage. I was extremely thirsty and eager to participate in this time-honored British ritual. Unfortunately, I did not know how to order tea. No one in all the political science literature I had perused ever ordered tea. The expression "May I have tea" was unknown to me, I did not know how to attract the waiter's attention, and English money was a dark mystery. So I was compelled to watch with increasing anguish how everyone else quenched his thirst while I was getting desperate. Finally, I just pulled at the waiter's sleeve when he passed by and said: "Tea, tea please!" He seemed to understand, but asked me a question—probably whether I wanted milk or lemon—which I did not understand. Frantically, I repeated the magic words: "Tea, please." The waiter apparently realized he was dealing with a foreigner and took pity on me. He brought the tea and selected the coins he felt I owed him from those I had in my hand. Only slowly did I learn to master the intricate ways by which the Anglo-Saxons make it difficult for foreigners to pronounce their language.

Still, my work on British electoral reforms, such as it was, added a small item to my brief list of linguistic accomplishments. It came in very handy when these were put to the test—by no less a person than Friedrich Adler. At this point, the story of my "academic achievements" rejoins the broad stream of European politics. For this, we must step back to 1918, the year of the Austrian revolution.

International Socialism

S hortly before the fall of the empire, Charles, the last emperor of
Austria-Hungary, granted unconditional amnesty to Friedrich
Adler. For some time Adler continued to play a predominant role
in Austrian politics. His love, however, was international affairs,
especially the international labor and socialist movements. Events in that
area were indeed exciting and of historic significance.

The Second International virtually disintegrated during the war. Rival
movements formed. Attempts to reestablish the International as a whole
failed. The disputes had been bitter, too bitter to permit a simple and
immediate reconstitution of the International once hostilities had ended.
Accusations had flown back and forth, not simply of misguided policies,
but also of treason, disloyalty, and the search for personal advantage.

Even before the Russian Revolution, Lenin had called for the creation
of a new revolutionary International. Now, victorious in Russia, he insisted upon the formation of a new Communist International, controlled by
him and his associates and committed to the policies and, even more
importantly, to the system of authoritarian organization and leadership that
he espoused. The first meeting of the Communist International (Comintern) was in Moscow in 1919. The nature of Communist strategy was
more clearly delineated at the second Comintern Congress in 1920. Lenin
and his close associate, Gregory Zinoviev, proclaimed the "twenty-one
conditions" as criteria for admission to the Communist International. All
candidate parties were required to become replicas of the Russian Bolshevik Party. They were to be authoritarian in their structure, expel all leaders
who were considered reformists rather than revolutionaries, and organize
trade union factions designed to combat the non-Communist union leader-

ship of their country and of the International Federation of Trade Unions. The last was perhaps the most fateful of the "twenty-one conditions." Without the support of the millions of organized workers, Lenin said, the Communists had no hope of establishing or maintaining a dictatorship anywhere.

By the summer of 1920 the old Second International had become dominated by the German Majority Socialists (SPD) and the British Labour Party. The other, more radical groups were now caught between the reformist parties of the Second International and the Soviet-dominated Comintern. In the fall and winter of 1920–21 the Comintern split the largest of these wavering radical groups, the French Socialists (SFIO), the Italian Socialists (PSI), and the German Independent Socialists (USPD). Of the major radical parties, only the Austrian Social Democrats avoided a split. The radical wings of the SFIO, PSI, and USPD became the bulk of the Western European Communist movement, and duly appeared at the Third Comintern Congress in the summer of 1921.

Friedrich Adler in turn helped to organize a new International, inspired by the principles of the "social internationalists." In February 1921, under his leadership, the Austrian socialists joined with what was left of the SFIO and USPD, along with some smaller parties such as the Swiss Social Democrats and the British Independent Labour Party (ILP) to form the International Working Union of Socialist Parties. It was often called the Viennese International, or International Two-and-a-Half, to mark Adler's politico-geographic location between the remnants of the old Second International, now in London, and Lenin's new organization in Moscow.

Adler saw his task as being the reconstitution of a real and unique Socialist International. In this endeavor his moral and political authority was the key question. His standing in the international socialist movement was higher than that of any other socialist leader except Lenin. And so the issue of reunification in fact boiled down to the question of whether Adler and Lenin could come to terms. An attempt was made to see whether this might be possible.

A meeting of the executive committee of the three existing partial Internationals was scheduled for Berlin. The conference took place in April 1922. Lenin did not appear. His absence was sufficient evidence that he had no desire to see the conference succeed. What he wanted was an International under his control, not a compromise in which he might share power with Adler and others. And the declaration which Clara Zetkin of the German Communist Party submitted on behalf of the Third International made it clear that the unification of the international socialist labor movement could not be a merger of the three existing organizations. That meant that it had to result from the victory of the Third International over the London and Vienna organizations. Conflict, not compromise, was Lenin's objective. The Berlin conference ended in utter failure.

In May 1923 the Second and the Two-and-a-Half Internationals met in Hamburg to constitute an international association which all socialist parties not affiliated with the Communist International were invited to join. Since this was essentially a merger of the two organizations, the decisions taken were compromises rendered possible by two facts: the issues created by the war were beginning to recede from the scene and the danger of Communist aggression upon the non-Communist left was great and acute. The simplest solution appeared to be the consolidation of the two organizations: the secretaries of both Internationals were appointed to be coordinate secretaries of the new Labor and Socialist International (LSI). Tom Shaw, an English Labourite who had held the position of secretary in the postwar Second International, retained his post, though only for a short while. Friedrich Adler was elected to be his colleague on an equal footing. The seat of the LSI was to be in London; thus the British Labour Party, soon to form the first Labour government in British history, was now the leading party of the International, taking the place formerly held by the German Social Democrats.

Friedrich Adler thus moved to London, accompanied by his assistant Oscar Pollak, one of the outstanding journalists of the Austrian Social Democratic Party and a first-rate linguist. Pollak's mastery of German and English and his good knowledge of French were, of course, important assets for work in an international organization, where all conferences and publications were produced in English, German, and French. These arrangements were, however, only short-lived. Tom Shaw left the Secretariat of the LSI to join the first British Labour government in 1924, leaving Adler as the only secretary. The former member parties of the Second International did not appoint a successor to Shaw. They were satisfied that the administration of the new organization could safely be left to Adler. Indeed, they agreed without too much resistance to Adler's wish that LSI headquarters be transferred to Zürich. Not only did this transfer correspond to Adler's own desire to return to the place where he had spent so many years as a student, scientist, and in party work, but Zürich also offered a favorable location for an international organization. It was near Geneva, seat of the League of Nations and of the International Labor Organization, both agencies with which the international labor and socialist organizations had intimate associations. Even though the Swiss police looked rather critically at the bunch of "radical" foreigners who now sought to establish themselves in Zürich, Switzerland's neutrality created an agreeable climate for the LSI.

The situation was complicated by the fact that the Swiss Social Democratic Party, led by Robert Grimm, Ernst Nobs, and Paul Graber, had refused to follow its colleagues of the Vienna Union into the merger with the Second International. Grimm had been one of the most outspoken critics of the "social patriots" during World War I, and Switzerland had offered hospitality to the two main conferences of antiwar socialists: the meetings held in Zimmerwald and Kienthal. Still, the leadership of the LSI included many of the most distinguished European personalities in the 1920s: men such as Arthur Henderson, formerly British foreign minister and later the president of the World Disarmament Conference called by the League of Nations; Émile Vandervelde, foreign minister of Belgium; Léon Blum, member of the French Chamber of Deputies and later twice prime minister of France; Hermann Müller, German chancellor in 1920 and again in 1928–30; Otto Bauer, Austrian foreign minister after the revolution of 1918; the list could be greatly extended. When the Swiss government was approached, it gave its consent and the Secretariat of the LSI, barely established in London after the congress of 1923, moved to Zürich in 1925.

For me, these were faraway events. I read about them, perhaps with a bit more interest than most of my colleagues since I had just accepted the position of secretary for a somewhat ephemeral international socialist student association. This relative indifference was to change dramatically in the summer of 1925.

The course of study which I was pursuing at the University of Vienna

culminated in two doctoral examinations following the successful comple-
tion of the dissertation. I had successfully passed the first *rigorosum*
(literally, "severe test") in the summer of 1925 and was busily preparing
for the second exam to follow a few weeks later. The second *rigorosum*
dealt with legal questions, and since I was not to be a lawyer I had paid
little attention to the subject. By relying on my good memory and reading
the voluminous civil law code, I hoped to get through the second examination with little effort. I was sitting in a park near the university in the
glorious sunshine of a late June day, when one of the junior faculty
members passed by, a philosopher whom I knew by way of my political
activities. He stopped and congratulated me; I assumed that he thought I
had passed the second examination and congratulated me for having
obtained the doctorate. "I have not yet taken the *rigorosum*," I responded.
"I am not talking about that," he said. "You are going to America, are you
not?" This was the first I had heard about the subject and so informed
Professor Kaufman. "Then you are the last person in Vienna to know.
Professor Francis Pribram, the European representative of the Rockefeller
Foundation, is looking for you. The foundation is considering you for a
fellowship at an American university. You had better get on the telephone
and arrange to see him."

My interview with Professor Pribram, a highly respected member of
the University of Vienna faculty, was exciting and surprising. I learned
that the foundation had a program in which every year two or three young
men of promise were sent to the United States for a year of study, which,
given favorable circumstances, could be extended to a second year. They
were then to return home and act as intellectual intermediaries between
their home country and the United States. I pointed out that my English,
most recently acquired, was at best of an elementary nature. He responded
that I could spend a few months in England, as part of my first year's
fellowship, to improve my English before proceeding to the United States.
Asked what I wanted to study in the United States, I was greatly embarrassed at not having an answer. This was the first day I had heard, not only
of my being considered for a fellowship of this kind, but even of the
existence of the program. I offered a somewhat noncommittal reply.
According to Professor Pribram's outline of this program, I would be
entitled not only to a monthly stipend for my living expenses, but also to a

certain amount per mile of travel. This appealed to me, of course. In the belief that research on American agriculture would justify a good deal of travel, I proposed to study some aspect of agricultural economics—a subject about which, to be frank, my knowledge came frighteningly close to zero. I was given plenty of time to reflect upon my ultimate choice, as Pribram pointed out that I was eligible for the fellowship until the age of thirty-two. Not yet being twenty-two years old, I was delighted to have this offer, and though nothing was put in writing, as far as I knew, the offer seemed pretty firm. A hint was dropped to the effect that my main sponsor had been Karl Renner, one of the outstanding party leaders I had met in the course of the efforts mentioned earlier to settle the divisions of the student movement.

While I was still pondering over this unexpected development, other minor job opportunities came my way. Hans Mayer, professor of economics at the University of Vienna, showed interest in my professional career. He referred me to a friend of his in city hall who held out hope for a job in the city administration. Another friend of Professor Mayer endeavored to place me in the administration of the social security system. What was remarkable about Mayer's interest was the fact that my political views, well known to him, did not prevent him from trying to help me, even though he was clearly opposed to my thinking. Perhaps it should also be pointed out that at this time Vienna was producing a crop of outstanding young economists: Gottfried von Haberler, Friedrich von Hayek, Oskar Morgenstern, Fritz Machlup, and others, in such numbers that it was clearly impossible to place them all in academic slots. Under the circumstances, Mayer's efforts on my behalf were truly remarkable.

In the end, however, neither Mayer's intervention nor the offer of a Rockefeller fellowship mattered. For out of the clear blue sky I received another offer which, to use current language, "I could not refuse," the more so since it appeared that I could still come back to the Rockefeller fellowship in due course. At the age of twenty-two, the age limit of thirty-two for the fellowship seemed eons away.

When the headquarters of the Labor and Socialist International was transferred to Switzerland, Oscar Pollak, Adler's main assistant, decided to accept an offer to become editor of the Viennese daily *Arbeiter Zeitung*, with the clear prospect of succeeding in due course to the post of editor-in-chief. Friedrich Austerlitz, the famed "commander" of the paper, was approaching an age when retirement could not be far away. Fritz Adler came to Vienna in 1925 to look for a replacement for Pollak. He turned for advice to Otto Bauer, his close friend and comrade-in-arms in the battles within the movement during the war.

At this point Helene Bauer remembered my ability to communicate in French and suggested to Otto and to Fritz Adler that I might be worth interviewing. There is no question that my competitors for the job—about whom I learned only much later—were far more qualified than I, by experience, work for the party, and past achievements. I was a youngster who had just received my doctorate and published my first book review. By no objective standard could I even faintly be compared with the other candidates for the job. My main merit, I suppose, was Helene and Otto Bauer's recommendation, which carried tremendous weight with Fritz Adler.

I still remember the surprise with which I received the news that I was to see the great Fritz Adler in connection with a job. It was Otto Bauer himself who told me to visit Fritz, who with his wife, Kathia, was engaged in liquidating his apartment in Vienna in preparation for the move to Zürich.

I, of course, was not in the running for the job. I did not know that the opening existed, had never met Adler, who in turn had hardly even heard of me, and I doubt that even under the best of circumstances would I have had the effrontery to compete for the job. Helene and Otto Bauer, however, must have felt that I at least deserved to be looked over by Adler. With the barest minimum of information about the job to be filled, I went to see Adler in his apartment in Vienna as he was getting ready to leave. This was about the end of the summer of 1925, a few weeks since I had obtained my diploma, and shortly before my twenty-second birthday.

The interview is still vivid in my memory. With trepidation I approached the great man who had made history and inspired an entire generation. Friedrich Adler combined the features of an artist with those of a scientist. He was fairly tall and slender; in his later years he gained quite a bit of weight. Behind his glasses, alert eyes peered with a benevolence that belied his sarcastic humor. He was surrounded by huge stacks of books that he obviously was sorting out for the mover. Toward the end of the hour-long conversation, Kathia Adler came in as well, to inspect the candidate for an assignment that would make him in effect the closest personal collaborator for her husband.

The interview had some of the more obvious elements of an examination. I was asked to translate orally a French newspaper that was lying on a table, into German and into English. The first I did rather well, if I may say so without appearing boastful. The translation into English left a good deal to be desired, and Adler did not hesitate to point this out. In turn, I translated another few sentences from a German paper into fairly good French. Then came a prolonged discussion of my work in the international student movement. I doubt that I was particularly brilliant, most of my knowledge having been acquired within the span of a few weeks. I remember that Adler was interested in what I knew of the Dutch student movement, a particularly tricky subject since Dutch students were organized according to religious as well as political allegiances, with the two occasionally overlapping or conflicting with one another.

Somehow I passed the exam to Adler's satisfaction, and in some mysterious fashion Kathia Adler must have learned of the result, for she indicated rather clearly that she expected to see me in Zürich. We did not discuss two topics: my assignment and my salary. The omissions were characteristic of the man and the times. Adler was always reluctant to establish clear lines of authority and outline definite responsibilities. More interesting for a contemporary reader may be the fact that I never asked, nor was I told what my salary would be. I was overwhelmed by the opportunity of working for Adler, and would have taken the job at almost any salary. My material requirements were quite modest, and I assumed without any conscious thought that my salary would cover that minimum. The Austrian socialist movement of that time was dominated by a spirit of Spartan simplicity in one's life-style. Most of its leaders were teetotalers. They did not have cars. When I accompanied Otto Bauer to huge mass meetings, his means of transportation was streetcars. Smoking was permitted, though Adler refrained from it. Any sign of luxury was frowned upon. Viktor Adler, the founder of the party, who came from a well-to-do family, had devoted a good deal of his private funds to party work, especially the financial support of its daily newspaper during its early years of struggle for survival. He was accordingly forgiven when he spent his annual vacation for many years in luxurious spas. He said that for a few days every year he wanted to be among people for whom material problems and misery did not exist.

I was thus simply behaving according to the standards of my peer group and of the leaders whom I most admired in not even considering the question of my salary. In fact, I learned the amount only when at the end of my first month of work I received the envelope containing four hundred Swiss francs. The amount was determined, I later discovered, by the allowance which Fritz Adler's father had sent him while he was a student in Zürich. A quarter of a century had passed, and prices and living standards even in such a basically conservative country as Switzerland had changed. My salary was frankly insufficient. Moreover, Fritz was not a practical man, especially in matters of finance. He had rented a double room for me, even though I was single. For Easter he took me to a lovely fishing village on the Lago Maggiore, Ascona, which since has become one of the most fashionable resorts in Switzerland. When I returned from the four-day vacation, I was broke and asked Adler for an advance on my salary. He was quite ready to acquiesce, but asked in fatherly concern, "Did you have any special expenditures?" I truthfully replied that I could not afford the kind of trip I had just undertaken with him. "But you must have vacations, if you work hard," was his reply. Mine was simply, "You don't have to convince me, Comrade Adler." My salary was then increased by a fair but still modest amount.

My financial stringency was accentuated by a debt I had incurred before leaving for Zürich. The responsibility for this trouble fell squarely upon the shoulders of the Swiss police for foreigners. My appointment had been official by the end of the summer of 1925, but before I could enter Switzerland and start the job I had to obtain an official permit from the Swiss government. The Bernese authorities obviously regarded me with the utmost suspicion, despite my youth and absence of any criminal past. The Swiss Embassy in Vienna was instructed to investigate me. The janitor in the house in which I lived was interviewed, as were my neighbors and one or two of my fellow students. All this was done with Swiss thoroughness and little sense of urgency. Thus one month after another passed without any reply from Bern. My appointment had been a minor sensation in Viennese party circles and farewell parties for me were numerous. I stayed on and on, a somewhat ridiculous figure, a bit resembling an umbrella that was left and forgotten. "You are still here?" became a most frequent form of greeting when friends saw me. It expressed a peculiar kind of disappointment in my failure to leave after the farewells.

Soon, financial worries arose. Expecting to depart momentarily, I neither looked for new assignments—for example, coaching students for their exams or assisting them in writing theses—nor could I in good faith accept any, since I might have to leave the work half done. My old jobs ran out, one after another, and so I finally turned to Oscar Pollak, who had already left the LSI and arrived in Vienna, with the request for a loan. He graciously provided the needed assistance, but the repayment after I started working and earning money in Zürich added to my money troubles.

It took the Swiss authorities close to four months to decide that I was unlikely to endanger the social and political order of Switzerland. Late in January 1926 I received a wire informing me that permission had been granted for me to enter Switzerland. Twenty-four hours later I was on the night train to Zürich. A new chapter in my life was due to begin, but my financial troubles lasted far into my new job.

The Labor and Socialist International

Work in the Secretariat of the LSI opened a new world for me. The staff itself was small, with four professionals in addition to Adler: one Englishman, one Norwegian, a part-time French translator, and myself. In addition, we had several typists and secretaries, a messenger, and—in due course—a woman, Martha Tausk, who combined bookkeeping with editing a women's supplement to the weekly bulletin that we published in English, French, and German. In periods preceding congresses or major conferences we added both temporary help for the preparation of the necessary documents and further assistance for oral interpretation at the meetings. Some conferences appointed several committees that met simultaneously and required a set of three interpreters each. Not all the people who did written translations were able to handle oral interpretation. There was not yet any simultaneous translation equipment in existence. A delegate would deliver his speech in his tongue, and then two interpreters in succession would present the same speech—as well as they could remember it—in the other two official languages. Each interpreter had his own method of note-taking and his own style.

Everyone who worked in the Secretariat of the LSI, Adler included, was supposed to be ready and willing to do anything that needed to be done, within the limits of one's abilities. This limitation referred primarily to the knowledge of foreign languages, since no amount of goodwill and dedication could serve as a substitute for that kind of competence. Even Adler himself would assist in folding letters and getting them ready for the mail when the Secretariat was under pressure. The rules, or rather the absence of rules, applied to him in full democratic equality. Only much later and with some reluctance did Adler openly acknowledge the distribution of assignments among the members of his small staff, and even then it was primarily done in terms of one's official designation.

My assignment was twofold to begin with, but other assignments were added later. I was editing the weekly news bulletin *International Information* and interpreting, mainly into German, occasionally into French, at the various meetings that the LSI organized. *International Information* was a mimeographed bulletin of some eight or ten pages published in the three official languages: English, French, and German. The editorial work was rather routine except for occasional flashes of interest, but for me it was all new and exciting. It would have become dull if Adler's reluctance to establish clear lines of authority and responsibility and the inevitable rivalries of any organization had not added spice to the normal life of the Secretariat.

Adler must have realized the difficulties which his reluctance provoked when I innocently and unintentionally caused a misunderstanding between the Secretariat and the highly respected leader of the Hungarian socialist émigrés, Sigmund Kunfi. One day while Adler was away on one of his many trips, Kunfi called on the phone from Vienna, where he lived, and asked whether an article of his about some event of importance—what it was, I do not remember any more—would be acceptable to *International Information*. No such authority had indeed been given to me by Adler. I reported the conversation to Fritz when he returned. He was unhappy because Kunfi was not easily induced to write, and any article of his would have been most welcome. This, among other incidents, led Adler to at least a minimum of clarification of duties in the Secretariat, which officially made life a bit easier for everyone. I was appointed editor of *International Information* and its supplements. When newspapers began to refer to me as the administrative secretary or assistant secretary of the Labor and Socialist International, this was not only unauthorized but incorrect, surely as regards administration.

It is true that as time went on at least some political work, especially the drafting of resolutions and reports, became more and more my task. My editorial responsibilities also tended to increase. This was brought home to me rather sharply when I printed one of Adler's own articles, signed by him, unchanged and unedited. It did not occur to me that I had the authority to change even one word in the manuscript. Adler was not one of the masters of languages, indeed of any language, contrary to his father's testimony at the trial that his son "mastered several languages." The article contained some rather clumsy turns of phrase, and when Fritz reread it, he was displeased. "Why did you not edit the manuscript?" he asked me. I naively but truthfully responded that I did not think I had the right to do so. "When I write something in German," Adler said smilingly, "it is not always German." I noted the admission for future reference.

A curious incident going back to my student days and ending a decade later occurred about that time (the late 1920s or early 1930s). One day, unexpectedly, I received a long-distance call from Frankfurt. Someone from the Institute of Social Research called and engaged me in a lengthy conversation culminating in the question of whether I would be interested in a position at the institute.

At an early stage of my university studies I had accidentally come into contact with the Frankfurt Institute of Social Research, or rather with a gentleman named Felix Weil. The occasion was an international congress of socialists held in Vienna, which had attracted my attention. As life dictated in Vienna in those days, a number of participants met one evening at the Café Reichsrat for a social gathering. I remember among those present Professor Hans Kelsen, the great legal scholar, author of the Austrian republican constitution, later professor at Harvard and Berkeley. Another participant was Louise Sommer, who taught economics at a popular university (no degrees) in Vienna. While still in high school I had taken a course with her and was greatly pleased when she asked me, after one of the class discussions, which university semester I was in. I also owe to her one of the most embarrassing introductions to a professor (i.e., Kelsen) I can remember. One evening I came to the Café Herrenhof—one of the "intellectual" cafés at the time—and saw Louise Sommer and Hans Kelsen sitting at one of the tables. She signaled me to come over and introduced me to my future law professor: "This is young Sturmthal whom I have mentioned to you. Er kann Sie schon heute in die Tasche stecken." ("Already today, he can put you in his pocket.") This was not only a colossal misstatement, but also a devastating introduction to my future professor. Fortunately for me, Kelsen did not take her praise very seriously.

To come back to the evening in the Reichsrat Café. As was customary in Vienna, when the party broke up people asked each other which way they were heading, so that little groups going the same way could be formed. I happened to be standing next to Felix Weil, and he told me that he was heading toward the Hotel Imperial, the most elegant hotel in Vienna. That was distinctly not my direction, but I found that Kelsen and I went at least part of the way in common. "The Frankfurt Institute," I said to Kelsen, "must be very well off if Weil can afford to stay at the Imperial." "You innocent angel," was Kelsen's reply, "Weil is the institute." He then proceeded to tell me the history of the Frankfurt Institute. While I have never checked on his report, I have no reason to question its veracity.

According to Kelsen, Weil's father, a German, had migrated to Argentina and there acquired a large fortune. Not satisfied with the scientific level of Argentine academia, he sent his son to Germany to study. Young Weil became so enamored of the German university way of life that he decided to stay on and become a German university professor. Unfortunately—for reasons that I can only guess at—no institution was found willing to grant him *Habilitation,* the traditional first step on the German university's ladder of success. "Don't worry," said Papa Weil, "I'll just buy a university for you." The result was, according to Kelsen, the Frankfurt Institute of Social Research. Still, it was not a university, nor even a part of a university. Solution: the Institute hired a director, the most distinguished Viennese professor Karl Grünberg, an economic historian of international reknown. The Goethe University in Frankfurt was delighted to have Grünberg on its faculty, and the institute had at least some modest connection with a German university. Soon, however, a new problem arose: too many people on the institute staff were "accused"—rightly or wrongly, I do not know—of being Communists or what were then called "fellow travelers." This endangered whatever standing Grünberg's appointment may have brought to the institute. Solution: hire a guaranteed, waterproof non-Communist.

For reasons that I am not familiar with, the choice fell upon me. I don't know what my standing as a social scientist was at the time, but as a member of the Secretariat of the LSI and close collaborator of Fritz Adler, my non-Communist status could hardly be questioned. And so, one day— I do not remember the date—I received a phone call from the institute, asking me to visit them in Frankfurt to discuss a possible appointment. After checking with Fritz and obtaining his agreement, I accepted the invitation and went to visit Weil in Frankfurt.

The trip was a revelation. Weil's house had beautiful arrangements of paintings, originals if I was not mistaken, especially French Impressionists. There must have been a fortune hanging on the walls, confirming that Weil could easily afford a stay in the Hotel Imperial in Vienna. I also met several members of the institute staff, including a man by the name of Friedrich Pollack. I soon discovered they were willing to give me maximum freedom, if I was willing to serve as kind of *Paradegoi,* a token object of the non-Communist character of the institute; this role I was not willing to play.

Years later the institute appeared in New York and once again sought affiliation with a university of high repute, this time Columbia. The result was not any better than in Frankfurt. Indeed, as receptive to foreign scholars as Robert Lynd, the great sociologist, was, he had little interest in the institute. The first issue of the periodical published by it started with an article on the sociology of music. "They are coming from one of the greatest catastrophes of mankind," Lynd said to me, "and instead of telling us what we can learn from the German experience, they are studying music!" In general, the institute at that time exerted little influence on American thought, though individual members, for some time, provided intellectual leadership for radical student movements.[1]

One of the main concerns of the Labor and Socialist International in the relatively quiet and prosperous years between 1925 and the onset of the Great Depression in 1929 was resisting the unceasing efforts of the Communists to organize "united front" activities jointly with socialists and non-Communist trade unionists. For the Communists these years of rela-

1. Editor's note: For a different assessment of the Frankfurt School, see Martin Jay, *The Dialectical Imagination: A History of the Frankfurt School and the Institute of Social Research, 1923–1950* (Boston: Little, Brown, 1973).

tive political stability and economic prosperity were a period of rapid decline. After the high tide of the German revolution had receded in the defeat of the Ruhr resistance, one setback followed another: the futile Hamburg rebellion of 1923, the rise of fascism in Italy, the legal prohibition of the Italian Communist Party, and the decline of the French Communist Party. The Third International responded with a strategy which directed the main struggle of the movement against the Social Democrats. They were the traitors without whose support capitalism could not survive in Europe.

By the end of 1927, membership in the Third International—including the Soviet Union—had dropped to one quarter of that of the LSI. Not counting the Soviet membership, the Communists stood at one-thirteenth of socialist membership. In terms of votes outside of Russia, the disproportion was still greater. Yet while the attacks were concentrated on the Social Democrats, the tactic of the united front was maintained. Originally devised by the Executive Committee of the Communist International as far back as December 1921, this tactical maneuver consisted of offers to individual Social Democrats, or groups of them (but never the party as such), to engage in joint actions. Once the unwary were so engaged, the Communists would take advantage of their cooperation to reveal "the traitorous character" of the socialist leaders and to attract the "masses by the most rapid means to the Communist camp." In the words of Lenin, the Communists were prepared to support the socialists the same way as "the rope supports the hanged."[2] In its first stages this maneuver went hand in hand with attempts at splitting the socialist parties.

Another concern of the LSI was to trace Communist-controlled front groups. At the center of these efforts was Willi Münzenberg, a German Communist who had spent part of his youth in Switzerland. He was undoubtedly one of the geniuses of organization who, had he been in business, would with any luck have ended as a tycoon. Münzenberg was a master at this deceptive game. The large funds which the Communist International put at his disposal, the moral support which many members of the intelligentsia gave the Soviet Union, and the expertise with which

2. V. I. Lenin, *"Left Wing" Communism: An Infantile Disorder* (New York: International Publishers, 1934), p. 68.

Münzenberg exploited a variety of sympathetic writers, artists, actors, musicians, and others, led to his creation of ever-new "front" organizations. Congresses against "war and fascism" and against "colonial oppression" followed each other at short intervals, sponsored by long lists of distinguished men and women, all of whom were steered from behind the scenes by the great manipulator.

One of my main assignments was to observe the various congresses of this kind, either by studying all the printed material connected with them or by attending them as a journalist. A Norwegian colleague, Finn Moe, seemingly had the same kind of assignment. We met not infrequently on such occasions and exchanged information and opinions. Together we acquired a peculiar kind of experience in identifying Münzenberg's operations and found him almost ubiquitous. No good progressive cause emerged anywhere in Europe, particularly during the rise of Hitler, without Münzenberg's assistance, whether solicited or not. And whenever he "assisted," he soon controlled and manipulated from behind the scenes.

Much later I met Münzenberg in Paris in the rue Cognac-Jay, in an apartment which Rudolf Breitscheid, the former chief spokesman of the German Social Democrats in the Reichstag, had been offered as temporary refuge from Hitler by, I believe, Pierre Cot, a minister in the French Popular Front government. By that time—it must have been sometime in 1936 or 1937—Münzenberg was no longer Moscow's fair-haired boy, for reasons that I have never understood. He probably had been on the "wrong" side in one of the Communists' unending factional disputes. He was frank and perhaps even a bit boastful about his achievements as an organizer of "front" maneuvers. We compared notes to see how successful my detective work had been. Münzenberg laughed when I finished my recitation of the organizations and people I identified as having been under his more or less secret control. "That's about half the real story," he said. And he gave me names of persons whom I had never suspected of being under his influence. As a detective, I scored not much better than 50 or 60 percent.

The most confusing cases were those card-carrying members of various socialist parties who lent themselves more or less knowingly to Münzenberg's operations. In many cases it was next to impossible to establish whether they knew the real purpose of the organization which they had joined or even that the great Willi was its guiding spirit. One of the perpetual sources of worry was Léon Nicole of Geneva, member of the Swiss Parliament and editor of the Geneva socialist daily. While I was personally convinced that he was a secret member of the Communist Party—with or without the membership card—I had no evidence whatsoever to prove it. In fact, he dominated the Geneva Socialist Party for many years and left it for the Communist Party only long after I had ceased to be interested in him.

Among the distinguished persons who operated in Münzenberg's network of organizations were the two great French writers Romain Rolland and Henri Barbusse. Their Olympian stature in the world of belles lettres gave them tremendous influence among French-speaking or French-reading intellectuals, and even beyond this circle. Münzenberg assured me, during one of our "confessional" sessions, that they had given him, once and for all, authority to use their names whenever he felt the need for their support. There was a long list of German and Austrian writers, British lawyers of distinction, and many others who belonged to Münzenberg's crowd, so that the mere appearance of their names on an appeal sufficed to indicate to the initiated that another of his ventures had been launched.

Once ousted from power by Moscow, Münzenberg had a tragic end. After the Hitler-Stalin pact in 1939, he lived a dangerous underground life in Nazi-occupied France. He was found dead in France in 1940; blame for his hanging remains unclear. Perhaps he was one of the many victims of the unbelievably immoral and illusionary policy by which Moscow tried to assuage the Nazis in the belief that the Teutonic furor could be diverted away from the Soviet Union and toward the West alone. This was, of course, simply the counterpart to the equally immoral and illusionary policy of Neville Chamberlain and Edouard Daladier, who, by making concessions to Hitler, hoped to turn his expansionist policy against the East as he himself had promised in *Mein Kampf*.

For me, Münzenberg's memory is also kept alive by a curious and unattractive but highly influential figure in West German journalism, William S. Schlamm. Born Siegmund Schlamm and educated at the same academic high school I had attended, Schlamm adopted the first name Willi out of admiration for Willi Münzenberg. He joined the Austrian

Communist Party and put his considerable journalistic talents at its disposal. Defeated in one of many factional disputes of the minuscule party, he started his move toward the political right. One of the early steps put him in charge of the highly respected leftist but non-Communist journal, *Die Weltbühne*. By the time he came to the United States and changed his first name again, this time to the English William, he had become the darling of Henry Luce, the founder of *Time* magazine. Luce seriously considered setting up a new magazine under Schlamm's direction, specifically aimed at converting the leftist intelligentsia in Europe to the conservative causes dear to Luce's heart. This project did not materialize, and after interludes in Paris and Vermont, Schlamm made his appearance in West Germany. He became one of the most articulate cold warriors: anti-Social Democratic Party, pro-Christian Democratic Union to the core; highly successful, hated by many, loved by few, but greatly admired for his journalistic skill and his ruthlessness in the political infighting that preceded the rise in 1969 of another Willy, Willy Brandt, to the chancellorship of West Germany.

The counterpart to Münzenberg's literary and artistic allies was—of all people—George Bernard Shaw. For reasons that I have never been able to understand, he became, if not an admirer, at least a supporter of Benito Mussolini. Perhaps this does an injustice to Shaw, one of the earliest advocates and probably the most persuasive spokesman of Fabian Socialism in Great Britain. What rankled him was the relentless but apparently totally unsuccessful campaign of Italian and other European socialists against the Italian dictator, who had spent a large part of his early life in the ranks of the Italian socialist movement. Shaw, impressed by the futility of this campaign, spoke out against it and advocated coming to terms with the regime which the Italian dictator had established. A correspondence developed between him and Friedrich Adler, which I published verbatim in *International Information*. I found it difficult to read more into Shaw's statements than his eternal desire to *épater les bourgeois* ("startle the bourgeois"). In spite of his worldwide literary reputation, George Bernard Shaw was in no way a spokesman for British Labour.

Some Socialists

Arthur Henderson was the Labour Party's main representative in the International. In view of the tremendous importance of the British Labour movement within the Socialist International, Henderson was elected its president and chairman of its Executive Committee during the twenties, except for the times (1924, 1929–31) when he was a member of the British government.

Henderson, an excellent chairman at meetings, rarely took part in the debates. A Methodist law preacher who still, whenever he could, went Sundays to his parish outside London to deliver the sermon, he undoubtedly felt a bit uncomfortable in these international gatherings in which highly trained intellectuals of various Marxian persuasions set the tone of the debates. But when he spoke he could count on a respectful audience, even when the majority disagreed with him. He was no impressive speaker but rather pedestrian, appealing to common sense and morality instead of involved theories.

A serious man of infinite patience, Henderson rarely lost his temper, but when he did he usually succeeded in searing his enemies. One such occasion arose when, in a rumor campaign, he was accused of nepotism because his son Will Henderson was made responsible for the administration of the British zone during the occupation of Germany after World War II. Will Henderson was never a member of the Cabinet, although he was a member of Parliament in 1923–24 and again in 1929–31. He never played an important role in the life of the party or the British government.

Arthur Henderson's main talent was organization; indeed, he could very well be described as the chief architect of the party organization. He had entered the House of Commons in 1903 and thus had extensive parliamentary experience before becoming foreign minister in the Labour government of 1929. He had been secretary of the Labour Party since 1911 and controlled the party machinery without fear of any competitor. While his socialism had its origin in his religious beliefs, he found it not difficult to cooperate with Sidney Webb, the Fabian Socialist. Together they were responsible for the party constitution of 1918 which made Labour a national party committed to socialism, though of a very moderate sort, to be achieved by gradual advances.

A Liberal early in his life, Arthur Henderson had committed himself entirely to the Labour Party after it came into existence. One could sense no rivalry between him and the leader of the party at the time. He acknowledged without hesitation that the top position in the party belonged to the far more brilliant, though less reliable, Ramsay MacDonald; but the credit for preserving the unity of the party in spite of its great internal diversity and cleavages was undoubtedly Henderson's. This became his crucial contribution to the survival and the recovery of the party after MacDonald and a few of his friends left the party during the great crisis of 1931.

It was almost a matter of course that Henderson was elected leader of the party after MacDonald was expelled. This was fair recognition of the fact that Henderson had "saved the character and the identity of the party to which he had already contributed so much."[1] Henderson limited his participation in the International's activities. This was partly because of the clause in the statutes of the International excluding government members from holding an LSI office. (Government members were, however, allowed to participate in meetings.) Moreover, after his defeat in the 1931 election, which was a disaster for the Labour Party, and after his election as president of the World Disarmament Conference (for which he won the Nobel Peace Prize in 1934), he withdrew from the International altogether. Nevertheless, he remained in contact through discussions with former colleagues. Since he spent a good deal of his time at the Disarmament Conference in Geneva, and one of my duties was to follow the activities of the League of Nations there, he would talk with me quite frequently, and I

1. Carl F. Brand, *The British Labour Party* (Stanford, Calif.: Stanford University Press, 1964), p. 159.

could do my share in bringing him up to date on our activities. Moreover, his closest collaborator, Philip Noel-Baker, often served as intermediary. Even though his position as president of the International was taken by the Belgian Émile Vandervelde, Henderson to the end of his days retained a lively interest in the problems of the LSI as Nazism continued its path of conquest.

Relations among the top leaders of the Labour Party were far from harmonious. Ramsay MacDonald, who was rarely seen at international labor and socialist gatherings, was far more conspicuous as a guest at house parties of the British aristocracy. His service as prime minister in the short-lived Labour government in 1924 had opened the doors of the most distinguished society to him. His social snobbishness alienated many of his colleagues. One of them told me that during the lifetime of the second Labour government (1929–31) not one of his fellow cabinet members was ever invited to Chequers, the prime minister's country residence, while members of the British aristocracy—Tories, as my informant disdainfully pointed out—were frequent guests. And Arthur Henderson, the grand old man of the party who saved it from destruction after MacDonald abandoned it in 1931, complained in a moment of weakness that the party leader had not even once expressed his thanks for Henderson's loyal support.

Henderson had not concealed his sorrow or even his reluctance to separate himself from his old comrade-in-arms, Ramsay MacDonald. But he realized, as he admitted in private conversation, that MacDonald had increasingly moved away from the party in search of more socially prestigious company. While there is—or at least was—a good deal of social snobbery among British workingmen (and even more so among workingwomen), some party leaders and the middle layers of the party machinery resented MacDonald's growing alienation from them. More important still was the fact that Henderson remained convinced that the very survival of the party depended upon its closeness to the unions, and few if any of them were prepared to follow MacDonald into the political wilderness. Only some fifteen Labour members of Parliament did follow him, but among them was Philip Snowden, whose cutting humor in parliamentary debates made him a major asset, but also a subject of considerable hostility from his peers. He, more than anyone else in the party, had been the most passionate defender of fiscal orthodoxy and, unfortunately, also the closest advisor of MacDonald in economic matters. The peculiar result of this was that the Liberal Party under Keynes's influence was to the left of the Labour Party on issues relating to public finance.

MacDonald had never played a significant role in the Labor and Socialist International. He participated in only very few of its meetings and even then had little to contribute. It was rather peculiar to see most if not all of the other member parties of the International represented in the LSI Executive by their outstanding leaders (Blum, Müller, and Vandervelde), while the Labour Party's leader almost never put in an appearance. True, the leaders of the Labour Party could not serve in the Executive while holding government positions. But as soon as they left the government other British leaders resumed their role in the International.

Under the circumstances, painful as the loss of its longtime leader MacDonald must have been for the party, the International was far less affected by his departure. Its main concern was the survival of its most important affiliate. Without an effective British Labour Party, and given the rapid decline of the German affiliate, the LSI would have lost most of whatever modest influence it had on European events.

Another who left the British Labour Party was Oswald Mosley, who for some time had been considered its rising star. His tremendous social prestige (which counted for so much in that peculiar mixture of social radicalism and reverence for feudal institutions that inspired the British working class) was raised even higher by his good looks and aristocratic arrogance and by his marriage to Lord Curzon's daughter, who appeared in expensive fur coats in working-class slums. His standing was so high that shortly after he joined the party he was regarded as a possible, if not probable, successor to Ramsay MacDonald.

I finally met him in London at an international socialist meeting some time before the victorious elections of 1929. In some ways this was a remarkable experience. Mosley and his wife, Lady Cynthia, gave an evening reception to the assembled socialist leaders. They had rented the house of Sidney and Beatrice Webb, which stood opposite Parliament. A bell was connected with the House of Commons so that Oswald Mosley could be called to the House if a vote was about to be taken. He could then just cross the street, enter the House, vote, and return.

I had met the Webbs only very briefly and have no real impression of their personalities except that they seemed somewhat reserved and perhaps a bit pedestrian. This is an uncertain judgment, but I feel quite confident in stating that Sir Oswald's reception was not in the style of the Webbs. I arrived at the evening reception with the leader of the Sudeten-German Social Democrats, Dr. Ludwig Czech (an odd coincidence that the spokesman of a German-speaking party in Czechoslovakia should have the name Czech). Czech and I had been on a subcommittee to draft a resolution for the next day's meeting. This had taken up so much of our time that we had to forego dinner. We hoped to make up for this at the Mosley reception.

Our hearts sank when we were received at the door by a liveried footman who tried desperately to announce our arrival and in the process distorted our names to the point that we ourselves could not recognize them. This was a brilliant assembly, full of leaders of the Labour Party and others whom I did not know. The buffet was huge and beautifully arranged. Both Czech and I were so impressed by all the splendor that we did not dare go after the delicacies that our empty stomachs required. One of us then came up with the clever solution that, while it would be ill-mannered on our part to take and eat as much as we wanted, no rule of good behavior prevented us from offering each other as much as we desired. After that the evening became a success. I remember a long conversation with Ellen Wilkinson, the future minister of education (diminutive, but a ball of fire), and others whose names escape me.

But the most impressive aspect of the evening was the feudal style and luxurious life of Mosley. I should not have been so surprised since my old friend, Egon Wertheimer, London correspondent of the German socialist press, had written in his *Portrait of the Labour Party,* published shortly before this reception, about the first Labour Party meeting at Empire Hall that he attended:

> There was a movement in the crowd, and a young man, with the face of the ruling class in Great Britain, but the gait of Douglas Fairbanks, thrust himself forward through the throng to the platform, followed by a lady in heavy, costly furs. There stood Oswald Mosley . . . a new recruit to the Socialist movement at his first London meeting. He was introduced to the audience, and even at that time, I remember, the song "For He's a Jolly Good Fellow" greeted the young man from

two thousand throats. . . . But then came something unexpected . . .
from the audience there came calls; they grew more urgent; and
suddenly the elegant lady in furs got up from her seat, and said a few
sympathetic words. . . . "Lady Cynthia Mosley," whispered in my
ear one of the armleted stewards who stood near me, excited, and
later, as though thinking he had not sufficiently impressed me, he
added, "Lord Curzon's daughter." His whole face beamed proudly.
All round the audience was still in uproar. . . .[2]

The evening told me a good deal about the degree to which class distinc-
tions in England not only persisted but were also fully accepted by a large
part, if not the majority, of the British working class. Indeed, even members of the Labour Party who were committed to a "classless society" felt
deeply honored by a member of the upper classes taking Labour's side.

Mosley felt superior to most of the Labour leaders, especially the old
guard. There is little doubt in my mind that in his conflicts with the party
leaders (especially with Philip Snowden, the most orthodox laissez-faire
liberal in the party) Mosley was nearer the truth than the old-timers, though
even he regarded the devaluation of the pound as an unmitigated disaster.
But Mosley, who was predestined to become a future Labour prime
minister, just could not wait. His impatience led to his doom. He became
the leader of the British fascists, an outcast during and after the war.

Curiously, he appeared much later on American television, on an
interview program with William Buckley, the most articulate spokesman
for American conservatives. There Mosley presented himself not as a
fascist but as a pacifist whose main aim had been to prevent the outbreak of
hostilities between England and Nazi Germany. I regret to add that Mr.
Buckley—rightly or wrongly—gave me the impression that he did not
know enough of Sir Oswald's speeches and activities during the crucial
years prior to 1939 to be able to reveal the actual face of Mosley the fascist.

A rare participant at international gatherings, but one of great stature
and influence, was Dr. Hugh Dalton. His standing within the Labour Party
was based not only on his impressive personality and competence but also
on the impact of his students on the movement. Hugh Gaitskell and Harold
Wilson were two of his outstanding disciples. In my own life Dalton

2. Egon Wertheimer, *Portrait of the Labour Party* (London, New York: G. P. Putnam's
Sons, 1929), pp. viii–x.

played a double role: he was not only a teacher but also an advisor at a crucial moment. I saw him while I was still in the throes of deciding which way to turn once I would leave the European continent. His advice, presented in witty and comradely terms, influenced me a good deal in the decision that I finally made. I shall report it in due course. At his own level Dalton was as competitive as the rest. Indeed, even though he denied aspiring to the leadership of the party, I had little doubt from a few conversations with him that he, perhaps unconsciously, expected to see himself some day in No. 10 Downing Street.

The first time I met Dalton was at the LSI Congress in 1928. He was a kind of junior delegate of the British Labour Party and not very conspicuous in the transactions of the congress. Philip Noel-Baker, who functioned a few years later as Arthur Henderson's principal assistant at the World Disarmament Conference sponsored by the League of Nations, held the limelight with a brilliant speech about the dangers of aerial warfare—a picture of demonic beauty, as he put it. I had the privilege of interpreting his speech into German—one of the three congress languages—and I seemed to have done well, probably because I was deeply moved by the speaker's performance. My interpretation was applauded.

Dalton did not belong to the top group of the "Big Five" (MacDonald, Henderson, Thomas, Clynes, and Snowden), but he was close to "Uncle" Henderson who guided his political career until he could stand on his own legs. Thus when Henderson became foreign minister in the Labour government of 1929, Dalton was appointed undersecretary. As Henderson's biographer, Mrs. Agnes Hamilton, put it: "The combination of the long-headed Trade Unionist and the brilliant product of Eton, King's, and the London School of Economics, worked admirably. It rested on entire mutual confidence and entire agreement both as to large aims and immediate methods."[3] Such close friendships were rare among the top leaders of the party. Henderson's willingness to subordinate his ambitions to the welfare of the party, and Dalton's junior status at the time, explain how this exception to the general rule of rivalry and mutual animosity came about.

3. Mary Agnes Hamilton, *Arthur Henderson: A Biography* (London: William Heinemann, 1938), p. 288.

A highly competent economist in his own right, Dalton was full of admiration for John Maynard Keynes, whom he later (after World War II) entrusted with vital financial discussions with the U.S. Treasury. At the same time Dalton never concealed his disdain for Professor Friedrich A. von Hayek, whose *Road to Serfdom* he described as a "silly-clever" book, not only in private conversations, but also publicly in his memoirs. Had Dalton still been alive, I am sure he would have been shocked to learn that Hayek was awarded a Nobel prize for economics in 1974.

Unfortunately, it is impossible to ignore the less-than-glorious role that Dalton played in the last years of the LSI. This occurred when Hitler, taking advantage of the West's weakness, cowardice, and highly civilized desire to avoid war at any price, advanced from victory to victory, spreading panicky fear throughout Europe. Socialist parties were no less affected than governments. Having advocated disarmament during most of their history, the labor movements found it impossible to reverse course. But the most important factor in their attitude toward foreign policy was fear accompanied by the hope that by keeping quiet, they and their countries might escape the wrath of the German Führer.

The mere existence of the LSI became a source of anxiety for some of the affiliates. The LSI embodied almost everything the German dictator hated: internationalism, Jewish leadership, antifascism. Fritz Adler represented socialist internationalism more than anyone else. To get rid of him became the main objective of Adler's opponents. Although Adler was willing to retire, he wanted his successor to be someone who would keep the International alive as a policy-making body. The candidate of his opponents was Bjarne Braatoy, a Norwegian journalist who had worked for some time in the Secretariat of the LSI, but who had resigned and become a correspondent in London for several newspapers. Adler's candidate was Max Buset, a Belgian socialist of considerable repute. As a result of Léon Blum's announcement that he was authorized by the French Socialist Party to vote for Adler and no one else, a stalemate developed. Hugh Dalton, who despaired of winning the battle to oust Adler with fair methods, attacked Adler's financial management in a hardly concealed manner. A special commission appointed to examine the books of the LSI came to the unanimous conclusion that no irregularities could be found.

The paralyzing conflict continued until the German occupation of

Belgium and Paris put an end to the LSI in 1940. Adler emigrated to New York, and Hugh Dalton became chancellor of the exchequer in the postwar Labour government. In 1947 Dalton lost this highly influential job as a result of violating a rather unimportant but traditionally sacred rule of British life. On budget day, equipped with the chancellor of the exchequer's age-old briefcase containing the important draft of his forthcoming speech, Dalton, walking along the corridors of the House of Commons, revealed to a member of the press the most important fact of this speech: the income tax rate the chancellor was to propose. This enabled the journalist to "scoop" his colleagues. They in turn attacked the chancellor, who was forced to resign.

The details of British representation in the International were in the hands of a short and highly active Scotsman by the name of William Gillies. He was a member of the Fabian Society and came from Glasgow. Being an appointed official, in charge of the party's small international department, he did not have the authority of an elected representative. Nevertheless, he was more familiar with the operations of the LSI than anyone else in the party. He spoke only when none of the elected delegates from England was present, or when one of them gave him special instructions to speak.

Gillies usually attended the meetings of the smallest executive body of the LSI, the so-called Bureau of the International. This group consisted of some ten members, all but one outstanding leaders of their parties, most of which were the largest and most influential parties affiliated with the LSI. Thus the German SPD, the French Socialists, the Austrians, Belgians, and Swedes were represented by the chairmen of these parties or at least members of the respective party executives. It was a rather strange spectacle to see Gillies in the middle of a group whose outstanding members were Otto Wels, chairman of the German Social Democrats; Alexandre Bracke (a pseudonym that the French Socialist leader Desrousseaux had adopted in order not to "put to shame" his distinguished family by his Socialist Party membership); Bauer; Vandervelde; Louis de Brouckère, Belgian delegate to the League of Nations; and many others of equal stature. To their honor, it must be said that they never pulled rank on Gillies and consistently treated him as their equal.

When Henderson was a member of a Labour government, his place was taken by the veteran Belgian socialist Émile Vandervelde who was president of the LSI from 1929 to 1936. Impressive not only because of his achievements but also because of his physical stature, Vandervelde dominated the meetings until he ran into the opposition of the left-wingers in the Executive who admired Otto Bauer. Once—it was a question of reporting the discussions of the Executive to congress—the insistence of the left was so strong that Vandervelde had to draw upon his diplomatic experience as Belgian foreign minister. He gave a brief report to the full meeting of the congress and then added: "For the rest, the Executive wants you to hear also Comrade Otto Bauer to supplement my report." Another "crisis" was solved.

Vandervelde had been president of the bureau of the pre-1914 Second International. One member of the Bureau, representing the Bolshevik wing of the Russian Social Democrats, had been Lenin. I once asked Vandervelde what he had thought at that time of the future dictator of Soviet Russia. Vandervelde's answer, undoubtedly truthful, was startling: "I thought of him as a bore whose endless speeches would needlessly delay the proceedings of the Bureau. So whenever I decently could, I would look away from him so as to disregard his raised hand, whenever he asked for the floor." Many observers have noted the endless speeches characteristic of Soviet party conferences. A great speech in Russia means, it would seem, a long speech. Some of Stalin's speeches continued from one day to the next. My pet theory for this phenomenon goes back to the long years of emigration or total impotence of the Bolshevik leaders. In the absence of great deeds, they took refuge in "great" speeches.

Vandervelde's power was greatly enhanced by the support he received from the Belgian Labor Party's second in command, Louis de Brouckère. A man of high standing in his party as well as in his country, coming from a distinguished family, de Brouckère could easily have aspired to first place in the party. But there never was, to my knowledge, the slightest suspicion of jealousy or competition between him and Vandervelde. Without hesitation, de Brouckère accepted second place behind his friend and comrade. Still, even in this position he played significant roles: Belgian delegate to the League of Nations, president of the LSI from 1936 to 1939 when neither Henderson nor Vandervelde could accept that role, speaker at mass meetings, and so forth. Tall and bearded, he looked the powerful leader that he was. He survived the Nazi dictatorship, and it was a great joy for me when I met him and his daughter after World War II in Paris for an excellent lunch in an open-air restaurant. He seemed in good health even though he had lost a good deal of weight, yet he must have been quite sick at that time because he passed away shortly after this last encounter.

Paul-Henri Spaak, who later became a leader of the Belgian party, had a checkered career. He started on the extreme left of the party and, thanks to his remarkable oratorical gifts, soon became that wing's main spokesman. I came to know him fairly well since I occasionally shared a ride with him on the Avenue Louise, the most elegant thoroughfare toward the center of Brussels. On one of these trips he asked me about the status of my U.S. visa; some time before this conversation I had told him of my plan to go to the United States. One of the requirements of the American consul in Antwerp (about whom I shall have more to say later in these recollections) was possession of a passport valid for at least six months beyond the date the visa was issued. The consul was unwilling to accept my Austrian passport for reasons I shall explain. Thus things were at a stalemate, and I accordingly answered Spaak's question. To my surprise, he told me not to worry. He would undertake to get me a Belgian passport for foreigners with the desired validity. And he kept his promise when the need for the passport arose.

Spaak's later political evolution, which led him to the far right of his party and made him the dominant figure of Belgian politics, occurred after the war. By then I had no further contact with him.

Camille Huysmans, socialist mayor of Antwerp, had been secretary of the Second International prior to 1914. Although he was still an influential member of his party, he played no significant role in the International after 1923. He was an elder statesman whose advice was occasionally sought by party colleagues (and whose assistance was greatly appreciated by my brother and his family when they fled Nazi-occupied Vienna), but beyond this he did not aspire to any national or international office.

Germany, of course, played an important role in the LSI: next to the British Labour Party, the SPD (Sozialdemokratische Partei Deutschlands, German Social Democratic Party) was the largest contingent. For historic reasons the party from 1932 to 1933 had three chairmen, two representing the dominant wing (the former "patriotic" majority) and the third representing the remnants of the Independent Social Democrats.

The first grouping emerged from the so-called Majority Socialists. Their left-wing opponents within the party called them "social patriots" since they had supported the Vaterland during World War I. The opponents finally broke away over the issue of support for the war and in 1917 established the Independent Social Democratic Party (in German, USPD). This rapidly growing party was split in 1920 over the issue of affiliation with the Communist International. The USPD majority joined the Communist Party of Germany (KPD) after the Halle Congress of October 1920. A minority led by Rudolf Hilferding retained until 1922 the identity of the USPD until it felt compelled to rejoin the Majority Socialists of the SPD.

In view of the relative strength of the two wings in the SPD the Majority Socialists provided two chairmen of the united party (Hermann Müller and Otto Wels), and the former Independents one (Artur Crispien). Given both the power relationship of the two partners in the merger and the personality of Crispien, he counted for very little in the decisions of the reconstituted SPD. The political leadership was in the hands of Hermann Müller, often referred to as Müller-Franken to designate the place of his origin and to distinguish him from the vast throng with whom he shared his name. The undisputed head of the huge organization of the party was Otto Wels. Müller was chancellor after the successful elections of 1928, though without parliamentary majority and therefore head of a coalition government in which Hilferding was minister of finance. Müller was a solid man, reliable and decent, but without any charisma. He spoke well but without inspiration. There was no rivalry between him and Wels.

Otto Wels came from the working class, and while conscious of his status as leader of the largest German party and successor of August Bebel and Friedrich Ebert, he was also aware of the limitations that his lack of a higher education imposed upon him in degree-conscious Germany. He regarded it as his main duty to keep the party in line behind Müller. In the LSI, Wels was the top representative of the SPD and as such had influence and deserved respect.

Unfortunately Otto Bauer, the main spokesman of the Austrian party, was not always aware of the need to treat Wels according to his status. I remember an incident in an Executive meeting of the LSI where by chance the two sat side by side. Bauer spoke in hardly concealed criticism of the German party. Wels interrupted him with a brief interjection. Bauer responded with a gesture of his hand similar to the motion with which one removes a nasty fly. Wels did not react except with a facial expression that indicated fury. Bauer's genius did not always extend to the area of human relations. He could be kind to young people of whom he expected future relations. Thus he steered me toward literature about the United States, giving me my first acquaintances with the country destined to be my home for the greater part of my life. But in his relations with equals—in status though rarely in intellectual power—he could be disdainful to the point of being cruel.

The idea men in the SPD were Rudolf Hilferding, the ex-Austrian who had applied Marxian thought to monopolistic market situations, and Rudolf Breitscheid, the chairman of the parliamentary group and main foreign affairs spokesman of the party. Hilferding, in his youth, was notoriously lazy. Viktor Adler sought out young men of promise and guided them in their work and development. Hilferding was one of Adler's protégés. While unwilling to sit at a desk and write books, Hilferding loved to talk. He was the ideal guest of a Viennese coffeehouse where according to local mores you could sit for hours with one cup of coffee and hold forth to friends or even strangers. It was in such a place that Hilferding began to develop the ideas enshrined in his major work, *Das Finanzkapital*, but at that time nothing had been put down on paper. After all attempts at persuasion had failed, Viktor Adler used the strongest weapon at his disposal. He ordered all friends of Hilferding to engage in a "conspiracy of silence"; that is, to refuse to converse with Hilferding in a café until he had finished the manuscript of his book. Driven to desperation, Hilferding capitulated and wrote the book that brought him international fame. Indeed, his prestige was so high that upon his move to Germany, he was disappointed not to be offered leadership of the SPD. Still, his influence in the party was undisputed—at least until the Great Depression of the thirties.

I had the privilege of being treated as a specially favored interlocutor of Hilferding, perhaps because I limited my own contributions to our discussions to such remarks as "Why?" "How?" "Interesting." Two minor incidents may illustrate this peculiar relationship. Hilferding, then

German Minister of Finance, was on a trip from Zürich to Geneva, where he had visited his friend Adler and a Zürich banker with whom he maintained personal and professional contacts. In Geneva he was to act as official German delegate to an international conference. I was sent to the same conference as observer for the LSI. Hilferding traveled, of course, in a first-class compartment, while I sat modestly in third class. A few minutes after the train's departure from Zürich, Hilferding appeared in my compartment, sat down, and stayed until we reached Geneva, engrossed in one of his typical but always interesting conversations. He needed listeners as other people need their daily bread.

This and many similar incidents produced, of course, a special relationship between the great man and me. One demonstration of this occurred during the same Geneva conference. I was invited to a party of a high functionary in the League of Nations where a dispute arose about the German attitude toward some issue that I do not remember any more. I suggested that the simplest solution to our "problem" was to phone Hilferding at the official residence of the German delegation, the Hotel Metropol. My proposal was received with general laughter since Hilferding was notoriously difficult to reach and even more unwilling to answer questions. Undisturbed by the skeptics, I went to the phone, reached Hilferding and got the desired answer—to the embarrassed and admiring silence of the assembled guests. My prestige has never been higher since. "This is the man who can talk to Hilferding any time," people would say, pointing me out, my fame acquired by my ability to listen.

One of Hilferding's weaknesses was his desire for a "good life." His second wife was a German society lady and, while not luxurious, his style of life grew better and better as he got older. He was not corrupt in any sense of the word, but as Otto Bauer once put it: "You remember, Rudolf's *Schnitzel* always had to be big."

My relationship to the SPD was friendly, but nothing prepared me for a surprise I had in early 1930 during a meeting of the International Executive in Zürich. Germany was represented by former chancellor Müller, Otto Wels, and Rudolf Breitscheid. One afternoon when the meeting ended a bit earlier than usual, the three of them asked me to join them at a café on the Limmat. Not suspecting anything of major importance behind the invitation, I gladly accepted. Since the weather was favorable, we sat at an outside table and had a pleasant conversation, which was suddenly interrupted by Hermann Müller's question: "How would you like to come and work for us?" My startled reply was, of course: "What do you want me to do?"

It appeared that the place for me had been carefully discussed among the three partners. In order to get my name known in Germany, I was to start as a special correspondent for the press service which the SPD maintained on a daily basis for its nearly two hundred daily newspapers (some being just local versions of a more central paper in the region). I would go to places of special interest which I was to select, and report from there, in addition to the regular correspondent whom the press service already maintained. My reports would be published under my name, which would establish what pollsters in the United States call "name recognition." Then, after two or three years of this, I would be ready for election to the Reichstag. I would serve as an additional spokesman for international affairs, substituting for Breitscheid when appropriate. And beyond that, an entirely new future seemed to be waiting for me.

I was taken aback by this sudden offer and asked for some time to think it over. Adler, with whom I discussed the matter, seemed to think the offer was surely worth considering. So I did—until the elections in September of that year (1930), with the gigantic Nazi advance, brought an end to these speculations as suddenly as they had arisen.

The younger generation of SPD leaders, whose role was still far in the future, was represented by three young men: Erich Ollenhauer, leader of the socialist youth, and Fritz Heine and Alfred Nau, both employees of the party Executive but clearly destined for higher office. They were close friends and, I believe, also friendly toward me. One early recollection I have is of two of them arriving in Zürich in 1933 in one of the party automobiles—then a rare and costly possession—in order to save it from immediate Nazi confiscation.

Another significant incident concerns Fritz Heine and took place at a French party conference shortly after the war. This was still a period in which the specter of "collective guilt" dominated the thinking of even many socialists in the formerly Nazi-occupied countries. It was painful for me to see Heine sitting alone on a bench in the conference hall as if he were an outcast. I knew, of course, that he had never been a Nazi or a Nazi supporter and, not being a believer in "collective guilt," I ostentatiously sat down next to him without even thinking about what others might feel. I am not sure whether he was aware of the symbolic meaning of my gesture, and I doubt that, even if he was, he remembers it. For me it was a necessary step.

I was aware that tensions developed between Adler and the SOPADE (the name of the SPD Executive in exile). The issue was mainly, though not exclusively, the relationship of both SOPADE and the International with a newly formed group called "New Beginning." Its founder was an unknown German businessman and political activist by the name of Walter Löwenheim, son of a Jewish merchant in Berlin, born in 1896. Around the end of 1933, the first year of the Nazi regime, he published a small pamphlet under the pseudonym Miles. The title was *New Beginning,* a name that was soon attached to a movement in Germany and abroad directed against the Nazis, which was critical of both the SPD leadership and the Communists. His pamphlet was first published in Czechoslovakia in the German language but was soon translated into a large number of foreign languages: English, French, Czech, and Yiddish. The author claimed to represent an active anti-Nazi underground group in Germany. I remember that the *Manchester Guardian* asked its distinguished Berlin correspondent F. A. Voigt, himself of German ancestry, to investigate. His reports gave a fascinating picture of "underground" work and greatly contributed to the prestige of Miles and "New Beginning." Perhaps Miles's main claim to glory was that he started work on his underground network in 1929 while all anti-Nazi political parties in Germany were still living in a world of fantasy. Equally remarkable was his absolute rejection of Soviet totalitarianism, which he dared to compare with the Italian and the early stages of German fascism. Until 1927 he had been a member of the Communist Party.

Miles established connections in Zürich with the LSI, with Vandervelde, and with my publisher Emil Oprecht, whose important role in the anti-Nazi struggle has so far not found its deserved recognition. I shall come back to him.

Unfortunately, Miles's influence was greatly impaired by a split in his group over his prediction that the end of Nazism could not be brought about by internal forces alone, but would result from a lost war. In this internal dispute secrets were either betrayed or revealed by neglect—factional disputes make it difficult to establish the truth—and Miles himself left Germany in 1935. "New Beginning" from then on was essentially an organization in exile. Löwenheim, who had adopted the Anglicized name of Walter Lowe, died in England in 1977.

Since "New Beginning" claimed a portion of the financial resources of the SPD abroad, a conflict became inevitable, and Adler was drawn into it. As is usual in such situations, he was unable to satisfy either side. SOPADE, in particular, was unhappy with his role in the dispute.

Among the French delegates Léon Blum was, of course, the outstanding personality. He was a distinguished man of letters, a member of the Conseil d'État, a kind of Supreme Court in administrative matters. In addition he was the undisputed leader of his party, the SFIO, which he led from near-oblivion to remarkable success and ultimate failure.

During World War I the patriotic wing of the SFIO under Albert Thomas and Pierre Renaudel gradually lost control of the party to a group led by Marx's son-in-law Jean Longuet; this group was dedicated to a peace without annexation or compensation. Blum maintained a compromise position in order to maintain party unity. The SFIO left the Second (Socialist) International, which in fact had ceased to function after the outbreak of the war. After 1917 a pro-Bolshevik trend emerged. When the Communist International was created in 1919, a strong group under Marcel Cachin, Ludovic-Oscar Frossard, and Albert Treint favored joining the Moscow organization. Blum and Renaudel united to oppose this step.

By then the left wing had obtained control of the party. At the Congress in Tours in 1920, on the basis of a report by Cachin and Frossard who had visited Moscow on behalf of the party, the great majority of the congress voted in favor of joining the Comintern. Blum emerged as the leader of the opposition and, after the party split, as one of the main spokesmen (together with Sembat, Bracke, and Renaudel) of the reconstituted Socialist Party. His main argument was that France was not ready for social transformation even if the left were to obtain political power by a revolution. Under his inspiration the reconstituted Socialist Party—far smaller than the Communists, but rapidly growing—joined Adler's Viennese International, which took an intermediary position between the reorganized Second International on the right and the revolutionary Third

International. Facetiously, it was called "International Two-and-a-Half."
When the merger between the Viennese International and the Second
International occurred in Hamburg in 1923, Blum became the main
spokesman of his party on the international scene.

It may be quite interesting to observe the political evolution of some
of these people. Cachin had been one of the leading "social patriots," a
supporter of the war against Imperial Germany. Indeed, it was he who
acted as an agent of the French General Staff in transmitting funds to
Benito Mussolini, the former Italian socialist, who during the war turned
into the leading advocate of Italy's entrance into the war against Germany
and Austria-Hungary. The funds were to establish a newspaper, *Il Popolo
d'Italia,* popularizing Mussolini's new stance. Having served the General
Staff, Cachin after 1917 became an admirer of Lenin and the chief advocate of the French Socialist Party's joining the newly established Third
(Communist) International. Ludovic-Oscar Frossard shared Cachin's attitude toward Moscow but left the Communist Party in 1923. From then on
he moved toward the right as did so many other former Communists. He
rejoined the Socialist Party, became editor of a highly successful moderate
newspaper, and ended his political career as a "sound conservative" and
member of the Pétain government—the government of capitulation
formed in 1940.

To find Blum and Renaudel on the same side was quite a surprise.
They were united, however, in their admiration for Jean Jaurès, the
socialist leader who was assassinated shortly before the outbreak of World
War I; they shared his unreserved dedication to democracy. Blum's other
teacher had been Lucien Herr, the librarian of the famous École Normale,
who earlier had converted Jaurès to socialism. But Blum's political career
did not start in earnest until the Dreyfus affair; he joined the socialist
movement out of a desire for justice. During the war Blum maintained a
compromise position. It was in the name of unity that he entered political
life wholeheartedly and became a member of Parliament for the first time
late in 1919. My acquaintance with him goes back to his work in the LSI
after I joined its Secretariat in January 1926.

Blum was not the orator to inspire great passion in a mass audience.
His speeches were well organized, clearly presented, almost delicate, and
appealed to the reasoning power rather than sentiments of his audience.

Jean Zyromski, who represented the left wing of the French party in the Executive of the LSI, was the exact opposite: a mass orator and rabble-rouser who manipulated his audience rather than convincing it by the logic of his arguments. Alexandre Bracke, the third representative of the French, rarely spoke. When he did, he was usually closer to Blum than to Zyromski: quiet and reasonable in his argumentation. When I saw him at a party congress in Paris after World War II, he shocked me by his reference to the mass of delegates: "More than half of them were collaborators with the Nazis, now they are all heroes of the Resistance."

Blum's decisive weakness was his inability to adjust to changing circumstances. The Hitler phenomenon was totally incomprehensible to him. Even though he had encountered and combated reactionaries and anti-Semites all his political life, or perhaps because he had, he fitted Hitler into the same category as Maurice Barrès and other French reactionaries. The monstrosity of the German phenomenon escaped him. Only gradually, beginning perhaps in 1935, did he admit that Germany's rearmament might force the party to reconsider its opposition to rearmament. Still, the contradiction between the desire to oppose aggression and the wish to abstain from action remained. Much later, after the war, he stated that the vote against military credits while Hitler was rearming stemmed from tradition, or even amounted to hypocrisy. That it merely bought a delay and thereby permitted Hitler to rearm even more thoroughly did not enter his mind.

The humanitarian ideas that dominated Blum's decisions emerged most clearly and with the most devastating effects when the Spanish Civil War broke out. He was fully aware that German and Italian intervention on Franco's side, as well as the international legal situation, permitted France to supply the legitimate government of Spain, i.e., the Republican government under José Giral, with weapons for its defense and survival. He was also made aware of the British Conservative government's refusal—with Winston Churchill's approval—to assist the Spanish Republicans. If France were to act, it would have to act alone. But the great majority of the French people opposed assistance. For the conservatives, even for many of the radicals that were represented in Blum's government, Franco was the lesser evil—if evil he was in their eyes—than the Spanish government which they identified with Moscow. His refusal to assist the Republican government of Spain, he openly admitted, gave him a mixed feeling of both shame and satisfaction, the latter because it kept France out of a conflict with Nazi Germany. Blum capitulated in the belief that peace at any price was preferable to war. In the end he had to accept war under far worse circumstances.

For me, the nonintervention policy meant that World War II was inevitable: if not at that time, then soon. I left the Secretariat of the LSI in 1936 and decided to apply for an immigration visa to the United States.

The last time I saw Blum was after World War II and his return from a Nazi camp. I happened to get to Paris on the day when a Socialist Party congress was taking place. My first impression was that the party had been taken over by new people; there was hardly anyone whom I knew. I was pleasantly surprised to see Bracke, who did not seem to have aged appreciably. He expressed his distrust for the "newcomers" who joined a government party for a variety of reasons, not all of which he regarded as legitimate. He took me to meet Blum who embraced me in front of the congress. I could hear the buzz of curious voices: "Who is he?" A brief conversation with Blum and then good-bye.

Italian Antifascists

I had occasion to become acquainted with some of the most distinguished spokesmen of the Italian antifascist movement, and played a small part in their survival or at least their escape from Italy after Mussolini's rise to power. The assassination of socialist deputy Giacomo Matteotti, on June 10, 1924, accelerated a trend which two years later led to the establishment of a totalitarian dictatorship. Compared to the wholesale slaughter during Hitler's regime a decade later, or to Stalin's terror, this was probably a fairly mild system of violence, but it was sufficiently effective to prevent the socialists from operating openly. Most of their leaders felt that their freedom was endangered, if not their very lives. They fled from Italy to more hospitable lands. One of my assignments was to assist them in their flight.

The actual organization of the escape was in the hands of an Italian-Swiss trade unionist, Valerio Agostinone, then secretary of the Camera del Lavoro (trade union city federation) of Lugano, Switzerland. Agostinone turned for help to the rather numerous professional smugglers who trafficked in tobacco and sugar between Switzerland and Italy. At one point, in Ponte Tresa, the border between the two countries was the small Tresa River running into the Lake of Lugano. The river was hardly 100 feet wide and was easily crossed, particularly when the water level was low. Passage by smugglers and political refugees across it was so easy that the fascist authorities felt compelled to erect an electrically charged fence, decorated with numerous little bells, along the river. That still left a passage across the mountains along the lake, where at night the smugglers came and went with rarely any disturbance from police forces.

For a modest fee, some of the smugglers were quite willing to take political refugees across the border. Once in Lugano, on the Swiss side of the border, Agostinone provided the refugees with the money and the information necessary to reach us. A fair number of socialist leaders from Italy thus passed through our offices to be sent on to their next destination. In most cases this was Paris, which offered hospitality and considerable freedom of expression to Italian refugees because a coalition of radicals and socialists formed the core of the governmental majority in the French Parliament at the time. So many Italians lived in France—by no means all of them political refugees—that a strongly antifascist Italian-language newspaper, the *Corriere degli Italiani,* was published in Paris; this greatly disturbed Mussolini. His protests were to no avail because the French government protected the publication.

Paris thus became the haven to which most of the Italian antifascist refugees flocked. One of the first I sent on his way was the socialist deputy Claudio Treves. He had forwarded some money to Switzerland for safe-keeping, which he withdrew while in Zürich. I remember the conspir-atorial way in which this transaction was carried out. We went together to the small private bank guarding his money. Treves presented a portion of a visiting card which had been cut with ragged edges, in an irregular pattern. The banker had the missing cardboard piece to be fitted to the one Treves presented. This served as identification, and Treves left the office with his money.

Transporting the refugees to France presented some difficulty because none of them, as known opponents of the fascist regime, had a valid Italian passport. A Swiss citizen of Russian origin, whose business quite often took him to France in his car, came to our rescue. He was so well known at the Franco-Swiss frontier that the officials on both sides never bothered to stop his car when he crossed the border. Once in France, the refugees could count upon the French authorities to grant them the necessary permits to reside and work in France and even to engage in political activities, something the Swiss authorities would never have dared to do— partly to protect their neutrality as they interpreted it, partly out of fear of their stronger and rather aggressive neighbor.

The arrival of Pietro Nenni stands out in my memory. He was one of the most interesting figures of the Italian antifascist movement. Originally a member of the Republican Party, Nenni switched to the Socialists and became one of the outstanding leaders of the left wing of the party, but a sharp critic of the Communists. A personal friend of his had been Benito Mussolini, who had belonged to the same group in the Socialist Party during the pre-World-War-I era. After Mussolini changed his views so radically, Pietro Nenni was no longer his friend and associate. Indeed, when Mussolini came to power Nenni had good reason to fear for his life, or at least for his freedom. And so he set out on his long journey into exile.

Nenni, too, crossed the mountains in the company of smugglers and then came to see me in Zürich. I still remember his visit. He wore elegant black-and-white shoes. Nothing in his appearance would have indicated that he had engaged in a nocturnal mountaineering expedition. He went on to Paris where he soon became a very active leader of the non-Communist antifascists. Giuseppe Modigliani, a relative of the famous painter, came too, distinguished not only by his impressive beard but also by his resolute antiwar activities in which Lenin and his associates had been involved. Independently from all of them, the foremost leader of the Italian Socialists, Filippo Turati, left Italy in secret—by means of a boat—and formed the center of the antifascist movement headquartered in France. Italian workers abroad and the growing number of antifascist refugees provided a sufficient core of members.

A special refugee case was that of Giuseppe Saragat, then a young bank clerk active in socialist politics. He arrived in Zürich by the same mountain-crossing route that Nenni and others had used, but instead of going on to France, he was headed for Vienna. It seems that the Italian bank for which he worked had an affiliate in Vienna, and arrangements had been made for Saragat to get a job there. This was good news, since the financial burden created by the arrival in France of unemployed and often almost unemployable refugees—who did not know the French language—was growing by leaps and bounds. Here at long last was one who could take care of himself, provided that we could get him to Vienna. Since Saragat, too, had no passport of any kind, this presented a little problem.

Fortunately, our influence with the government authorities in Vienna at this time was still very strong, even though the Austrian Social Democratic Party was in opposition to the conservative government of Monsignor Ignaz Seipel. The issuance of passports was at least partly controlled by the then police president of Vienna, Johannes Schober, with whom the party maintained reasonably good relations. The party official in charge of the liaison with Schober was Karl Heinz, the secretary general of the Republican Defense Corps, who later died in exile in California. I thus turned to Heinz by telephone on Saragat's behalf. A few days later Saragat and I went to see the Austrian consul general in Zürich to get the precious document. The consul was most accommodating and started filling out the necessary forms until he reached the crucial question of nationality. Saragat responded that he was an Italian citizen. "Then why do you expect to get an Austrian passport?", the surprised consul asked. I intervened: "Did you not yet get instructions regarding Signor Saragat from Vienna?" The consul checked, looked at the day's mail, but found no message. "In that case," I said, "we shall come back in a few days." Indeed, three or four days later I had a phone call from the highly bewildered consul, informing me that he had received the extraordinary order to hand over a valid Austrian passport to the Italian citizen Giuseppe Saragat.

Thus equipped, Saragat went off to Vienna and his job. He did not stay there very long, for he too was called to Paris to help edit the Italian émigré paper published there. This was to be the beginning of a distinguished political career which much later led Saragat to the presidency of post-Mussolini Italy.

Another distinguished Italian whom I met at the time, even though he did not need assistance, was Ignazio Silone (real name: Secondo Tranquilli), then just at the threshold of his great literary fame and fortune. Between 1930 and 1945, as a literary critic recently pointed out, Giuseppe Antonio Borgese (who emigrated to the United States in 1933) and Silone (who went to Switzerland) were the only major Italian writers who lived in exile so that their works could be published and reach a wider audience. The others, Alberto Moravia, Vitaliano Brancati, and Cesare Pavese, stayed "in exile" in Italy: they were forbidden to write or publish or were sent to supervised villages—the Italian counterpart of czarist banishment to Siberia. Silone had been one of the founders of the Italian Communist Party at the Congress of Livorno in 1921, was a member of its Central Committee, and represented the party on various occasions in Moscow. There he encountered the great men who led the Bolshevik revolution: Lenin, Trotsky, Bukharin, Zinoviev, and Stalin. It was a clash with Stalin in 1927 that led Silone to withdraw from the party. At a meeting in Moscow Stalin asked the foreign delegates, among them Silone, to condemn a letter Trotsky had addressed to the meeting, but which Stalin refused to submit to the participants. While Silone and Palmiro Togliatti, the leader of the Italian Communists, protested, the other delegates agreed to Stalin's outrageous demand: to condemn a letter that no one had even seen. This was the last push needed to induce Silone to turn away from the party. The official expulsion followed in 1931. By that time Silone and his wife lived in Zürich, in a small pension belonging to a Russian who had long before emigrated to Switzerland. My office being just across the street, I regularly ate luncheon in the pension and met Silone and his wife, with whom I conversed rather freely without knowing of Silone's Communist past.

What tied us together was not only the pension, but also a common publisher. My first major book—*Die grosse Krise (The Great Crisis)*, on the Great Depression—was published by Emil Oprecht, a publisher in Zürich who was head of the Europa Verlag (which still exists). Silone's *Fontamara, Bread and Wine,* and other writings appeared first in German translations in Oprecht's publishing house before beginning their phenomenal sales around the world. It is perhaps interesting to note that Silone's stature in liberated Italy, to which he returned after World War II, has not equaled the fame he enjoyed abroad. Although his later books were published in Italian by the Mondadori publishing house, he did not belong to the circles, nor write in the periodicals, which dominate Italian literature. To the literary hierarchy, predominantly Communist in its orientation, he remains an outcast, a renegade, even though the official party leadership asserts time and again its independence from Moscow and especially from the Stalinist past against which Silone rebelled. The postwar literary style that appealed to the Italian public is neorealistic and documentary, different from Silone's novels published in the 1950s. It seems to have been Silone's fate never to fit into the mold that prevailed at any given time.

Emil Oprecht, our common publisher, exerted a major influence on the antifascist and later the anti-Nazi movement. He was by far the most important publisher of German-language books outside Nazi or Austro-fascist control during the long dark night that descended upon the European continent. His bookstore and his home became the social centers for all of Hitler's opponents who managed to reach Zürich. Oprecht and his wife, Emmy, were helpful in arranging innumerable details of life for the refugees, from food and clothing to assistance with the Swiss authorities. The latter were not too happy about the influx of men and women whom the powerful neighbors to the north and to the south regarded as arch-enemies. Still more important was the possibility which Emil Oprecht's Europa Verlag provided for the émigrés to carry on their literary work. Oprecht founded this publishing house with Kurt Düby, later federal judge, and Friedrich Heeb, the father of Solzhenitsyn's Swiss lawyer. Thomas Mann; Hermann Rauschning, a German conservative opponent of Hitler; Konrad Heiden, the first and most brilliant biographer of Hitler; and many others found Oprecht receptive to their manuscripts, even when outlets for German-language anti-Nazi books were highly limited and the publishing house had permanent financial and political difficulties.

During the war Oprecht was to play a different but equally important role in the anti-Nazi struggle. Allen Dulles, head of the American intelligence service in Switzerland, met Oprecht shortly after his arrival in the country. Both Dulles and Elizabeth Wiskemann, a distinguished British historian who headed the intelligence section in the British Embassy in Berne during the war, took advantage of Oprecht's far-flung network of acquaintances among refugees to obtain contacts and information of value to the Allies. Dulles also regularly met the Swiss intelligence officer Major Hans Hausamann in Oprecht's house on the Hirschengraben in Zürich, just across the street from the offices of the German Consulate General. This was also the location of Allen Dulles's secret negotiations concerning surrender of the German armies in Italy. Indeed, Dulles used Oprecht's home as his headquarters in Zürich.

My own modest antifascist activities were the cause of a somewhat amusing little incident in my life. Unbeknownst to me, my name appeared—with all details about my father's name, my date of birth, residence, and so forth—on the ill-famed "black list" of the Italian government. Whether my assistance to Treves, Nenni, Saragat, and others had become known to the Italian government and whether this was the cause of

my being enshrined on that list of honor, I do not know. My own guess is
that it was quite a different fact that brought me to the attention of the
fascist authorities.

Margherita Sarfatti, Mussolini's mistress at that time, had published a
book about her hero. A Swiss magazine of no earth-shattering significance
asked me to review it. I undertook to do so, paying less attention to
whatever literary merits the book may or may not have possessed than to
the political views and misdeeds of its subject. It is not unfair to point out
that I was biased in my judgment, and my review was very critical and
negative. Undoubtedly, given the periodical's small circulation, its impact
upon a wider public was likely to be insignificant. However, the newspaper of the Italian antifascist émigrés in Paris, *Corriere degli Italiani,* got
hold of the magazine, translated my review into Italian, and published it.
Published it, that is, on its front page. This, of course, could not escape the
attention of the secret police in Rome, and since my article was signed, the
author, if not known before to Mussolini's agents, was surely no longer
unknown to them.

In my innocence I never thought about this connection which tied
Zürich to Paris and Paris to Rome. The Rome secret police kept a "black
list" of names of persons whose presence on Italian soil was regarded by
the fascist officials as highly undesirable. I knew of the existence of the
list, but it never occurred to me that I could be regarded as important
enough to appear on it. Rather unexpectedly I was made aware of my
error.

One day in September, shortly before the League of Nations Assembly was to meet in Geneva, I found myself on a brief vacation in the
Ticino, the southernmost, Italian-speaking canton of Switzerland. A message reached me from my office in Zürich instructing me to go to Geneva
and arrange a meeting of the socialist members of the various national
delegations to the League meeting. There were two ways to go from
Locarno to Geneva; one meant taking the Centovalli train, which crossed a
brief Italian tongue of land around Domodossola and returned to Swiss
territory; the other meant going north by train to Lucerne and then west to
Geneva, a far longer route but entirely inside Swiss territory. Without
hesitation I chose the first of the alternatives.

Shortly after the train (really a glorified streetcar which leads through the Centovalli) had crossed the Italian border, Italian officials appeared and collected the passports of all the passengers. A while later, after the train had gone about one-third of the way across the Italian insert, the same officials returned and distributed the passports to their rightful owners—all except mine. Mine remained firmly in the hands of the passport officer who quietly stayed in the middle of the car. I waited for a while, still without suspicion, and then got out of my seat, approached the dignitary and claimed my travel document. Suddenly coming alive, he asked me to pick up my luggage and follow him. He took me into another car where a compartment was apparently reserved for the use of the control officials. Two of them accompanied me into the compartment; two *bersaglieri* in their theatrical uniforms, with a coat draped over their shoulders and long feathers on their hats, took up positions at the door: one inside, one outside the compartment. I was searched, with special attention focused on my fountain pen. No secret weapons were found, for the simple reason that I did not possess any—and if I had had any, I would not have known how to use them.

The failure to find anything incriminating on my person and in my luggage started a rapid-fire discussion in Italian among the dignitaries. It resulted in their handing me the infamous black list. They pointed at my name: there it was, correctly spelled, with my birth date and birthplace, even the names of my parents. Apparently they expected a much more dangerous-looking man and could not quite make up their minds whether I, looking far younger than my age and rather harmless, could really be the suspicious character that would belong on that list of "enemies of the state." So they proceeded to ask me for my opinion. I did not think that I was under any obligation, legal or moral, to assist them in their work, and simply refused to answer. "This is your job, not mine." This set off another rapid-fire exchange of words among the dignitaries, in an Italian dialect which I could only partly follow. The conclusion, however, was perfectly comprehensible. *È lui, è lui* ("it is he, it is he").

While this was going on, the train had moved on and was by then about halfway across the Italian territory, on the way to the safe borders of Switzerland. I ventured to suggest to the representatives of Italian sovereignty that under the circumstances, if I were to be refused admission, they might as well expel me in the direction in which I intended to travel.

This proposal, perfectly reasonable though it seemed to me, met with an instantaneous refusal and within a few minutes the police officers had stopped the train in the midst of nowhere, simply by pulling the emergency brake. Accompanied by one of the civilians and the two martial-looking *bersaglieri*, I found myself standing next to the track while the train, gathering speed, went gaily on toward the Swiss border, free of the dangerous freight it had been carrying a few minutes before.

Soon, a train running in the opposite direction (back to Locarno) appeared on the horizon and was promptly stopped by hand signals from my escort. All four of us stepped onto the train, the civilian sitting next to me and the two *bersaglieri* standing guard outside the compartment door.

A rather bizarre conversation in a mixture of French and Italian developed between my companion and myself, soon after the train had resumed its journey toward Locarno. "You understand, don't you," said my guardian, "that I have nothing against you." "Of course," I responded, pretending not to understand the double meaning of the conversation. "After all, a few minutes ago, you did not know me at all. Why should you be personally hostile?" To which my neighbor reacted, "You don't understand. What I mean is, I personally do not object to you!" I was in a quandary. This could be a barely concealed intimation that at the bottom of his heart he was on my side. More probably, it was just a ploy to get me to talk and possibly reveal some secret. Unfortunately for my talkative neighbor, I not only had no particular secrets to reveal, but I also felt that it was wise to remain uncommunicative. I pretended not to understand, and he finally gave up, complaining that I just did not understand him. To this day, I do not know what the little incident really meant, but my guess is still that an attempt was being made to obtain some interesting information from me—interesting, that is, for the fascist police.

My expulsion was duly reported in the newspapers, protested by the Association of Journalists accredited with the League of Nations, and no further action was taken by anyone. I traveled the "long way" on to Geneva.

Stalin's Trials

One of the most curious incidents during my work at the headquarters of the Socialist International involved me in the terrorist aspects of Stalin's regime. Beginning in June 1928 the Soviet dictator organized a series of trials with a double purpose. One was to throw responsibility for the terrible deprivations, which the hothouse industrialization of the country imposed upon the Russian people, upon saboteurs—real or alleged—rather than upon the regime itself. Stalin, Lenin's successor, had as his second objective the elimination of all of his great predecessor's friends and associates: potential rivals for ultimate power in the vast country.

Thus in June 1928 fifty-three defendants, mostly engineers and technicians in the Shakhty district of the Donbass basin, were put on trial for "economic counterrevolution." They were accused of having formed "the Counterrevolutionary Organization of Engineers in the Coal Industry of the Soviet Union," which allegedly had a "Charkov center" and a "Moscow center." Eleven defendants were sentenced to death, five were actually executed, and more than 130 years of prison were imposed. Then, toward the end of 1930, eight high officials of the economic administration, headed by Professor Ramzin, were charged with "sabotage." They were supposed to have founded a "Union of Engineers' Organizations," which was described in the indictment as an "Industrial Party"—whatever that was supposed to indicate. Although five defendants were sentenced to death, all were, in the end, simply imprisoned. Another trial in this series was the one in which I was to play a modest but not negligible role. It opened my eyes to the possibilities of abuse that absolute power offered, and also to the possibility that even all-powerful men can stumble over minor errors. In a sense I was such an error, or at least a witness to an error of some historic significance.

In the so-called "Menshevik trial" of March 1931 fourteen defendants stood before the court. They were accused of forming an "All-Union Bureau" engaged in a conspiracy to overthrow the Bolshevik regime and assassinate Stalin and some of his associates in the Politburo. Prior to World War I the Mensheviks, a wing of the Russian Social Democratic Party, had split with the Bolsheviks, partly over the issue of a minority dictatorship which the Mensheviks rejected in favor of the democratic strategy pursued by the German Social Democratic Party. Stalin's vendetta was carried on with special bitterness and with no regard for the most elementary requirements of truth or justice.

There were many common features in all these trials. For instance, in all of them the evidence consisted merely of the confessions of the defendants, without any other proof of their guilt. The confessions were usually couched in extravagant language such as: "We are all counterrevolutionary murderers and deserve nothing better than death." It was difficult not to be suspicious of the methods by which such dramatic self-denigrations were obtained during the long period of investigation and incarceration that preceded the trial. What threats against the lives of family members, what forms of physical or psychological torture were used to induce upright men to make such confessions? We do not know, but in at least one case—and, later, in another one—we could easily ascertain that the confessions were untrue. The Moscow prosecutors—perhaps poorly trained when compared with the subsequent Nazi prosecutors—extorted false, fabricated confessions from the defendants. I cannot assert this with certainty as to the first two trials which I mentioned, but I can bear witness in the Menshevik trial.

In that case a clandestine visit, or rather the alleged visit of the distinguished Menshevik leader Raphael Abramovitch to the Soviet Union, was the central piece of evidence in the trial. As usual, the defendants made full confessions of their sins, the principal one being their meetings and conversations with Abramovitch in Russia in August 1928. Abramovitch himself was not among the defendants. Indeed, he could not be, since he had not been arrested. And he could not be arrested since he had not set foot on Soviet soil for many years, especially not during the crucial days of August 1928.

What the Soviet prosecutors had overlooked—an unforgivable technical error—was that precisely at the time of the alleged meetings with the defendants in Russia, Abramovitch was in Brussels. He attended meetings of the International Socialist Bureau as the official representative of the Menshevik Party, and following these meetings he attended the sessions of the International Socialist Congress which were also held in Brussels. Since I kept the records of the attendance and the discussions at the International Socialist Bureau, I was in an excellent position to testify that Abramovitch, whom I had known very well for several years, had been sitting opposite me in Brussels and could not at the same time and on the same day have engaged in any kind of conspiracy and oral discussions with anyone in the Soviet Union. Not even jet planes, had they then existed, could have made possible this kind of miracle.

Moreover, there is a photograph: part of a large picture taken of the delegates present at the International Socialist Congress in Brussels in August 1928. The front row shows the delegates Vliegen from Holland; Jean Longuet, representing France; Alexandre Bracke, the veteran socialist leader from France; Émile Vandervelde, former Belgian foreign minister; Friedrich Adler, the secretary of the Social International; Arthur Henderson, due to become the British foreign minister the next year; the Belgian Joseph van Roosbroeck, the treasurer of the International; and Filippo Turati, the veteran Italian socialist leader. And between Vandervelde and Adler there appears quite unmistakably, in the second row, the head of Abramovitch. The testimony of the defendants in the trial against the Mensheviks was pure invention and by poor workmanship or negligence the prosecutors had selected a date for the meeting in Russia which allowed hundreds of congress participants, and thousands of readers of the congress report with its photograph, to ascertain the falsehood of both accusations and confessions.

It might be of some interest to the reader to know that this trial was followed by others of the same type. Perhaps the most shocking was that of August 1936 which was directed against Zinoviev, Kamenev, and others, who were elite members of the original Lenin circle and were some of his most immediate collaborators during the Bolshevik revolution of 1917.[1] In this trial, too, the "evidence" consisted of the confession of one of the defendants, Holtzman, who, according to the official report of the trials, expressed himself as follows: "Here in the dock beside me is a gang of murderers, not only murderers, but Fascist murderers. I do not ask for mercy." And just as in the trial involving Abramovitch, the prosecutor made a mistake of a "technical" nature which helps in understanding the character of these trials.

According to Holtzman, he personally received instructions from Leon Trotsky in 1932 regarding terrorist acts against the leaders of the Communist Party of the Soviet Union and of the Soviet government. He gave details of the circumstances under which he received these instructions. He met Trotsky's son Sedov who took him to his father in Copenhagen. During the conversation that ensued, Trotsky—to quote Holtzman—plainly told "him that the fundamental task now (fall of 1932) [was] to assassinate Comrade Stalin." The circumstances of this conversation were described by Holtzman as follows: "I arranged with Sedov to be in Copenhagen within two or three days, to put up at the Hotel Bristol and meet him there. I went to the hotel straight from the station and in the lounge met Sedov. About 10:00 A.M. we went to Trotsky. . . ."[2] Unfortunately for the prosecutor, the Hotel Bristol, which in prewar editions of the guidebooks is given prominence among the Copenhagen hotels, did not exist any longer in 1932 and did not appear in guidebooks of the time. It had been torn down in 1917 and had not yet been rebuilt in 1932. This fact, which of course the Copenhagen press noted as soon as the Soviet government revealed the "confession" of Holtzman, came too late to save him or his codefendants. By that time they had all been executed. Nor did it help when Sedov revealed that he had never in his life visited Copenhagen.

1. On the trial, Friedrich Adler wrote a thirty-six-page pamphlet, *The Witchcraft Trial in Moscow*, issued in November 1936 by the Commission of Enquiry into the Conditions of Political Prisoners. The Menshevik trial was critically examined by Adler, Abramovitch, Léon Blum, and Émile Vandervelde in *The Moscow Trial and the Labor and Socialist International*, published by the Labour Publications Department (London, 1931).
2. Adler, *The Witchcraft Trial*, p. 14.

For me, the trial of the Mensheviks came as a revelation which forever protected me against excessive confidence in the decency and truthfulness of governments in general, and of the Soviet government in particular. To learn this at an early stage of one's life was an advantage that not too many young men or women enjoyed.

1933

The year 1933 brought radical changes in my life, as it did—to a far greater extent—to tens of millions of people in Europe and, eventually, America and the Far East. In fact, the change began in 1929, the last year of the boom that followed World War I. But as far as I knew, no one, surely no one in the European labor and socialist movement, foresaw the severity and duration of the economic crisis which started in the fall of 1929. The development of the social sciences and especially of economics may have made it possible for the experts in business cycle theory to forecast what they politely called a "downswing" for the fall of 1929. No scientific theory[1] existed which permitted forecasting the economic blizzard that was to sweep across the world. It was even less possible for human knowledge to anticipate the frightful political and social consequences of the catastrophe. I, at least, freely confess that I did not expect much more than an ordinary economic recession: an increase in unemployment by a reasonable percentage, some bankruptcies, a temporary deterioration of the political situation of governments in power, and then recovery and return to what was accepted as normal in Europe in the late 1920s.

Unfortunately, two major parties affiliated with the Socialist International were represented in the governments of their countries at the time; indeed, they were primarily responsible for government policy. The British Labour Party had taken over the British government as a result of elections held in May 1929. Though it did not hold an absolute majority of

1. The closest to such a theory would have been the Kondratieff theory of long cycles. I had come across it during work on my doctoral thesis on business cycles, but failed to connect it with the long and severe depression which began in 1929. Mea culpa.

the seats in the House of Commons, Labour was the strongest party and could govern with the support of the Liberal Party against a weakened Conservative opposition. Ramsay MacDonald thus became prime minister again, and Philip Snowden was chancellor of the exchequer. In Germany the Social Democrats gained considerably in the elections of May 1928 and took the lead in forming a coalition government with a number of middle-class parties. The head of the government was Hermann Müller, a Social Democrat; the crucial Ministry of Finance was in the hands of Rudolf Hilferding.

The Great Depression thus hit west central Europe at a time when two of the most important countries were governed by administrations of social democratic inspiration. The policies of both governments followed the same course, even though British Labour was free of Marxian theoretical influence and in Germany Hilferding represented Marxian views, though with a good deal of moderation. Whether inspired by British classical laissez-faire liberal thought or Marxian rejection of all "tinkering with money," both governments obeyed the rules of strict fiscal orthodoxy. Balancing the budget and defense of the gold parity of the national currency were the lodestars toward which their policies were directed. In a period of declining business and, consequently, shrinking government revenues, a balanced budget required cutting expenditures. This in turn depressed business even further, causing more reductions in government services in a never-ending, descending spiral. The recession turned into a depression, growing ever more severe. Defending the gold parity of one's currency added additional impetus to this race into the abyss. The United States, with the severest depression, set the pace for all the rest. Its prices fell further and faster, encouraging exports and discouraging imports. To preserve their own trade balances from continuous deterioration, other countries had to remain competitive on the world markets. This meant that they had to depress their prices as much as or more than the leading deflationist country. Competition in reducing prices, wages, and business forced one country after another into a race whose "winner" was the one with the severest depression. This phenomenon is discussed in my *The Tragedy of European Labor, 1918–1939*.[2]

2. New York: Columbia University Press, 1943.

For those who still live in the world of ideas shaped by John Maynard Keynes—another epoch having passed—the spectacle of labor-sponsored governments taking the lead in reducing wages, unemployment benefits, and other social services must appear like a story out of *Alice in Wonderland.*

Rudolf Hilferding was the main advocate of several ideas: that a crisis simply had to be gone through, that measures taken to resist it would only lead to stronger setbacks, even that the crisis fulfilled a useful function by eliminating the least efficient businesses. After the publication of his *Finance Capital,* the former physician had become the leading Marxist economist in the German labor movement. His authority was undisputed; the party and trade unions followed his directions. Helping the victims of the crisis was perceived as natural, but the crisis itself had to take its course.

Only gradually, as the situation worsened increasingly, did opposition to Hilferding appear. It was led by three men: by the old Russian Menshevik Wladimir Woytinsky, the trade unionist Fritz Tarnow, and Fritz Baade. Baade worked for the research institute of the trade unions, in which the SPD was represented as well; Woytinsky was a consultant to this institute. Baade's main interest was agriculture, but during this critical period he showed particular talent in a different field, that of macroeconomic policy (the general structure of the economy). With Woytinsky and Tarnow, Baade was an advocate of the so-called WTB plan, named after the initials of the three authors. The essential point of this plan, which will probably not seem particularly revolutionary to today's readers, was that in periods of economic crisis, a deficit in the government's budget would be advantageous.

As even today many people equate the state's budget with that of a private citizen, it was normally the custom during the 1920s and even the 1930s to balance the budget. To diverge from this principle appeared to most contemporaries as a great evil that would lead to inflation. And, since Germany had just emerged from the terrible inflation following the end of World War I, every claim that a budget deficit would have inflationary effects sufficed to make citizens reject such ideas on principle and with dread.

Even among social democrats and trade unionists, this idea remained undisputed for a long time. Unfortunately, the opponents of a counter-cyclical financial policy, led by Hilferding, could refer to Marx (but only if they overlooked the circumstances that were decisive for him). Marx competed intellectually with a number of people who wanted to battle the social evils of early capitalism through monetary reforms. For the American people who are familiar with the Populist struggle against gold currency, Marx's rejection of countercyclical ideas will come as no surprise. At any rate, this has nothing to do with the question of how national budget policy could be used in the struggle against an economic crisis. In the early 1930s, of course, few people were familiar with this idea, and a conscious and intentional budget deficit would have appeared as economic suicide to the overwhelming majority. The fear of inflation still dominated.

When Hilferding rejected a policy of public works financed by loans, he was, according to his own honest conviction, in complete accordance with Marx's ideas. To the SPD, it was more important that a careful policy of deflation—also advocated by the nonsocialist parties under the leadership of Müller's successor, Chancellor Heinrich Brüning—be followed as a guarantee against inflation. Together with the undisputed authority Hilferding possessed, this mood was decisive. Of course, alternatives were not made easy for the SPD. When Johannes Popitz, state secretary at the Finance Ministry, wanted a foreign loan (which could not possibly have been regarded as inflationary), Hjalmar Schacht, president of the Reichsbank, opposed him with a public declaration which accused Popitz of inflationary tendencies. That was enough to put an end to the plan, which perhaps would have somewhat alleviated the crisis and the growing unemployment.

While the SPD insisted on its downright suicidal policy, the trade unions began to have doubts. They looked into alternatives to Hilferding's deflationary policy. In this task the economists felt as though they were pioneers. Keynes's investigations were unknown to them; his main work had not yet been published. Of course, the Swedish Social Democrats developed new ideas, Ernst Wigforss in particular. He proceeded from the idea that annual balancing of the budget was economically pointless. It would be much more reasonable, he said, to adapt the balancing of the budget to the period of one economic cycle, consisting of boom and depression. During the depression there would be deficits in the state budget, which would lead to an increasing demand for goods and services. This would alleviate the acuteness of the crisis. During the boom there would be a surplus in the budget, which should compensate for the deficits of the period of crisis. These ideas, which led the Swedish Social Democrats from one victory to another, were unknown in Germany.

Accordingly, the three men who opposed the SPD's deflationary policy had to develop their own ideas. As Woytinsky described it, two goals were foremost in his mind: raising prices and developing public works. Higher prices would restore the profitability of business and diminish debts. Public works would help to fight unemployment. The main point was the struggle against deflation. Every step on the path of deflation led, as they viewed it and as the events showed, to more unemployment and to the advance of the Nazis and the Communists.

The ideas of the three men, in the form of the WTB plan, made progress with the trade unions but not with the party. The SPD, however, was essential, since this was a question of measures that needed legislation. The result of this paralysis of the labor movement is common knowledge: Hitler's victory and the establishment of his dictatorship.

I do not want to say that the failure of the labor movement in the field of economic policy alone was sufficient to bring about the catastrophe. But it can hardly be denied that the economic collapse of Germany was an important, perhaps the most important, factor leading to the victory of the Nazis. I myself advocated ideas similar to those of Hilferding in my book, *Die grosse Krise*. In that respect, I share the guilt.

The nations suffering through the vicissitudes of the late 1920s and early 1930s had the correct feeling that a world was coming to an end. The events of the Nazi period turned many ordinary citizens into victims of unbelievable tortures, or into adventurers. Everyday life became a sequence of nightmares and cops-and-robbers stories which an Edgar Wallace or an Agent 007 might have designed and weathered. My own life soon fell into this fantastic pattern.

I was on a skiing holiday in Zürs in the Arlberg, one of the most attractive winter resorts of Austria, on that fateful day in February 1933 when the news of the Reichstag fire reached me. Not knowing any details, but realizing that the event might prove to be of historic importance, I decided immediately to end my trip and return to my office in Zürich. I phoned ahead, with the result that Friedrich Adler, holding a suitcase of "civilian clothes" and a ticket to Berlin, was waiting for me at the railroad station. I barely had time to exchange a few words with Adler before my train left again. I was secretly hoping that it would never reach Berlin: I was sure that a general strike protesting against the terror which the Nazis had begun to unleash after the Reichstag fire would unfailingly stop the railroad traffic, including my own train. In that case I would attempt to reach Berlin by any other means that I could find in order to carry out my instructions. They were simply to assist those who wanted to flee Germany by providing them with money and whatever advice I could offer, and to see how party and union property could be protected from confiscation by Nazi authorities. How great was my disappointment when I woke up the next morning and found the train peacefully moving toward Berlin. I saw no general strike, no visible signs of resistance against the rising tide of Nazi terror, swastikas all over the landscape, and life going on as routine dictated.

My stay in Berlin was brief because many party and union leaders were taking refuge wherever they could, or had already left for the only part of Germany not yet under Nazi control—Bavaria. This stronghold of the Catholic Center Party managed to resist Nazi control for a few days longer than any other part of Germany. Other Social Democratic Party dignitaries refused to believe that law and order in so orderly a country as Germany could indeed come to an end under a regime committed to "law and order"—as it understood these terms. I came across one rather sad, yet amusing, example of this kind of refusal to see the world as it really was.

When I found myself unable to conclude my business without further consultations in Zürich, I tried to arrange some innocuous way of maintaining contact with one of the party dignitaries who had decided to remain in Berlin. I asked him to give me a cover address for further correspondence. "What for?" he asked angrily. "We are in Germany; the postal service is not in danger." I was in no mood to argue with the venerable gentleman and responded: "Just do it, please. I would feel safer if I did not have to address my letters to a man of political renown." "Well," was the answer, "if you insist, you may send your mail to my mother-in-law." He gave me her name. "What is the address?" I asked. "Care of myself," he said proudly. I gave up on the idea of carrying on any conspiratorial correspondence with my interlocutor.

That same evening I took the train to Munich, hoping to find there partners of greater insight and power of imagination. But before leaving Berlin I had dinner in the railroad restaurant with two old personal friends, skiing companions on several vacations in the Swiss Alps, husband and wife. He was the son of a well-known German painter, but—for reasons that were never fully clear to me—had been adopted by one of Germany's leading steel magnates. Although my friend shared my political views, his adopted father was a man of great influence in the new regime. This fact was the key to the surprising revelations which my friend disclosed during our meal.

He worked, thanks to his adopted father, in an agency which, according to him, functioned secretly as a kind of General Staff office of the German Army. According to the Treaty of Versailles, Germany was prohibited from having a General Staff. Apparently, an institution performing substantially the services of a General Staff had nevertheless been established under cover some time ago and was in full operation when Hitler became chancellor. It included a secret service which maintained a network of intelligence agents. What role my friend performed in this organization was left unspecified, and the situation in which we all found ourselves was not one to encourage excessive confidences. If I had known the expression, I would have spoken of limiting information to those with a "need to know."

Among the confidences which my friend thought I needed to know was a somewhat fantastic-sounding story involving a double or triple agent—whose name I vaguely remember as something like Mütterer or some similar name of Austrian provincial origin—and relating to the Republican Defense Corps of the Austrian province of Carinthia, as well as to Yugoslavia.

To understand the story, it is necessary to refer to the political problems of Yugoslavia, Carinthia's neighbor. It was a country born of the upheavals created by the breakup of the Austro-Hungarian empire at the end of World War I. Serbia, whose conflict with the Hapsburg empire had been the spark that set off the conflagration, was at the heart of the new country. Added to it were Croatia and Slovenia, the Dalmatian Coast,

Montenegro, slices of southern Hungary, and a big part of Carinthia. From its birth the country was at odds with practically all its neighbors who contested the loss of all or parts of their own territory. The "Little Entente," an alliance of Yugoslavia, Czechoslovakia, and Romania, was formed to offset the pressure of Hungary, Italy, and certain groups in Austria clamoring for a revision of the peace treaty. While the "Little Entente" represented an impressive military force, it was poorly equipped to deal with the second congenital defect of Yugoslavia: its internal cleavages.

This is not the place for an extensive analysis of the history and causes of these cleavages, for they go back to the division of the Roman empire into a western and an eastern part, separated by religious and cultural differences for almost a millenium. What is perhaps more relevant is the difference in the degree of economic development and per capita income among the various parts of the country. Slovenia and Croatia were the most advanced industrial areas, while the south and east were poor and primitive agricultural areas. I remember receiving a delegation of Croat politicians who had come to see us in our Zürich office, apparently simply for the purpose of informing us of the underlying causes of the conflict between them and the dictatorial system established by the Serbian king in the face of the persistent and almost unanimous opposition of the Croats and Slovenes to the regime. Obviously, they were hoping to obtain Western socialist and labor support in their struggle. It was they who described as a division between two worlds the deep cleavages between those Roman Catholic parts of Yugoslavia formerly in the Western Roman empire and those under the rule of Byzantium (which became the Greek Orthodox Church).

We were not too flattered by the visit of the Croat delegation, nor excessively impressed by their arguments. This was partly because similar Croat groups were openly vying for the support of the Italian fascist government and of other right-wing extremist groups, so that to an outsider the rebellion of the Croats against the dictatorial regime in Belgrade appeared to be a conflict between rival right-wing groups. To some extent our indifference resulted from our belief that the breakup of Yugoslavia might very well be the beginning of a much larger international conflagration. The assassination of King Alexander in Marseilles in 1934 by professional killers hired by right-wing Croats tended to confirm our view that the real complaints of the Croats were overshadowed or exploited by conflicts between different fascist groups.

I was therefore not too surprised when I learned, at the dinner in the Berlin restaurant, of an international conspiracy designed to take advantage of the internal cleavages of Yugoslavia in order to split the country for the benefit of its various neighbors. Yet there were some horrifying aspects of this conspiracy which my friend revealed to me, so frightful that I accepted his report with a certain amount of skepticism.

What had happened, according to him, was that a formal treaty about the dismemberment of Yugoslavia had been concluded a few weeks before our dinner meeting; the partners to the agreement were a Croat nationalist movement, the fascist government of Italy, and the Republican Defense Corps of Carinthia.

The Corps, too, requires explanation. Neither the German nor the Austrian republics in the 1920s was firmly based on the democratic will of the overwhelming majority of the people. Hankering for the past glory of the empires created a climate of hatred and contempt for the "new system" among those who suffered from the loss of age-old privileges. Fear of the rise of the "unwashed and unkempt," who for so long had been suppressed, was sharpened by the events in the Soviet Union and the attempts in 1919 to establish dictatorships of the proletariat in Hungary and Bavaria. The police and the armed forces soon came to be regarded as instruments of antidemocratic adventurers. Their use in the suppression of Communist coups in the early days following the proclamation of democratic republics in central Europe, and even more their behavior during the right-wing Kapp Putsch[3] seemed to furnish ample evidence of the antidemocratic attitude of the armed forces in Germany and—with some delay—in Austria.

In response to these threats, private armed defense organizations

3. In July 1919 Captain Waldemar Pabst had unsuccessfully attempted to march into Berlin to oust the government. This was followed in March 1920 by a "regular" large-scale putsch attempt under the leadership of a rather unknown east-Prussian politician named Wolfgang Kapp. He succeeded in driving the republican government into flight to Stuttgart while the armed forces of the republic stood by without intervening. A general strike soon brought an end to the adventure but unleashed in return Communist attempts to overthrow the government.

were established in Germany and Austria. In Germany, the SPD established the *Reichsbanner Schwarz-Rot-Gold* corps, named for the colors of the Weimar Republic flag. In Austria, the corresponding organization was the *Schutzbund* (Republican Defense Corps), under tight socialist control.

At first sight it might appear to the reader that a political party has no business setting up an armed defense corps under party command. In any civilized country the democratically elected government, and it alone, has the right to organize and command armed forces. But neither Germany nor Austria in the 1920s was a normal civilized country. The revolution of November 1918 had changed the institutions of both countries too suddenly to call forth a wide consensus on the fundamentals of social and political life. The workers in particular, treated as outcasts not so long ago, were not yet integrated into society. They led a life of their own, separate from the official institutions of the country.

> This explains the profusion of forms in which the (socialist) movement manifested itself. Almost every field of activity of the individual was integrated in the party. Cyclists and lovers of music, amateur botanists, chess-players, and mountaineers, bird-fanciers, football players, wrestlers, and singers formed groups of their own within the movement. Tens of thousands of children belonged to the groups of "Children's Friends" and "Red Falcons."[4]

The *Schutzbund* served primarily to protect party and trade union meetings against the attacks of radical opponents from the right. There was little need for a similar service against the extreme left because the Communist Party was an insignificant sect, unable to elect a single deputy to Parliament or even to the city council of any of the major cities of the country. Maintaining the unity of the working class within the framework of the Social Democratic Party had been the major objective of Viktor Adler, and in this task the party had always succeeded. The Republican Defense Corps was a moderately armed guard of the party whose existence was justified by the attacks of manifold fascist organizations upon workers' demonstrations and party offices in various towns. While government propaganda tried to make it appear that the Corps was a means of establish-

4. Julius Braunthal, *In Search of the Millenium* (London: Victor Gollancz, 1945), pp. 253–54.

ing a "proletarian dictatorship" in the country, no objective observer could detect even the faintest threat to democracy in the Corps, and its inadequate equipment alone would have been sufficient to make aggressive moves on its part against the police or the armed forces of the republic a suicidal mission. Karl Heinz, the secretary general of the Corps, was prudence and caution embodied, and any adventure was alien to his nature.

It was difficult to conceive of the Corps as an armed force capable of resisting the regular army of the republic. However, during the first years after the 1918 revolution, the army was not yet thought of as an antidemocratic weapon in Austria as it was in Germany. Later, when the Christian Social Party dominated the Ministry of National Defense and gradually transformed the spirit and the personnel of the armed forces in an antidemocratic direction, the Social Democrats developed the theory that the Defense Corps would operate in coordination with a general strike in the case of a fascist coup. In this way the mobility and the communications of the army would be paralyzed to the point where the Corps, assisted by masses of striking workers, could operate effectively.

Needless to say, in Germany and Austria large antidemocratic organizations existed on the right. Led by former officers of the prerevolutionary armed forces, they consisted of soldiers deprived of a professional career by the disarmament clauses of the peace treaties of 1919, and of mercenaries and adventurers led by antidemocratic politicians but also supported, not too secretly, by the official troops of the German Republic. In Austria their political leadership was divided between men hankering for the return of the Hapsburg dynasty and pan-German politicians, some of whom soon entered into an understanding with the German Nazis. The former group could count in due course upon the support of the Italian dictator Mussolini, as well as that of the Hungarian leader, Admiral Horthy, who had defeated the Red Republic proclaimed by Béla Kun in 1919.

Now to return to my friend's revelations that evening in Berlin at the Anhalt railroad station. It appeared that one section of the Republican Defense Corps, that of the province of Carinthia, had engaged in a foreign policy of its own. Carinthia borders on Yugoslavia. In 1918 a sizable portion of Carinthia as well as of neighboring Styria had been passed on to

Yugoslavia by the victorious allies. The Carinthians, regardless of party affiliation, looked at this as an unjust violation of the self-determination principle put forward by Woodrow Wilson. In their view these were German-language territories and thus ought to belong to Austria as they had before the war. Cities like Marburg, renamed Maribor by the Yugoslavs, were, they claimed, old German settlements. On the other side, it is also true that many Carinthians were Germanized Slavs. The Carinthians were thus ready to take advantage of a possible breakup of Yugoslavia to return their former territory to the Austrian Republic.

My friend continued his story. An Austrian who claimed to represent a powerful Croat separatist organization had offered the Carinthian *Schutzbund* leaders a formal treaty of alliance. In exchange for mutual support the Croats undertook to return to Carinthia some of the territory that had become part of Yugoslavia after World War I. The *Schutzbund* leaders, believing they were dealing with Croat patriots who, like the socialists, opposed the dictatorial Serb regime, had accepted. My friend in Berlin read out loud, from a document he held in his hand, the text of a formal treaty that sounded like an international agreement concluded between two sovereign powers. Its objective was the breakup of Yugoslavia and the redistribution of its pieces: some were to return to Austria, some were to become an independent Croatia.

What the *Schutzbund* leaders did not know, my friend pointed out to me, was that this agreement was part of a much larger conspiracy. The conspiracy involved fascist Italy as well, and apparently Germany had gotten wind of it. Italy had aspirations regarding Istria, the coastal area beyond Trieste on the Adriatic Sea. Italian troops were to support the Croat rebellion in exchange for the cession of Istria. Thus unbeknownst to them, the *Schutzbund* leaders, who fought at home against fascist organizations supported by the Italian government, were allies of that same government in the struggle for the spoils of Yugoslavia in the throes of disintegration. And to top it all, the good Austrian patriot who had arranged the deal between the *Schutzbund* and the Croats happened to be a paid agent of Mussolini.

The whole story sounded like a spy novel to me, and, I confess, I listened with a good deal of skepticism. But 1933 was a year in which anything seemed possible, and the most unlikely event became the most probable one. I decided that, fantastic as the story was, I should at least take notice and investigate.[5] I hastily took notes of the various articles of the treaty concluded between the *Schutzbund* in Carinthia and the Croats. Upon reflection, however, I decided that possession of these notes, if I were to be arrested by Nazi authorities, would provide them with at least the appearance of a case of international espionage against me. This might endanger the more important mission upon which I was engaged. I apologized to my guests, withdrew to the men's room, reread my notes hastily to impress them upon my memory, and flushed the torn pieces of paper down the toilet.

When I returned to Zürich—a trip about which more will have to be said—I phoned Otto Bauer. I reported, in a somewhat amused fashion, the incredible story I had heard in Berlin. To my surprise, Bauer took my report quite seriously and asked me for a written statement in detail. Fritz Adler, who overheard our conversation, added on his own that "things of this kind happen in periods of monumental unrest." I followed instructions, wrote my report, and sent it to Vienna. These were the halycon days when one still trusted the post office to preserve the secrecy of mail.

I heard a few weeks later that Bauer had called in the *Schutzbund* leaders of Carinthia, informed them of the true character of their partner in the negotiations, and ordered them to abstain from any initiatives in foreign policy without authorization of the party Executive, especially initiatives of a nationalist and basically reactionary nature such as the one in which they had been involved.

My trip from Berlin to Munich started with a minor surprise. When I climbed into my berth in the sleeping car, I found a briefcase in it. A

5. Many years later I encountered my friend again. He was then a professor at the University of Bremen. In a little book he revealed the way in which he had obtained knowledge of the treaty mentioned above. A leading German industrialist, who had been his patron for several years, obtained a job for him in the office of a Dr. Hahn, who was close to a group of industrial leaders. One of the tasks of this office, it appeared, was to obtain information of a diplomatic or military nature that could be of interest to the leaders of German industry. In some sense this could be described as a preliminary, secret, and modest stage of a General Staff which, under the Versailles Treaty, Germany was forbidden to establish. Even though my friend had a low-level job in that office, he saw and heard a great deal which was of more than passing interest to people involved in politics and international affairs. Needless to say, his personal views were quite different from those of his contemporaries.

visiting card attached to it indicated the case belonged to Gustav Stolper, the distinguished editor of a weekly economic affairs journal in Berlin. From the Nazi point of view, Stolper committed the double crime of being Jewish and a supporter of democratic views. No wonder that he took advantage of the remnant of freedom that survived for a few brief days in southern Germany. He later went to the United States where one of his sons became a distinguished professor of economics at the University of Michigan. The briefcase in question had simply wandered by error into my sleeping quarters in the train.

Gustav Stolper was not the only refugee from Nazi terror on the train. When I got up in the morning, shortly before we pulled into the Munich railroad station, I discovered in the corridor two old friends of mine: Rudolf Breitscheid, the chief spokesman of the Social Democrats in the German Parliament, and his wife. Breitscheid, originally a member of the German Liberal Party, had joined the socialist movement mainly because it was closer to his antiwar feelings. An excellent speaker, he was pre-destined for a career in the Reichstag where he spoke primarily on matters of foreign policy. When in 1928 a cabinet was formed under Social Democratic leadership, Breitscheid became chairman of the parliamentary group of the party. This, of course, was sufficient to make him a leading target for the Nazis in their search for opponents.

Breitscheid was a master of wry humor. When in 1928 I asked him what his official role would be in the new Social Democratic government, he responded: "I am to be the *Zetzler* of the Reich government." Bewildered by an expression I had never heard, I asked for an explanation. "It's simple," Breitscheid answered. "Whenever anyone in the government makes a speech, I'll be standing by and expressing my admiration: Tse, Tse, Tse, Tse!" Compared to the average German politician, who took himself seriously at all times, Breitscheid was a refreshing exception. Tall and handsome, the highly articulate Breitscheid looked the ideal "Aryan" with perhaps a bit of an aristocratic vision. I often thought that Hitler might have wished to look a bit more like Breitscheid, but if he had, he might not have had the popular appeal to the common man. In any case, Breitscheid's death during the war, after his capture in France by Nazi police, removed one of the most appealing figures from the German political scene.

The Breitscheids and I walked together to the editorial offices of the Munich Social Democratic daily, one of the few of its kind, perhaps the only one, that could still be published in Germany. Along the way he made a comment which has remained engraved in my memory. Better than any long sociological or psychological dissertation, it illustrated the weakness, but also the moral strength of the socialist movement at the time. "What I am most afraid of," he said, "is not what the Nazis are doing to us now, but rather what our people will do to them when things change." I confess that I was startled. That a man fleeing for his life from the cruelest opponents should at that time worry about future revenge by his friends and associates seemed to me almost superhuman in its humanity. I for one could not share his feelings.

My business in Munich was rapidly completed and, as soon as I could, I took the train back to Zürich. I carried with me all kinds of documents relating to the possible transfer of party and union funds to some safe place abroad, and I was somewhat worried about the fact that I was carrying them with me. Quite apart from the political implications, the transfer of German funds to a foreign country was a violation of the stern foreign exchange control laws then in force in Germany. I could readily imagine how the Nazis would have exploited my arrest while I was in possession of these documents. Mine would not have been simply a political crime, but one of the most despicable crimes. Obviously they would have presented me as engaged in foreign exchange speculation for my benefit and to the detriment of the German people.

Fear drove me to an act for which I never quite forgave myself. At the Munich railroad station a pretty young girl joined me in my compartment after saying a tearful good-bye to a young man on the platform outside my window. He was to all appearances a foreign student close to the heart of the young lady who bade him farewell. Still, a few minutes after the train had left Munich on its way to the Swiss frontier, she was quite willing to engage in conversation with me, rapidly becoming friendlier and friendlier; so friendly indeed that when at one of the stops along the way a stranger opened the door to our compartment and saw us together, he discreetly withdrew to leave us alone. The frontier, which we reached in a matter of hours, was already occupied by Nazi storm troopers. Everything depended now on passing through a careful search of our luggage.

As a precautionary measure I mixed my luggage with that of the girl's, opened the window toward the station platform, and both of us, arm in arm, leaned out the window—to all appearances a happy young couple concerned with each other rather than with politics or other serious matters. The ruse worked; perhaps it was not necessary. In any case, no storm trooper entered our compartment, and the man who controlled the passports was a Swiss frontier guard. Apparently, no serious exit control existed yet.

The story, as far as the young lady was concerned, ended at the Zürich railroad station. She of course was not aware of the danger to which my behavior had exposed her, and we parted as good friends.

There is a small postscript to this happy ending. A few days later the man who had so sensitively reacted to the situation in our railroad compartment appeared at my office in Zürich. He was a leading Social Democratic lawyer in Munich who had decided to leave Germany for what he hoped would be a few weeks until the Nazi nightmare would pass. To his great amusement, he recognized me, and I thought it wiser not to tell him the sinister background of my amorous interlude: an example of the extent to which "underground" work makes for the habit of discretion.

February 1934

The Nazi victory in Germany in early 1933 had profound repercussions in Austria, which was intimately tied to Germany by language, history, trade, and a feeling of national solidarity. German money started to flow across the border, as did Nazi agents. The Austrian Nazi Party, until quite recently a weak organization, grew by leaps and bounds.

With the rise of the Nazis in Germany, Austria became the scene of a three-front struggle, with survival as the issue for each of the three parties: first, the Nazis, eager to absorb Austria into the Third Reich; second, the Christian Social government of Chancellor Engelbert Dollfuss, never a reliable supporter of democratic institutions and now, under the pressure from Nazi rivals, turning more and more toward dictatorial methods for its very survival; and, finally, the Social Democrats, still a power to be reckoned with thanks to the support of the strong trade unions associated with the party, and still in control of the Vienna city administration, but slowly losing prestige and popular support.

Each party was equipped with physical weapons: this was not simply an electoral battle, but one fought with private armies. The government had not only the official army and the police at its disposal (even though some parts of these were likely to be at least as loyal to the Nazis as to the government), but also two other auxiliary organizations: a broad-gauged fascist party, patterned after Italian and German models and called the Fatherland Front, and an armed guard, the *Heimwehr*. The latter had its origin in a traditional popular armed force of the province of Tyrol; but it had spread throughout the entire republic. A *Heimwehr* leader, Prince Ernst Starhemberg, who had inherited a distinguished name in Austrian history and a large landed estate, was both a supporter of the government and a rival of Chancellor Dollfuss for the leadership of the Austrian fascist movement. The Austrian Nazis had their German-style storm troopers, the s.a., amply supplied with arms, money, and the prestige of Hitler's victory in neighboring Germany. On the side of the democratic republic there was only the *Schutzbund,* the Republican Defense Corps under the political leadership of Julius Deutsch of the Social Democratic Party.

Each of these forces had its foreign support. For the Nazis, the term "command" would be more appropriate. The Nazi Party had designated Austria as a Gau of Germany (Gau is the old German term for province), and appointed a Gauleiter (provincial commander), Theo Habicht, who resided, for the time being, in Munich—a short distance from Salzburg and the Austrian border.

The Social Democrats received help from Czechoslovakia and from France, as long as a reasonably progressive government was in charge in the latter country—that is, until February 6, 1934.

Chancellor Dollfuss had put himself under the protectorate of Benito Mussolini, the Duce of Italy who, though allied to Germany, was interested in keeping the powerful and aggressive Germans at a distance from the Italian border. To have Austria as a buffer between Italy and Germany made life considerably easier for the Duce. He thus gave whatever support he could to Dollfuss in his effort to maintain an independent Austria.

Mussolini also pursued other objectives. The Austrian Social Democrats had long been a thorn in his side. Italy's main enemy was Yugoslavia, whose dismemberment, as we have seen, was one of Mussolini's principal foreign policy objectives. A natural ally in this endeavor was Hungary, which had territorial claims on Yugoslavia. To strengthen his ally, Mussolini sent arms and ammunition to Hungary in violation of the Trianon Peace Treaty concluded at the end of World War I between the Allied powers and Hungary. Since Italy had no common border with Hungary, these shipments went by train via Austrian territory. That was a fundamental weakness in Mussolini's strategic design.

On January 8, 1933, the Vienna socialist newspaper, the *Arbeiter Zeitung,* revealed the famous Hirtenberg affair. Hirtenberg, site of an Austrian ammunition factory, was located not far from the Austro-Hungarian border. According to the press report, some forty carloads from

Italy had arrived at the plant. While being unloaded, one of the boxes had accidentally dropped to the ground and broken open; it was found to contain arms. The paper claimed that the arms were destined for Hungary. Chancellor Dollfuss denied this, but to little avail. France, Czechoslovakia, Romania, Yugoslavia—the three latter countries allied in a defensive combination against Hungarian territorial claims—protested, indicating thereby that they refused to accept the Austrian chancellor's claim that the arms were merely to be repaired in Austria and then returned to their Italian owners. Even the British government got into the act and joined the French in protesting in the sharpest terms. In the end, Italy had to take the arms back.

No friend of the socialists, Mussolini was now doubly determined to destroy the Austrian trade unions and socialists. His support for Dollfuss increased. On the other hand, Czechoslovakia and France resolved to maintain their assistance to the democratic forces in Austria. Arms and ammunition for the socialist *Schutzbund* came mainly from Czechoslovakia and were kept in hiding places—which were all too often known to the police.

Perhaps this provides some background for the following incident. A few weeks after I returned from my German trip, a strange visitor was announced to me, Fritz Adler being out of town. It was none other than Mr. Mütterer, the intermediary who had negotiated with the Carinthian *Schutzbund*, allegedly in behalf of the Croat nationalist and separatist movement. Short and stocky, he looked far more like an innkeeper in a Tyrolean village than like the movie model of a spy. I assumed that he did not know I was aware of his true vocation as Mussolini's agent, but the course of our conversation was such that I am to this day unsure whether this assumption was correct. In any case he betrayed no surprise when I made it clear that I knew of his connections with Rome and the Italian secret service. Nor was I quite certain of the purpose of his visit. The stated objective was his apparent concern with the survival of Austria and Austrian democracy.

A vast amount of underground and espionage activity took place in and around Austria. The man who came to see me was only one of a large crowd of agents paid by one or more of the powers involved in the struggle for control of the country. My friend in Berlin had reported to me that my visitor was in the pay of the Italian secret service. His talk made him appear in a different light. He urged me, and through me the Austrian Social Democratic Party, to resist any further encroachments on democracy in the country. To put it bluntly, he advised civil war in Austria in which the Republican Defense Corps and the Socialists would oppose the forces of the Dollfuss government.

That advice was not necessarily bad. Dollfuss engaged in a war of attrition against the Social Democrats and democratic institutions in general. Taking advantage of the antidemocratic sentiments sweeping Europe, he used a minor parliamentary incident in order to dissolve Parliament altogether in March 1933. He then proceeded to establish his dictatorial regime buttressed by his party militia, as well as by the Fatherland Front, the police, and the army, in slow and easy steps. He took care not to resort to any measures likely to arouse mass protests, but instead kept digging away at the foundations of the Social Democratic Party and trade unions. He was restrained not only by his fear of armed workers' resistance, but also by diplomatic considerations. He needed French acquiescence to an international loan to revive the stagnating Austrian economy, and the French government with the moderate independent Socialist Joseph Paul-Boncour as foreign minister for a time was unwilling to assist a government engaged in suppressing the labor movement and the Social Democratic Party.

Still, the gradual undermining of working-class power demoralized precisely those activist elements in the party upon whom socialists and unions would have to rely most in the case of armed resistance. There was a continuous soul-searching within the labor movement concerning when and under what conditions resort to armed force was justifiable and necessary. The Nazis, as the laughing third party, were standing by, hoping that the two other parties, the Catholic fascists and the Social Democrats, would devour each other so that the Nazis could emerge as the victors of this struggle.

My strange visitor had advice to offer. There was no time to lose, he said, in taking up arms against the Dollfuss regime lest the workers be so demoralized by continued retreats that armed resistance would be impossible at all. Knowing who he was, I was taken aback by his words. Could he as an agent of the Italian secret service have any interest in a civil war in Austria? Was it not, on the contrary, better from that point of view for the slow, wearing-down tactic to continue to avoid any armed clash that could only help the Nazis? I decided to take the bull by the horns. "On whose behalf are you speaking?" I asked my visitor. "What is your interest in the socialists' strategy?" He was taken aback. "I am just trying to prevent the breakdown of Austrian democracy," he said. "Don't you work for the Italian government?" "Yes, from time to time, but not now." "For whom are you working at this time?" He was obviously embarrassed and replied, "I have some business for the Austrian government, but this conversation has nothing to do with that. I am just stopping off on my way to Munich where my son is a student." Zürich is not exactly en route from Austria to Munich. Thus his answer was not quite convincing, the more so as Munich was the headquarters of the Nazi Party. Could the Nazis be naive enough to use a triple agent—working for Rome, Vienna, and Munich—in order to stir up civil war in Austria? Could they think that on a matter of such importance the opinion of an outsider—even if he were not known as an agent—would have any influence? Or was the agent acting on his own, hoping to curry favor with one of his several "business" contacts?

I shall never know the answer to these questions and just have to be satisfied with the contact with a professional spy about whom I knew more than he expected. As a postscript to this story: Perhaps there is a bit of higher justice in the fact that Yugoslavia outlived Italian fascism—as well as the Carinthian Republican Defense Corps.

The financial situation of Austria was desperate. In 1932 Chancellor Dollfuss managed to obtain from England, Italy, Belgium, and a reluctant France the promise of a substantial loan in exchange for commitments including the maintenance of Austrian independence—this term was a polite way to prohibit Anschluss. With Hitler's specter rising on the horizon, this was not a difficult promise for Dollfuss or the Social Democrats. However, the affair of the arms shipment threatened to delay the loan, even though the governments of England, France, and Italy had finally ratified the loan agreement. The French Socialists refused to vote the necessary appropriation until the arms affair was cleared up, and without their votes no majority for the appropriation could be found. So desperate was Dollfuss to obtain the funds that he started secret negotiations with the German government by way of the German vice-chancellor, Franz von Papen, to let Germany take France's share of the loan. This effort failed because Hitler insisted upon Austrian Nazis entering the cabinet in exchange for his financial support.

The attitude of the French Socialists stiffened even more after Dollfuss proceeded to destroy the parliamentary regime in Austria. *Populaire,* the Paris daily of the French Socialist Party, declared the full solidarity of French Socialists with their Austrian comrades and stated that the Socialists had originally voted for the loan treaty only on the express condition that a democratic and parliamentary regime be maintained in Austria. Abruptly, French Foreign Minister Paul-Boncour changed his stand in August 1933, and Dollfuss at last received the funds of the Lausanne loan.[1]

Nevertheless, Paul-Boncour's attitude toward the Dollfuss government remained a crucial factor, because the Austrian chancellor had solemnly promised Paul-Boncour that he would rule in a democratic spirit and in particular that he would not use force against the Austrian labor movement. Unable or unwilling to keep this promise, Dollfuss now endeavored to convince the French statesman that the Austrian workers were no longer following their Social Democratic leaders, but had instead swung over to Dollfuss's supra-party organization, the Fatherland Front. In proceeding against the Social Democratic Party he was thus not fighting against the workers and their interests, but merely opposing former political leaders now without a working-class following. Moreover, these same leaders had until quite recently—i.e., the rise of Hitler—favored Austria's joining Germany as one of her federal provinces. The chancellor simply failed to point out that the Social Democrats had solemnly rejected Anschluss with a Nazified Germany; thereby he made it appear that Otto

---

1. Charles A. Gulick reports an interesting exchange between himself and Paul-Boncour on the circumstances of French yielding on the loan. "During the time Joseph Paul-Boncour was in San Francisco for the organization meeting of the United States I asked him by letter why his country and England did not make it a condition of the final flotation of the loan that Dollfuss reassemble the *Nationalrat* [lower house of the Austrian Parliament] and reactivate the Constitutional Court. His written reply reports in one short paragraph a perfect example of that attitude which was to lead to the rape of Austria, to Munich, and to World War II: 'Obviously, in retrospect, it would have been better to attach this condition to the loan. At that time it was not thought necessary to do so to save Austria from financial disaster and to avoid throwing her into the arms of Germany.' " (Charles A. Gulick, *Austria from Habsburg to Hitler* [Berkeley: University of California Press, 1948], vol. 2, p. 1098.

Bauer and his socialist associates were, at best, unreliable allies in the struggle against the Nazis.

I was involved in an effort to refute Dollfuss's allegations. In the ordinary course of events, no special effort should have been required. France had an embassy in Vienna and its reports on Austrian domestic political developments should have been sufficient to clarify the socialist stand on the Anschluss and its repudiation since Hitler took power. Unfortunately for the sake of truth and a proper French policy, the ambassador was an outspoken partisan of Dollfuss, and his reports faithfully reflected the official government line as regards both the Nazis and the Socialists. The latter thus depended on unofficial channels of information to counteract the antisocialist reports which the French government received from many sides, including its own ambassador.

One day, in what must have been September 1933, I was in Geneva, the seat of the League of Nations. Walking along the beautiful quay which runs along the lakeshore, I met Salomon Grumbach, an Alsatian socialist and journalist whom I had known for many years. We stopped to exchange greetings and news. His most interesting item was that on that very day Dollfuss was to have luncheon with Paul-Boncour in Geneva. That information was sufficiently important for me to get to the nearest telephone in order to pass the news on to Adler in Zürich and, if he felt it desirable, through him to Otto Bauer in Vienna. At the same time I asked Adler whether there was any new information he wanted me to bring to the notice of Paul-Boncour, whom I hoped to see immediately. "Indeed, there is news," said Adler. "Last night there was a demonstration of some government employees, especially postal clerks, in front of the Chancellery. It was a demonstration in favor of Dollfuss, and I am willing to bet he will tell Paul-Boncour about it. It will serve Dollfuss to prove that the workers are no longer supporting the Social Democrats, but have gone over to his Fatherland Front. What Dollfuss will not tell the French minister is that the office chiefs kept lists of their employees and marked off the names of those who did not attend."[2] The threat of disciplinary measures, perhaps

2. Gulick reports a similar episode in which lists were distributed on which those who were willing to participate in uniform could write their names. Since the response was unsatisfactory, the director of the Vienna post office issued an order stating: "I expect, in consideration of the reduced time on duty that has been granted, that the unbroken ranks of

dismissal, in a period of mass unemployment was of course a very effective device to obtain full participation in demonstrations or even to force people to join the Fatherland Front.[3]

I hastened to telephone Paul-Boncour to make sure that I could talk with him before his luncheon. He was ready to see me immediately, and I rushed to his hotel, full of news and in particular of information about the "spontaneous" demonstration of the day before in Vienna. The value of my ability to communicate with Paul-Boncour was enhanced by the fact that the French ambassador in Vienna was unlikely to inform the French Foreign Office of the true circumstances of this particular demonstration or, in fact, the Austrian political situation in general.

I left Paul-Boncour after a brief conversation, literally at the same time that Dollfuss entered by a different door. I still remember a brief exchange with Paul-Boncour on that occasion because it was so characteristic of the inability of Western politicians, and Western democrats in general, to understand the nature of their fascist opponents. At one point in my report I told Paul-Boncour that Dollfuss would undoubtedly refer to the demonstration as evidence that the Austrian workers were abandoning the Social Democrats and turning toward him, even though participation in the meeting in front of the Chancellery was far from voluntary. "You don't mean to say that the chancellor of Austria will lie to me?" said Paul-Boncour. "That is precisely what I am trying to tell you," I responded.

I do not know exactly what happened at the luncheon. But I had some inkling of the general trend of the conversation between the two statesmen from a report of a member of the Austrian group at the League of Nations, who was a personal friend of mine, although his political sympathies were closer to Dollfuss's party than to the Social Democrats. He was in close

---

uniformed postal employees participate in this patriotic demonstration that is organized in conformity with the intentions of the government, and that no spirit of opposition to participation in this patriotic demonstration will be created." (Gulick, *Austria from Habsburg to Hitler*, vol. 2, p. 1128.)

3. A classic story that made the rounds of the Vienna coffeehouses at that time reports that Chancellor Dollfuss, upon a visit to a small town in Styria (one of the Austrian provinces), inquired into the political views of the population. "Thirty percent vote the government party, forty percent are Nazis, and thirty percent are Social Democrats," was the answer. "Only thirty percent are in the Fatherland Front?" the chancellor asked in surprise. "Oh no," he was told, "all of them are in the Fatherland Front!"

contact with the Austrian delegation to the League of Nations and apparently saw Dollfuss right after he returned to the Austrian headquarters after his luncheon with Paul-Boncour. As my friend put it, the Austrian chancellor was pale and trembling, crushed by the reception he had received from the French foreign minister. "He talked to me," said Dollfuss, "as if he were an Austro-Marxist." Austro-Marxist was the term by which Dollfuss and his associates designated the Social Democrats in an effort to associate them as closely as possible with the Communists—against whom of course any action, legal or otherwise, was permitted.[4] Dollfuss, apparently, had been confronted by Paul-Boncour with the true story of the demonstration the day before, just as I had assumed, and was startled to discover that the Frenchman knew the way this "spontaneous" demonstration had been organized.[5]

Apart from causing the Austrian chancellor an unpleasant hour or two, the incident was to have major consequences for me. I assume, without knowing it, that Dollfuss tried to find out how the story had traveled so rapidly from Vienna to Paul-Boncour in Geneva. Unquestionably, it was not by regular diplomatic channels since the French embassy in Vienna would certainly not have transmitted the true or full story. It had to be an "Austro-Marxist" in Geneva, and far and wide I was the only one around. Quite possibly and innocently, the same man who reported to me on Dollfuss's reaction to his luncheon host had told Dollfuss about me and my presence in Geneva. I had met the chancellor only once, quite briefly, at some kind of diplomatic function, and I doubt that he remembered that meeting. But he certainly knew who I was and what roles I performed, and he must have read my name repeatedly in Austrian publications.

In any case, I went down on his list of "enemies" and, as events were to prove, he patiently waited for the day when new circumstances permitted him to repay me for the unpleasantness I had caused him. That time came a few months later.

4. The Austrian Social Democrats also called themselves Austro-Marxists. [Ed.]
5. It is worth recording that Dollfuss's action against the Austrian Social Democrats occurred on February 12, 1934; six days before, there were street riots in Paris directed against the government of which Paul-Boncour was a member. The government fell and was replaced by a conservative government without Paul-Boncour. Dollfuss took advantage of this change to inform the French ambassador in Vienna that he no longer felt bound by his promise to respect the democratic constitution.

In the meantime, the chancellor and his allies dug away slowly and gradually at what was left of the democratic institutions in Austria whose main—practically sole—support was the power of the Social Democrats and the trade unions. There have been endless debates ever since concerning whether the ultimate outcome would have been different had the Social Democrats called upon their supporters to revolt at an earlier stage, in the course of 1933. Perhaps a major event such as the government's armed intervention to prevent a meeting of parliament might have provided an effective stimulus for mass resistance against the increasingly provocative authoritarian regime. As it was, the government's step-by-step strategy in destroying the democratic institutions, as well as in undermining the self-confidence of the workers, led the Social Democrats from retreat to retreat until the last remnants of the once so powerful labor organizations rebelled in a confused and disorganized fashion on February 12, 1934, and went down to bloody defeat. Dollfuss and his fascist allies took revenge on their opponents, hanging several of them, including Koloman Wallisch who had been so badly wounded in the fighting that he had to be supported on his way to the gallows.

On May 1, 1934, Dollfuss proceeded to establish his Catholic version of fascism, a mixture of medieval institutions—the "estates"—with more modern patterns of dictatorship. However, lacking even the semblance of mass support—with the workers in sullen opposition and the Nazis gaining ground every day—his regime never acquired the status or the prestige of Italian fascism or German Nazism. Indeed, his victory over the Social Democrats was only the last stage of his life-or-death struggle against the Nazis, for him in the most literal sense of the words: on July 25, 1934, he was killed in an unsuccessful Nazi coup.

I Lose My Citizenship

In the midst of his trials and tribulations, Dollfuss did not forget his defeated enemies. I learned of one of his petty acts of revenge in March 1934, shortly after the February upheaval. All this time I had stayed in Zürich, serving as a telephone contact with the party and the unions during the critical days in February and transmitting the news to Western newspapers, which otherwise depended only on official government news bulletins.

One evening in March I went to one of the Zürich literary and political cafés with a group of friends. Just like Vienna and other central European cities, Zürich had a number of cafés, each of which had its special regular clientele. If you wanted to meet a particular group of people, you knew which café to visit. This time, it was the Odeon—which I understand has since radically changed its character. On the way I stopped to buy the morning edition of the world-renowned Zürich newspaper, the *Neue Zürcher Zeitung,* which by peculiar timing is published in Zürich late in the evening so as to reach all parts of Switzerland the following morning. Hence its designation as the "morning edition."

Because I was in company I did not open or read the paper in the café but put it away for future consumption, folded, on the table around which we—some five or six persons—were sitting. Still, a few minutes later, in the course of the conversation, my eyes passed over a part of the front page of the paper, and I had the impression that I saw my name. I picked up the paper and looked again. Yes, there was my name, together with four others: it was a list of people whom Dollfuss, by decree, had deprived of their Austrian citizenship, regardless of the fact that no law existed which would have permitted such an action. Respect for law and order had been discarded by those who in the past had been its most ardent advocates. After the civil war of February, it was now clearly established that the government was dictatorial, regardless—or perhaps precisely because— of the fact that it commanded the respect and support of only a small fraction of the people. Its power was deprived from the basic division of the opposition—Social Democrats and Nazis—who hated each other even more than they hated the government, and from the somewhat fragile loyalty of police and army.

The list of those deprived of their citizenship was a bit strange. It consisted of names that obviously belonged on that list—if such a list was established at all—and was surprising in that my name appeared in company that vastly exceeded my own standing in the party, or my importance. There were Otto Bauer and Julius Deutsch, the two foremost leaders of the party and members of its executive committee; Berthold Koenig, chairman of the railwaymen's union whose strike was intended to paralyze the movement of the government's armed forces but which had failed miserably; and Karl Heinz, the general secretary of the Republican Defense Corps. These four could be held closely connected with preparations for resistance to the government's dictatorial aspirations, even though they were not responsible for the actual outbreak of fighting on February 12, 1934. Indeed, they had made a last-minute attempt to delay the beginning of the armed resistance movement in Linz in Upper Austria, where the Republican Defense Corps leader Bernaschek had decided the time had come to resist before the last democratic power positions had been destroyed. How my name got on to that list, God and Dollfuss alone know. I had no connection whatsoever with the Corps, with the general strike call that followed the outbreak in Linz, and did not even know the name Bernaschek until February 12. Nor did I belong to the political leadership of the party, and to put me on the same level as Bauer and Deutsch as far as my political role and influence went was plainly ridiculous. So I was left to guess the reason I had acquired the honor to be linked with them. And the most plausible explanation was the incident in Geneva, involving the Dollfuss/Paul-Boncour luncheon.

The official explanation was a simple statement to the effect that I had engaged in anti-Austrian activities, the terminology typical of authoritarian governments which tend to identify themselves with the country as a whole. An attack upon the government, even a verbal one, thus becomes an act of hostility toward the country itself. In order to clarify the situation as best I could, I wrote a letter to the chancellor offering to return to Vienna and stand trial for whatever violations of any law I was alleged to have committed. I put down only one condition: that the trial be public and foreign press representatives be freely admitted. There was, of course, no law that I had violated. My visit with Paul-Boncour was no crime, and the speeches I had made in public assemblies during the civil war in February contained attacks upon the government, not upon the country itself. Under the circumstances, however, I was not surprised to receive an official notification from Vienna rejecting my "appeal." That was a further mis-representation of facts and law because I had not appealed. No verdict existed against which an appeal could have been directed.

Thus I found myself in the somewhat difficult position of being re-garded as a "stateless" person. My Austrian passport was valid, according to its text, until the fall of 1934, but the Austrian government denied its va-lidity as of the middle of March. Any other government could do the same. I had no legal recourse against an illegal action. For the moment this caused me no trouble because the control agents at the various borders—apart from the Austrian border—did not check whatever lists of "expatriates" the government in Vienna had established. The numbers of these lists increased rapidly as the first was followed by lists of lesser "enemies" of Austria. For someone like me, whose job involved extensive travel in a part of the world full of borders, the possession of a valid passport was essen-tial. I thus began to consider ways by which I could continue my travels.

Actually, I had two problems to solve. One was to obtain, if possible, an extension of the apparent validity of my Austrian passport. The other still greater difficulty was created by the geography of the European continent. There were now three countries eager to get hold of me: Nazi Germany, Austria, and fascist Italy. Europe was thus divided for me by a bloc of states running north and south and separating friendly France, Switzerland, and England from equally hospitable Czechoslovakia. There was one flight daily, I believe, nonstop from Paris to Prague; I could use that flight, but if unfavorable weather or any other unforeseeable circum-stance should compel the plane to land in Germany, my fate was only too clear to me. Travel, however, was essential for me in my occupation.

Thus these were the two tasks which presented themselves to me: how to get my Austrian passport renewed so as to make it usable in Switzerland and other friendly countries, and how to obtain a passport that would enable me to travel with a minimum of danger in the hostile countries.

The first required an intricate maneuver. Before my Austrian passport expired, thus before the fall of 1934, I had to locate an Austrian consulate that would not know of my loss of citizenship. Some out-of-the-way Austrian consular office, preferably headed by an honorary non-Austrian consul, might be the right one. Upon some investigating, I found what I thought was the appropriate kind of consulate: the one in Marseilles. It was listed as having an honorary consul, a Frenchman, who thus could reasonably be expected not to know the details of Austrian politics, especially the names of people deprived of their citizenship. This was all the more plausible since other names kept being added to the original list of five. I do not know the exact number, but it surely exceeded the original five by at least a few dozen who had fled Austria after the civil war.

Apart from having a Frenchman as Austrian consul, Marseilles had another advantage: I had an influential friend, Senator Léon Bon of the Bouches-du-Rhône department of which Marseilles is the capital. Bon was a socialist and knew some of the personnel of the Socialist International because one of its early congresses had been held in Marseilles. I felt confident that I could count upon his assistance.

So, one day in the summer of 1934, I set out for the city on the Mediterranean, equipped with my Austrian passport which, at least in appearance and in my own view, was still valid. To be on the safe side, I also procured another document whose nature I shall describe.

Upon my arrival in Marseilles, I went to visit the senator with whom I had arranged an interview in advance. I told him my story and asked whether he could help me in dealing with the consul. My idea was that an introduction by the senator to the consul would so impress the latter that it would not even occur to him to check any possible lists or make any sort of investigation. Bon had a better plan. He would get the prefect of the department to intervene in my behalf.

For the benefit of readers not familiar with France, I need to describe at least briefly the role and status of a French prefect. He is not only the chief administrative officer of the area (*Départment*) but also the personal representative of the central government. Because the latter is the major power center in the country, its glory is reflected upon the prefect. In the particular case in question, that of the tapestry merchant who acted as Austrian consul in Marseilles, what mattered most was that the prefect is responsible for recommending candidates for various decorations—such as the Legion of Honor—to the central government in Paris. As I was told in due course, the consul was eager to receive a decoration, and, therefore, to please the prefect.

The next step was thus my introduction to the prefect by the senator. There was only one question that seemed to matter to the prefect: whether I had been involved in any ordinary criminal activity. As soon as the senator assured him that only political issues were involved in my loss of citizenship, the prefect was not only willing but eager to assist me. A slight reference in passing to my acquaintance with Paul-Boncour may also have been of some help in persuading him. He began to look at the matter as a kind of juvenile prank in which he was most willing to participate. Not only did he know the consul, but he was also aware of the latter's interest in being proposed for a decoration. Without any further ado, the prefect called the Austrian consul on the telephone to tell him that an Austrian citizen, a close friend of the prefect, needed an extension of the validity of his passport in some hurry as he was due to leave on a prolonged trip.

The consul responded as expected and asked that I just present myself at his home where he would settle the matter without delay. I took a taxi straight to the consul's home where I was received as an honored guest. Some powerful Turkish coffee was served. The conversation was polite and essentially no more than small talk until we finally got to the real business of my visit. And then I had a most unpleasant surprise. "Follow me to the consular office," said my host, "and I shall introduce you to the chancellor of the consulate." This person, it immediately developed, was not only an Austrian, but obviously a civil servant, thus likely to be familiar with at least the main political events in the country. To top it all, he had on his desk, right in front of me, a folder entitled "List of those deprived of their nationality." The consul introduced me to the chancellor, adding that I was the person the prefect had called about, and withdrew. I sat down next to the desk. As a protective move, I put my hat right on the folder, hoping this would be a physical handicap to his checking my name on the blacklist. This seemed to work, for the time being. The only rather modest complaint of the chancellor was that I, an Austrian, had turned to the French for assistance. I explained, as well as I could, that the prefect, an old friend of mine, had acted on his own in calling the consul, just to speed up the matter since I had to undertake a long journey quite unexpectedly and immediately.

This seemed to satisfy the chancellor. He took up my passport, made some record of the impending transaction on some official-looking documents, and then turned abruptly to me: "Where are the photos?" "What photos?" I asked. "We need two passport pictures for a prolongation of the validity of a passport. If you don't have them, there is an automat in the big shop in town where you can get them in a few minutes." I was terrified. Leaving the office, with my passport on his desk, would give the chancellor an opportunity to consult his file and to find my name on the blacklist. Yet, there was no alternative. Without the photos, my whole plan would collapse. If I managed to get the pictures in a hurry, I might still have a chance.

Leaving my passport and my hat behind, I rushed out of his office, ran as fast as I could to the store, used the machine, got the photos, and returned to the consulate—all in less than half an hour. The office door was closed. I knocked. The chancellor opened the door, glanced hastily at me through his thick eyeglasses, and said: "Sorry, the office is closed for some time."

Convinced that he had discovered the "true" nature of his visitor, I slowly turned away, pondering what to do about the passport I had left on his desk. Should I force my way into the office, grab my passport, and run, or should I proceed as if nothing had happened and wait for the chancellor's return? As it was, with its validity to expire in a few weeks, the passport was not worth very much, surely not the possibility of being sentenced for breaking and entering. I decided to remain calm and wait for developments. In the meantime, I slowly started to walk down the stairs leading from the consular office to the street.

Suddenly, the door behind me opened and the consular official appeared with a little package in his hand. He recognized me and apologized for his brusque behavior. Being nearsighted he had not identified me. "I just received a package," he added, "that I am to bring to the prefect." And then: "I am new here and have never met the prefect. He is your friend, is he not? Why don't you come along and introduce me to him?" I was relieved and frightened at the same time: relieved because the request indicated that I was still in the good graces of the authorities, and terrified at the thought that the prefect might not recognize me or remember the story the senator and I had told him. Still, unless I was to endanger my plan, I had to go along with the chancellor's invitation, hoping desperately that somehow I could give the prefect a signal to remind him of the incident that had led me to him.

As events soon proved, I had worried needlessly. We arrived at the prefect's office in a taxi and were immediately admitted to his office. When he saw me, he came across the large room to embrace me: "How are you, old friend?" I presented the chancellor, who was obviously deeply impressed by the cordial reception I had received. The package was handed over and, after a few minutes of small talk, we left.

A taxi ride and a few minutes later, we were back at the consulate. I presented my photos and the funny part of the proceedings began. "I can give you the extension free of charge, but that is only intended for poor persons and as it is noted on the passport, this may embarrass you." I magnanimously refused his kind offer and paid my full fee. Indeed, as there was a bit of small change left, I grandiosely donated it to the poor of the Austrian colony in Marseilles. "Normally, the validity of a passport can be extended only for two years, but in special cases, I am authorized to grant an extension for five years," the consular official told me. "I would greatly appreciate a five-year extension," I said, "because it would save me future inconvenience." And so my passport was provided with an endorsement extending its validity into late 1939. It outlasted by more than a year the life of the government that had illegally deprived me of my citizenship, for the very existence of the Austrian Republic came to an end when Hitler occupied Austria in March 1938 and transformed it into the *Ostmark,* one of the provinces of Greater Germany.

This was not yet the end of the humorous part of the proceedings. The official asked me whether I was a member of the Fatherland Front. I pretended not to know what this, Dollfuss's fascist organization, was. "If it has anything to do with politics, I would rather abstain," I said. "Oh, no," the answer was, "this is simply a social body in which the gentlemen of the Austrian colony meet." The emphasis was on the term "gentlemen," in German *die Herren,* a term that clearly separates the upper classes from the "common people," the *Männer.* "Certainly," I said, "we shall talk about this when I return." I had to use the word "return" since I had claimed residence in the area so as to come within the competency of the Marseilles consulate. Having spent a delightful weekend at the Hotel "Les Roches Blanches" in Cassis, on the Mediterranean, I had simply invented a street address in that lovely town as my home.

One last request from the official: "I am new here," he repeated, "and I am supposed to report on economic, social, and political events in the area. Can you help me by introducing me to some of the leading personalities around here, since you are so well acquainted with them?" I assured him of my willingness to assist him in any way I could, as soon as I would return. "Good, you just call me and we shall have luncheon in a beautifully located restaurant on the Corniche, the road that overlooks the harbor and the islands off the coast." "Agreed," I said and took my departure.

I confess to a slight embarrassment at the thought of all the trouble I may have created for the consular dignitary. He was not the youngest any more and was obviously extremely nearsighted. If he lost his job for having granted me the passport extension, he might have met great difficulties in finding another. I was all set to write to the Austrian Foreign Office and explain the trickery of which the consular official had been the innocent victim. Perhaps that would help him, I thought. But then again, it was quite possible that no one in Vienna had detected the egregious mistake, and that my letter would create the very difficulties for the victim of my intrigue that I wanted to avert. And, after all, in a conflict with a fascist, lawbreaking government, I was entitled, was I not, to use my halfway reasonable device to counter the moves of the enemy?

A year or so later I made an attempt to find out whether the incident had produced any serious consequences for the consular official in question, but my effort failed. To this day I do not know whether my trickery was ever discovered.

By now I had solved one of my personal problems. This still left me with the question of how to obtain a false passport for travel in "enemy territory." That, of course, was a problem I had in common with many other people, although my case was perhaps a bit more difficult than the average because I was persona non grata in three different countries at the same time. Still, false passports carried an especially high value since neutral Switzerland was universally respected.

Fortunately for me, the Swiss procedure for obtaining a passport made it extremely easy to achieve my objective. The Swiss authorities at the time did not require that an applicant for a travel document appear in person at the passport office. Someone else could submit the documents proving his nationality, provide the necessary photos, and pay the fee. As the birth certificate—proof of Swiss nationality—did not contain a photo, it was not difficult to substitute someone else's photograph for that of the rightful owner of the birth certificate. All that was necessary was thus to find a Swiss citizen of approximately my age who was willing, in the interests of the cause, to hand over his birth certificate to a messenger who in turn would submit certificate and photos to the Swiss authorities. Given public sympathy for the anti-Nazi and the anti-Dollfuss cause, we encountered few problems in locating the necessary "donors."

Our office messenger, a Swiss citizen who was later to play an important, if less than glorious, role in shaping the course of my life, undertook to submit the necessary forms and documents to the Swiss authorities and to obtain the passports for a select few who were in need of such documents. Fritz Adler established the short list of those eligible for the privilege of a "safe" passport, and I was among them. I traveled a few times under my assumed Swiss name—let me call my "donor" by the name of Sieber so as not to compromise anyone still alive. The only major difficulty was my inability to speak Swiss-German, a language, or better, a dialect impossible to learn after one's childhood. It followed that I could not present my Swiss passport at the Swiss border upon my return from Germany, Italy, or Austria, but had to use my rejuvenated Austrian travel documents. This meant that I had to carry both passports with me and rapidly change from Austrian to Swiss while the train was moving from one border station to the next. Flying was a bit more complicated since the airlines in Europe recorded one's nationality and wanted to see the visa permitting the traveler to enter the country of his destination. Fortunately, as I mentioned, just then one of the airlines introduced a nonstop flight from Paris to Prague which permitted me and countless others to fly over Nazi territory—unless something untoward happened.

A flight from Copenhagen to Amsterdam and Brussels which I used fairly often also crossed over a small insert of German territory without touching down. One day I sat peacefully in that plane on my return from a meeting in Copenhagen. I was heading for Brussels where I was stationed at the time for reasons to be detailed below. Just about the time the plane was approaching German territory, it descended rather rapidly. I watched this maneuver with growing unhappiness as it appeared to be the prelude to a landing on German soil. As the weather was quite bad, an emergency landing at a German airport seemed a distinct possibility, even though I had no idea whether there was an airport in the vicinity or where it could be located. As the plane continued to fly rather close to the ground, I became increasingly anxious. Obviously there was little I could do if weather conditions were to force the pilot to decide on an emergency landing in Germany. Still, I could not sit patiently and wait for things to develop. My nervous system was not equipped for such patience. Perhaps if I knew what was in store for me and the other passengers on the plane, I would destroy whatever personal or "incriminating" papers I carried with me. Some such vague idea must have crossed my mind. In any case, I had to know. I called the stewardess and asked her to find out whether for any reason the captain was planning to land in Germany. The young lady was kind enough to transmit my query to the pilot. A few seconds later she reappeared, carrying a small sheet of paper. The captain, obviously guessing correctly the reason behind my curiosity, responded: "Do not worry. We shall not land in Germany; it's simply that the weather is better close to the ground."

A few minutes later we landed in Amsterdam, and I changed to a plane for Brussels. The other plane was to go on to Paris. It crashed on takeoff; no one survived. My "understanding" pilot and my friendly stewardess were dead.

My passport story continued without difficulty for quite some time. Then fate intervened abruptly to bring an end to this valuable document. The final chapter began in 1935 with the move of the Secretariat of the Labor and Socialist International to Brussels.

Our presence in Switzerland had become increasingly burdensome for the Swiss government. Three of the country's neighbors resented our mere existence and made their feelings clear to the Swiss authorities: Nazi Germany, Austria under Dollfuss and his successor Kurt von Schuschnigg, and, last but not least, Mussolini's Italy. Informal suggestions that we leave the country before the situation became untenable came more and more frequently and urgently our way. Without waiting for any official action which the Swiss might feel compelled to take, we decided to transfer the Secretariat to a country somewhat less exposed by geography, and perhaps less susceptible to extreme right-wing pressures. Belgium offered us hospitality, and Brussels became our new headquarters.

The Belgian capital, which since has become a thriving metropolis and the capital of the European Economic Community, was far from being so lively then. Its bilingual character was a handicap to its cultural and intellectual aspirations: audiences for theater performances in French were limited; the Free, that is, nonreligious, University of Brussels took second place to the tradition-rich Catholic University of Louvain. But life was pleasant, the food was excellent, the landscape from the ocean shore to the Ardennes Mountains offered great variety, and there was always the "Micheline," the rubber-tired nonstop express train to Paris.

Most of the staff transferred from Zürich to Brussels, including our Swiss messenger who had been so helpful in arranging for protective travel documents. However, a few changes did occur and local staff was hired. More importantly, the Belgian Treasurer of the LSI, Joseph van Roosbroeck, took over and proceeded with a careful and detailed audit of our accounts. This included our not inconsiderable postage expenditures, the record of which was kept in a small book, year by year.

Van Roosbroeck was a 100 percent product of the Belgian labor movement. Illiterate when he started work at an early age, he joined the budding trade union movement, which at the time was part of the Belgian Labor Party in a somewhat similar fashion as most British trade unions are still affiliated with the British Labour Party. A devoted union and party member, he attracted the attention of some of the leaders who recognized his loyalty and his talents.

There had been a tremendous lack of educated workers in Belgium in the nineteenth century, and one of the functions of the labor movement had been to remedy this situation. Workers' education became one of the central assignments of labor's activity. The top leaders of the movement devoted themselves to the task of turning illiterate workers into persons capable of following the literature of the movement and participating in the cultural life of the nation. Émile Vandervelde, the leader of the Belgian Labor Party and many times a cabinet member, performed this duty, as did Louis de Brouckère, scion of one of the most distinguished families of the country, professor at the Free University of Brussels and for many years Belgium's representative to the League of Nations.

Van Roosbroeck had gone through one of the party's schools and had learned how to read and write. This entitled him to serve as a judge on the three-man labor courts deciding grievances under either the labor law or, where they existed, the collective contracts. He went on to become a member of the Senate of Belgium and the treasurer of the LSI. The latter was not much more than a symbolic appointment as long as the Secretariat was located in Switzerland. With the transfer to Brussels, van Roosbroeck's role changed. He took his assignment as treasurer seriously enough to proceed to a careful examination of our books and records.

One of the most voluminous books that he examined was a record of our mail. Not only had we written lots of letters, we also issued weekly publications that were sent out in three languages—German, French, and English—and in several hundreds if not thousands of copies. Postage was paid from a cash fund administered by one of the employees, a Swiss man whose whole behavior—quiet, steadfast—inspired confidence. He was to record each piece of mail and the postage paid in a little book. For the first time in many years these books were now checked by someone, namely the treasurer. To his surprise, van Roosbroeck discovered that on every single page there was a small error of addition, always ending with a larger total expenditure than justified. This went on page after page, and while each provided only a small amount of difference, over the months and years the total "errors" added up to a significant amount. Confronted with this fact, the employee broke down and admitted his guilt.

The first I knew of this incident was when the employee came to see me and pleaded with me to intervene in his favor. Apparently, he was not satisfied with the result of my plea in his behalf or with the action taken by the secretary, who dismissed the guilty employee but waived criminal prosecution. I frankly thought that dismissal was indeed the minimum punishment for fraud that had extended over several years. The fact that until our move to Brussels no one had even bothered to check on the cash fund records may have served as a partial excuse, as did the unquestionable loyalty of the man in all other respects. That he was involved in a somewhat messy love affair hardly mattered since his acts of fraud started much earlier than when that affair began.

Still, the employee—whom I shall refer to as Hans—felt deep resentment toward us, as his subsequent actions indicated. Apparently, he informed the Nazi authorities of the existence of "our" Swiss passports and the names under which we traveled, thus making the travel documents unusable and endangering anyone who would use them. He also reported in some unknown way the same facts to the Swiss authorities and provided them with a full list of the names on the passports and those of the actual holders of the documents. The Swiss authorities were compelled to take action against us, but the gentle and halfhearted way in which they proceeded indicated quite clearly that, at least at this stage, their sympathies were clearly on our side. Indeed, I have some reason—based on information which I obtained quite recently—to believe that some of the Swiss functionaries and elected officials knew of our scheme and quietly and secretly tolerated or even actively supported it. This was 1936 and Nazi pressure on Switzerland, though by no means negligible, was not yet as formidable or threatening as it became later.

A Trip to Eastern Europe

I was engaged in a tour of Eastern Europe when Hans's betrayal became known. The consequences would soon appear. I had visited Czechoslovakia, Hungary, Romania, Bulgaria, and—very briefly—Athens, giving lectures and collecting material for a book on Eastern Europe. The trip itself was exceedingly interesting and educational.

In Czechoslovakia, a new nation born of the disintegration of the Austro-Hungarian empire in 1918, I learned a good deal about the Sudeten-German problem. The Sudeten-Germans were the German-speaking people of Czechoslovakia, known by the name of the frontier region they inhabited. Traditionally, many of them were German nationalists who looked with disdain upon the "lower forms of human life" represented, in their view, by the Slavs. All Slavs, whether Czechs, Slovaks, Poles, or Russians, were regarded as inferior races. To expel or destroy them was the right, nay the duty, of the "higher" races such as the Germans.

My primary purpose was to establish, as best I could, what might be the chances for the survival of Czech democracy. That meant, I then naively believed, to study the internal forms of cohesion and disintegration in the country. I was convinced that France and England would come to the rescue of Czech democracy if it were threatened by outside forces. My only excuse for this optimistic view was that by 1936–37, when I undertook my trip, no country had yet been absorbed by Nazi Germany, even though threats and pressures and open violence had occurred in Austria.

Perhaps I should have been more suspicious than I was: the friction between Britain and France was intense, and in fact some pacifist currents, especially in the British Labour Party, quite openly indicated their sympathy for Nazi Germany and their hostility toward France—they held France at least partly responsible for the rise of Hitler. "France," they said, "had it coming!" It was indeed a historic fact that French pressure on the Weimar Republic had contributed to its downfall. It was difficult, however, to follow the logic which led some of the Labourites (including the Labour newspaper *Daily Herald*) to see with some glee the rising Nazi danger to France while overlooking the destruction of German democracy, socialism, and trade unions.

A small excursion into an incident illustrating the inability of British Labourites to understand the nature of the Nazi regime may be permitted, even at risk of diverting the flow of the main story. In September 1933 the new Nazi masters of Germany decided to attend the annual Assembly of the League of Nations. I do not remember whether Foreign Minister Baron von Neurath and Josef Goebbels themselves came to Geneva, but in any case this was the first appearance of the Nazis on the world scene. The young diplomat and Rhodes scholar Adam von Trott zu Solz was in this delegation; he later became one of the conspirators in the attempt on Hitler's life in July 1944 and ended on the gallows. (A simple cross in Hesse serves as a memorial for him.) The Nazi delegates called a press conference to be arranged by the Association of Journalists accredited to the League of Nations. A number of anti-Nazi journalists were members, including myself. I approached some of them with a suggestion to turn the press conference into a demonstration against Nazi terror and the destruction of freedom of the press and of German democracy. I found a generally favorable response until I talked to Norman Ewer, the Geneva correspondent of the *Daily Herald*. To my surprise and discomfort his answer was: "The German delegates are our guests. If any journalists, whether you or anyone else, treat them with disrespect, I shall publicly denounce and try to remove these journalists physically."

This response prevented any action, desirable as it might have been. Obviously, I could not permit a public demonstration of the split between the representative of the *Daily Herald* and the anti-Nazi journalists. The best we could do was to stay away altogether from the press conference. What remained firmly anchored in my mind was the—now almost unbelievable—naïveté of many British Labourites, who out of pacifist convictions or hatred of France or simple stupidity treated the Nazis as if they were a political party like any other, deserving respect and politeness on the part of those whom, if they were Germans, the Nazis would have happily sent to a concentration camp.

It was this same attitude, this mixture of motivations, which later caused Britain to regard the annexation of Austria as a kind of "internal affair of Germans," and Nazi Germany's dismemberment of Czechoslovakia, including the annexation of the Sudeten-German areas, as the proper exercise of the democratic right of national self-determination. The result was the abstruse defense by the Western democracies of the indefensible and authoritarian regime of Poland in contrast with the equanimity with which the same democracies had watched the destruction of democratic Czechoslovakia.

Czechoslovakia, which I visited on my trip in 1937, was still a well-functioning democracy, though greatly concerned with the fate of Austria. The geographic situation of the country was such that of its neighbors only Austria was a friend. Hungary, Poland, and of course Germany were enemies. Hungary had territorial claims on Slovak territory; Poland, in addition to aspiring to acquire some small disputed territory, despised the democratic leadership of Czechoslovakia; and Nazi Germany knew that to carry out Hitler's gigantic plans for the German colonization of Eastern Europe, Czechoslovakia—and in due course Poland—would have to be destroyed.

Hungary, the next station on my trip through Eastern Europe, looked like an early nineteenth-century relic straggling into the twentieth century. A little joke and a small scene remain fixed in my memory to illustrate how much the feudal mores of pre-1848 Hungary still remained. Friends, including Emanuel (Manó) Buchinger, a deputy to the Hungarian parody of a parliament, took me to the resplendent Parliament building, partly so that I could meet other Hungarian political leaders and partly so that they, just like other Liberals and Social Democrats, could perform their function. This function was to act as if there were an effective opposition in order to make the regime appear democratic. A standard joke of the time was that one day the "opposition" refused to oppose unless it was granted certain concessions. Count Bethlen, the former prime minister under president-dictator Admiral Horthy, was greatly upset. Without opposition, how could he pretend that his was a decent, honorable, ordinary democratic-parliamentary system? The opposition persisted in its refusal to oppose. Finally, Bethlen capitulated, conceded jobs and import quotas, and the oppositionists took their seats in Parliament again. Immediately, they started once again to shout: "Crooks, imposters, liars, resign!" The "honor" of the regime was reestablished: it was, in appearance, a democracy with a functioning opposition.

One little incident in Parliament was less amusing but more characteristic of the feudal nature of the regime. Count Bethlen appeared in the corridor to speak with some of his friends and admirers. Without a single glance backward, he took off his hat and his overcoat and let them slide off his head and his shoulders; he knew that behind him would be servants ready to catch and take care of them. There were.

Romania, my next stop, lived up to its reputation as the sharpest trading nation in the Balkans. I stepped off the sleeping car early in the morning in Bucharest. Since there was no bank anywhere in sight, I had no Romanian currency and thus no way of getting from the station into town. But when I mentioned my problem to the sleeping car conductor and added that I had Swiss franc bank notes, my difficulties rapidly disappeared. Sleeping car conductors, other passengers, and bystanders offered to change francs into Romanian leu. Indeed, so eager were they—not to help me but to get Swiss currency—that a regular auction developed with everyone outbidding everyone else. Well equipped with the national currency, I left the railroad station for my hotel. The taxis were elegant American cars, but the roads into town were poorly maintained country roads with plenty of rain-filled holes. Along the way were little huts with small gardens, with chickens, geese, and children playing in a confused mix.

Romania is situated in the Eastern European time zone, but this was then the only point in which it conceded to being Eastern European. In all other respects it regarded itself as an outpost of Western civilization, the advance guard of Latin culture against the barbarian hordes from the East, especially Asia. France was traditionally the cultural motherland of Romania, and educated Romanians spoke French, read French books, and dreamed of going to Paris. This began to change with the rise of National Socialism in Germany. Gradually the relatively small part of the population that took any interest in political matters split into two factions: the

Francophiles more or less dedicated to democratic ideas, and the pro-German faction committed to the establishment of a dictatorship. In the end it was the latter faction that won out, carried forward by the tide of Hitlerism on the continent.

There was an inkling of things to come when, leaving Romania and crossing the Danube, we entered Bulgaria at the town of Ruse: from the roof of a modern house a giant swastika flag offered its greetings. It was a German high school, or rather a high school established and maintained by the German government for the benefit of Bulgarian youngsters. Relying on the German origin of Bulgarian royalty and the fact that Bulgaria had been an ally of Germany in World War I, the Nazis counted on their ability to conquer the country without firing a shot, by "boring from within," Communist-style. No less important was Germany's almost complete control of Bulgarian foreign trade. More than half of that trade was with Germany, thus making the country almost totally dependent on its large trading partner for whom trade with Bulgaria represented barely 1 percent of its foreign commerce. The loss of the German market would be an economic catastrophe for Bulgaria. Germany not only had decisive influence on the Bulgarian economy to which it could dictate what and how to produce; Germany could also favor certain groups, discriminate against others, influence individual newspapers, etc. Bulgaria, for all intents and purposes, had become a German colony. France, with only 2 percent of Bulgaria's foreign trade, played a comparatively negligible role.

Various fascist organizations did spring up in these years in Bulgaria; the most curious of them, *Rodna Zaschtita* (Home Guard), campaigned against Jews and Freemasons in a country where Jews played an insignificant role both in numbers and in influence, while Alexander Tsankov, the man designated by Hitler himself as the head of the fascist movement, was a Freemason.

The final stop on my trip was Yugoslavia, next to Czechoslovakia the most important country in the area. My trip started in Sarajevo—the capital of Bosnia, one of the provinces of Yugoslavia, and the city in which one of the preludes to World War I took place. I remember a street corner in Sarajevo. On the house at the corner hung a memorial tablet crowned by greenery. One half of it had torn loose from the tablet and hung diagonally across it. I managed to decipher the inscription. It read: "On this spot on June 28, 1914 Gavrilo Princip proclaimed liberty."[1]

It was more than pure accident that my exploration of Yugoslavia started at this historic spot. Very soon the fate of the country, indeed of the world, was again to be at stake, and Yugoslavia was to be one of the keys to the unfolding tragedy.

On June 28, 1914, Gavrilo Princip, a young Serbian student, killed Archduke Franz Ferdinand, successor to the throne of the Austro-Hungarian monarchy, and his wife, the duchess of Hohenberg. The event provided the war party in Vienna and Budapest with the desired reason—or pretext—to attack Serbia, whose independence and nationalism gave impetus to nationalist movements in the southern Slav provinces of the Hapsburg empire. Because they enjoyed the support of Russia, these movements represented a real danger to the cohesion and the survival of the Austro-Hungarian empire. In truth, the conflict involved Germany and Austria-Hungary on one side, czarist Russia on the other. It was this fact and the involvement of other great powers—France, Great Britain—by way of a system of alliances that turned the conflict between Vienna and Belgrade into a worldwide conflagration.

The suspicion that Vienna only waited for a pretext to start military operations against Serbia was very much alive in the minds of objective observers at the time. There was first, the sad and ill-famed Friedjung affair: in 1909 the Austrian historian Friedjung published documents which had been transmitted to him by the Foreign Ministry and which were to prove that the leaders of the most important Serb and Croatian parties in the monarchy were agents of Belgrade, indeed paid agents. Soon, however, it became clear that outright forgeries were involved, and that Friedjung had been deceived. Thomas Masaryk, later president of Czecho-slovakia, demonstrated that the forgeries had been produced in the building of the Austro-Hungarian legation in Belgrade. A second comparable incident was that of the Austro-Hungarian consul in Prizren (Serbia). In

1. It must be remembered that in 1389, on St. Vitus's day in the Greek calendar ("Vidov-dan" in Serbian), the Serbs on the Amselfield were defeated by the troops of the Turkish Sultan Murad. On the evening of that fateful day, Milos Obilic, a young Serb, entered the tent of the victorious Turkish general and stabbed him to death. The end of the Serb freedom was avenged. On Vidovdan 1914 a new chapter in world history began.

November 1912 Viennese newspapers and some papers in Budapest reported that Consul Prohaska had been attacked by Serbian officers in Prizren. He had been beaten up and castrated, the newspapers indicated. The Austrian Foreign Office soon learned that nothing of the kind had in fact occurred, but preferred to let the attack in the newspapers continue as long as the idea of a preventive strike against Serbia had not been definitively abandoned.

When Thomas Masaryk (already before World War I a distinguished person) attempted—in agreement with the Serbian Prime Minister Pasic— to mediate between Vienna and Belgrade, Count Berchtold (the Austrian foreign minister) rejected the attempt disdainfully. In his view Masaryk was "a poor devil who probably wants to earn a commission for his mediation." A short while later, insightful Austrians may have regretted not having taken advantage of this opportunity. In the Balkan war, Austria's ally Bulgaria had lost badly while Serbia had emerged as the victorious leader of the southern Slavs. And this meant increasing prestige and power for Serbia among the southern Slavs of the Hapsburg empire who included the Slovenes, Croats, and even the Muslim inhabitants of Bosnia-Herzegovina, whose capital was Sarajevo, the city in which the Austrian archduke and his wife were assassinated.

Yugoslavia, when I visited, was far from a democratic regime. The merger of the formerly Austro-Hungarian parts of the country—Slovenia, Croatia, Dalmatia, and Bosnia—with the Serbs and with the formerly independent little kingdom of Montenegro had created as many problems as it had solved. The friction between the Croats and Slovenes on the one hand, and between the Croats and Serbs on the other, made the country practically ungovernable. With the exception of Bosnia the newly acquired areas were Roman Catholic, but Serbia was Greek Orthodox. Although the languages are closely related, the script is different: Roman versus Cyrillic. Add to this the two or three million Muslims in Bosnia, the Bulgarians, Germans, and Hungarians, as well as people who trace their origin to Albania, Montenegro, and Macedonia, and you have a picture of the diversity of the citizens of the new country that emerged from the ashes of World War I.

Perhaps still more important is an historical fact frequently overlooked by observers. While there is some degree of southern Slav solidarity, the fact is that for close to a thousand years the political and social development of Serbs and Croats had gone different ways. I still remember the skepticism and the surprise with which I once heard the spokesman for a delegation of Croat politicians assert: "Serbs and Croats have nothing in common. The Una-Sava and Danube rivers formed for a thousand years the boundary between the eastern and the western Roman empires and later the western limit of Turkish rule. Only twice did the Turks attempt to move farther west and both times—in 1529 and 1683—they suffered severe defeats. Croats and Serbs have no common history, share no common experiences. We do not belong together."

Experts on Yugoslavia today know how deep-seated are the distrust and rivalry between the two major parts of the country, and how differently the two areas behaved in the face of the Nazi enemy. The internal tension dividing the country was, and remains, one of the main dangers threatening the entire area, and indeed, the relationship between East and West. Tito's independent communism was ready-made for this situation: an effort to keep the country, at least to some degree, away from the rivalries of the superpowers. The establishment of a royal dictatorship in 1929 had been a desperate attempt to preserve the unity of the country, just as was Tito's dictatorship at a later stage. No wonder, therefore, that Croat conspirators hired a professional killer who removed King Alexander of Yugoslavia from the scene, a few minutes after he had landed in Marseilles on October 9, 1934, to visit French Foreign Minister Louis Barthou.

Yugoslavia, the cornerstone of the French foreign policy designed to stabilize the Balkans and to put a stop to Hungarian revisionist designs, was a weak pillar on which to base hopes for peace and stability. My trip confirmed my view that little help could be expected for anti-Nazi resistance from that corner of the world.

I went from Sarajevo to Dubrovnik, the Yugoslav beauty spot on the Dalmatian coast, using the narrow-gauge military railroad which the Austrians had built during their occupation of the region after they had driven out the Turks. It was to be a period combined of work and rest, permitting me to catch up on sleep (which had been badly neglected during my trip of several weeks) and to organize my notes for the book on Eastern Europe that I was preparing. Dubrovnik, a delightful place that combined a medieval city with some reasonable modern hotels, seemed the ideal location for what I had set out to do. For a few days things went as planned. I worked in the morning and swam in the crystal-clear water of the Adriatic in the afternoon. I also recovered from a bad stomach upset. A meal eaten at a station restaurant at one of the frequent stops had made me quite ill.

I thoroughly enjoyed a few days of pleasure and work after the whirlwind of travel and interviews of the preceding three months. But this was not to last very long. For out of the blue I received a telegram from Friedrich Adler. In slightly concealed language, he informed me that it would be unwise for me to return to Switzerland and asked me to telephone home from Prague on my way back west. (For those familiar with European geography I would hasten to add that the shortest route west would, of course, have taken me through Austria. For political reasons, that might have turned out to be a very long trip. So once again I had to use my favorite nonstop flight from Prague to Paris.) Although I still had a few free days at my disposal, the telegram made me hurry to find out what had happened.

The facts, which I learned upon reaching the Czech capital, were simple but stupefying. Our employee, the one who had been dismissed for having defrauded our petty cash account, had taken his revenge. One might have expected him to be grateful for our failure to prosecute him under the law and our decision simply to discharge him. Not so. Our former associate, in whom we had placed so much trust, was out to take revenge. And the method he had chosen was unbelievably traitorous. As noted earlier, having handled the procurement of Swiss passports for a dozen or fifteen people whose lives would have been in danger if they had been caught and identified by the Nazis, he handed a list of their names to the German authorities. They in turn duly informed the Swiss government of the existence of these unlawful travel documents. And Switzerland immediately started legal proceedings against the evildoers, including— probably very much to his surprise—our Swiss employee himself.

This was the status of things when I learned about them in Prague. I still had large quantities of books and papers stored with a friend in Zürich and had rented a small attic room to preserve a residence in Switzerland. I intended to keep open the possibility of becoming a permanent resident of Switzerland. All that was now impossible, out of my reach. An old friend—later a federal judge—took over as my attorney. But there was little to be salvaged from the wreckage created by the denunciations of my former colleague Hans. The facts were obvious and could not be denied. The only issue of any legal significance that remained to be settled was whether the Swiss passport had in fact been used.

Hans claimed he had seen my passport with entry and departure stamps of several foreign countries, indicating that I had made extensive use of the document. My lawyer produced my Austrian passport which I had indeed used on my Eastern European journey since I had succeeded in having its validity extended. It contained a most impressive variety of visas and entry and departure stamps. My Swiss passport had been destroyed as soon as the news of Hans's betrayal reached Adler, who had possession of the document. There was thus no evidence of whether it had ever been used or not. I was not available to answer any questions since I stayed away from Switzerland, and my lawyer simply did not know.

The Swiss authorities responded by prohibiting my entry into the country for an indefinite period beginning on October 20, 1937. My lawyer appealed the decision without questioning the facts. On August 1, 1938, the Swiss authorities limited the prohibition of entry into Switzerland to a period of three years. The official reply of the Swiss Ministry of Justice, dated August 1, 1938—the Swiss national holiday—summarized the case as follows:

> In the spring of 1934, Sturmthal requested from Hans . . . a Swiss passport with Sturmthal's photographic picture. For this purpose he gave Hans a passport picture. Soon afterward Hans gave the accused a Swiss passport in the name of Paul Sieber, born 1902 in Herisau, made out by the State office of the Canton of Zürich on March 27, 1934, under Number . . . and containing the photograph of Dr. Sturmthal. The accused, thereby, has made himself guilty of having induced, or at least assisted in, procuring a false identity paper from the police for foreigners. However, . . . the statute of limitations excludes any prosecution on this score. . . . The same applies to the question whether the Swiss passport was used or not.

The legal battle ended, prohibiting me from entering Switzerland without special permit for three years. In the meantime, I had received an extraordinary permit to enter and stay in Switzerland to collect at least my most essential possessions and take care of personal matters. Many years later I had an occasion to discuss the matter with high judicial authorities in Switzerland, and it was made quite plain to me that official sympathy had been on my side and that, given the international situation, the minimum possible punishment was inflicted upon me.

Shortly after the end of the war in Europe I planned a visit to Switzerland: I had business to attend to in London, Paris, and Germany. I wrote a friend, then a member of the Federal Court in Lausanne, to inquire whether I would encounter any difficulties in attempting to enter Switzerland. "You will not only be welcome," he replied, "but will be honored if you can bring a wagonload of rice along." Dependent upon food imports, Switzerland during most of the war needed both Allied and German permits to import food. The ships had to pass the Allied blockade in the Mediterranean, and the freight trains went through German control on the way from the ports—Genoa or Marseilles—to Swiss territory. Allied principle was to grant such permits only to the extent that the supplies met Swiss requirements without any surplus being available for German or Italian needs. Even after the end of hostilities in Europe, the Swiss had difficulties in replenishing their empty granaries. Unfortunately, I could not provide any rice for them at the time, although during the war I was occasionally consulted by officials of the U.S. Board of Economic Warfare on the advisability of permitting the passage of ships with freight destined for Switzerland. Still, I had no problem in crossing the border at Basel and visiting old friends.

To return to events prior to the war. The only passport which I could now use was my Austrian passport whose validity had been extended until October 1939. Long before any of these events took place, I had decided to leave Europe and, if possible, live in the United States. The circumstances which caused me to make this decision are perhaps of some interest.

The rise of Nazi power in Europe had met with little resistance. In Germany the democratic forces had capitulated when, on July 20, 1932, Chancellor von Papen ousted the Social Democratic state government in Prussia of Prime Minister Otto Braun and Interior Minister Carl Severing. The violation of the constitution by Chancellor Hitler, who used the February 1933 Reichstag fire as a pretext to arrest political opponents and Jews and to deprive the elected Communist deputies of their seats in the Reichstag, aroused no organized resistance—nor did the spectacle of the

German Parliament meeting in a hall guarded by armed Nazi storm troopers. In 1936 German troops, in violation of the peace treaties, marched into the Rhineland, thus protecting the western flank of the Reich so as to gain freedom of maneuver against Austria and the East. The French government failed to react, partly because a mobilization of its armed forces would have unbalanced the French budget!

The conclusive evidence, however, that the Western democracies were unwilling or unable to act against Hitler while Nazi Germany was still unready to fight on a world scale came a second time in 1936. The Spanish Civil War erupted: a rebellion of armed fascist forces against a democratically elected government. While Germany and fascist Italy came to the support of General Francisco Franco in his rebellion, France and Britain declared and maintained a policy of nonintervention. The Nazi Condor division flew fighter planes against the Spanish Republican forces, thus acquiring the experience which later proved so effective against France and England—but the two democratic countries stood by, with little more than some minimal and unofficial help for Spanish democracy. Léon Blum played a very unhappy role in this vital conflict.

It was this nonintervention in Spain that induced me to leave Europe and go overseas. War now seemed inevitable; if not immediately, then under worse conditions for the democracies and just a few years away. I thought the issue would be Czechoslovakia. Undoubtedly the Nazis, having protected their western flank by the occupation of the Rhineland and trained their new air force and tested their military equipment in Spain, would begin implementing Hitler's program of expanding the German *Lebensraum* (living space). The three million German-speaking inhabitants of Czechoslovakia would offer a first-rate pretext; they would support German claims on the Prague government. Once the Czech army was out of the way, the last major bulwark of democracy in central Europe would be destroyed.

The Prague government was fully aware of the growing danger and prepared itself as best it could. The armed forces were well equipped, well trained, and well led. They would have acquitted themselves honorably. But it was obvious that, left alone, they could not hold out long against the vastly superior numbers which the Germans could mobilize against them. Czechoslovakia had to be able to count upon massive outside support if it was to survive. While the Czech alliance with Romania and Yugoslavia was designed to neutralize Hungary and her territorial ambitions against all three countries, Czech diplomacy counted on France and England to offset the German threat. And frankly I could not believe, in spite of all disappointments, that the Western powers would be so stupid or cowardly as to abandon Czechoslovakia and her not inconsiderable military might the way they had given up the unfortified Rhineland and Republican Spain.

In any case, whether over the issue of Czechoslovakia or some other Nazi aggression, war on an enormous scale seemed inevitable to me. This would not be a minor altercation as might have occurred if the French had resisted the German military occupation of the Rhineland. Nor would it be limited to a war by proxy as could be expected if the Western powers had come to the aid of the Spanish Republic against the German and Italian military aid to Franco. No, the war I saw coming would be a world war, similar to World War I, if not more devastating in sacrifices and consequences.

Emigration

What was to be my role or duty in this conflict? Obviously, all my sympathies were on the side of the democracies and opposed to Hitler and his supporters. Cowardly and self-defeating as the governments of France and Great Britain were, simple human decency and all values of democracy were on the side of the Western countries. Nor could I shift all the blame to the governments of Britain and France. In both countries the socialist labor movements as well as the Communists had to bear a large share of guilt. Even as farsighted a socialist leader as Blum accepted the capitulation of the Western democracies in the face of Nazi-fascist aggression.

As for me, although I was willing to serve in the armed forces of any democratic country resisting the aggressors, I did not think that this would be the most effective way in which I could contribute to the anti-Nazi cause. I was past the age which the U.S. armed forces declared the most desirable for service on the battlefield. More important perhaps was the fact that my knowledge of languages, foreign countries, and their institutions made other kinds of service more rational from the point of view of the democratic cause. Later events were to confirm this reasoning.

In the course of 1936 I thus decided to leave the continent. The main issue then became the choice of the country to which I wanted to go, and, of course, to which I could be admitted. The question of getting a visa became now one of the most important, and most bothersome, as I soon discovered.

My first choice was England. I had numerous friends there, British as well as Austrian and German. There was the British Labour Party, among whose leaders I had many friends and acquaintances. I would be in a milieu which, although still foreign, would not be as strange to me as, say, Mexico, the United States, or other obvious choices. And, last but in fact first, I would not be too far from the continent and from the dramatic events that I expected would unfold there before long.

Among my acquaintances in England was Elizabeth Wiskemann, political analyst and expert in international relations who just then was working on a book for Chatham House, the home of the distinguished Royal Institute of International Affairs in London. The book was later published as *Czechs and Germans;* it dealt with the rapidly developing tensions between the two language groups in Czechoslovakia, which led in due course to the breakup of the country and its absorption in one form or another by Hitler. She inquired on my behalf at Chatham House, with no success. There was no opening.

Another acquaintance I consulted was Dr. Hugh Dalton, one of the few Englishmen who used his doctor's title without being a physician. He had been a top assistant to Arthur Henderson in the British Labour government, and became chancellor of the exchequer when Labour returned to power in 1945. Dalton was a highly respected economist and had of course excellent connections with British universities, in one of which I hoped eventually to find a little place for myself. When I went to see him at his home in London, he was a man of high repute and tremendous influence. It was clearly in his power to help me with advice and by way of his ample connections. However, all he offered was advice: go to the United States. When I complained that this was too far from Europe and the exciting events that I expected to happen there in the near future, Dalton replied: "On the contrary, you would be much nearer to the continent." My facial expression must have shown my total lack of comprehension, for he continued: "I measure distance in money, not in miles, and you will be earning much more money in the United States than you could in England!"

I took his advice, with one small reservation: I wanted to explore the possibilities of Mexico. Under the presidency of Lázaro Cárdenas, Mexico had acquired the reputation of being a highly progressive and interesting country; and the beautiful landscape I had heard about from various sources added to its charm. Émile Vandervelde knew the Mexican ambassador to Brussels rather well and provided me with an introduction.

My conversation with the ambassador was my first introduction to the art of diplomacy, which combined what I believe to be a Latin American ability to say a lot without saying anything. Charming and inviting, he expressed his confidence that my presence in Mexico would greatly contribute to the cultural enrichment of the country. He intimated that a friend of Émile Vandervelde would of course be especially welcome and that he, personally, would be as helpful as he could in facilitating my entry into the country. Nevertheless, there would of course be all kinds of bureaucratic formalities, and as to jobs the prospects at the time were not too good. Universities in particular had very few full-time faculty members, and part-time lecturers were usually so poorly paid that practically all of them had other full-time jobs to maintain themselves—an observation which I later found to be absolutely correct. All in all, at the end of the conversation, I was impressed by the ambassador's charm, but I did not know any more about my personal prospects in Mexico than I had before.

Fritz Adler strongly urged me to go to the United States, and my experience with the Mexican ambassador appeared to reinforce Fritz's recommendation. I thus turned to the U.S. consul in Antwerp in the hope of settling my business in the rapid and efficient manner that people are told everywhere is the hallmark of the United States. My experience with the worthy gentleman was soon to teach me to add a good portion of skepticism to that well-worn cliché.

Sometime in late 1936 or early 1937—I am not sure of the exact date—I went from Brussels to Antwerp to visit the U.S. consulate, which was authorized to issue visas. I was well equipped with copies of the two books and some of the articles I had published by then, in the hope that my literary output would make a favorable impression upon the gentleman in charge of issuing visas.

Unfortunately, the consul had little interest in my literary output, most of which was published in languages he did not understand and dealt with problems with which he had only a modicum of concern. His interest was aroused, however, when I told him about the Austrian government's decree depriving me of my citizenship. The fact that this decree was unconstitutional, and that I had nevertheless obtained an extension of my Austrian passport made no impression on him. He listened to my attempts to explain what happened with ill-concealed impatience. "I don't know anything about Austrian politics," he said; "I have served the last ten years in Latin America and have had no occasion to follow events in Austria. I can only assume that you have committed a most serious crime which justified taking away your citizenship." He then asked me to translate into English the German language documents referring to my loss of citizenship and to add whatever comments I cared to make to explain my position. "In any case," he added, "I doubt very much that I can make a decision in a case of this kind. I fear I shall have to refer it to the State Department, in which case you may have to wait many months, if not years, for a decision. You may prefer to withdraw your application rather than waste your time waiting for a decision from Washington." This phrase became a kind of recurrent refrain in our conversations—of which there were several—as was my standard answer, "Oh, no, I shall not withdraw my application under any circumstances. My friends in the United States surely want to know whether the United States refuses admission to someone because he is in favor of democracy." This answer made the consul a bit uncertain in his attitude. A man who writes books and articles may well have influential friends in the United States, and a rejection of my request might cause some trouble for the unlucky consul. On the other hand, I might indeed be a dubious character, and to respond favorably to my request might easily get him into difficulties as well. The best solution from his angle was obviously for me to withdraw my application. Thus he endlessly repeated his refrain: "This case may take years to decide. It would be best if you withdraw your application." To which I responded patiently that I would not even consider this course of action, because of my friends in the United States. In fact, at the time I had barely a few of them, mostly newspaper people whom I had met in Geneva at the League of Nations.

I had no alternative but to follow his request and write a lengthy paper, translating the official documents of the Austrian government and then trying to explain the intricate diplomatic and political history of the Austrian Republic from 1918 to 1934 to someone who claimed not to know anything about it. This proved to be a lengthy document. Not only was it a major chore to make central European politics halfway comprehensible to an outsider who confessed total ignorance of the subject; I also had to document my story by referring to sources that would appear

reliable and unbiased to a U.S. government official. After some deliberations with friends, I decided to rely primarily on one source, which had the
double advantage of being American and totally sympathetic to my own
views: the reports of the Vienna correspondent of the *New York Times,*
G. E. R. Gedye.

Gedye was not only profoundly antifascist, but he hated Dollfuss
with a good mixture of contempt, inspired perhaps by the narrow-minded-
ness of this would-be mini-Mussolini. Gedye, like John Gunther, another
distinguished American journalist in Austria, had admiration for the Austrian Social Democrats, especially for the outstanding work they had done
in Vienna. Gunther expressed his views not only in his writings, but also
participated actively in the underground that the Social Democrats set up
after February 1934, whereas Gedye demonstrated his feelings primarily
in his reports to the *New York Times.* His hatred and contempt for Dollfuss
exceeded even mine, although he was convinced that cooperation between
Dollfuss and the Social Democrats might have enabled Austria to resist
Nazi pressure. In his view, Dollfuss, inadequate to realize his historical
potential and driven by blind hatred (especially for the socialist leader Otto
Bauer who was vastly superior to him in intelligence and eloquence), had
left the doors wide open to Hitler as well as to Mussolini.

Gedye was thus an excellent witness for my cause. The fact that he
was a correspondent for the most influential American newspaper added
considerable prestige to his reports. I added some fairly spicy comments
from as respectable a source as Chatham House. Its annual report on
events of 1934 was critical of Dollfuss, in unusually sharp terms for such a
stodgy publication. I hoped that criticism from Chatham House, which no
one in his right mind could label "radical," was bound to impress the
highly conservative State Department official.

Still, all I received from the consul was an acknowledgment of the
receipt of the document, accompanied by the usual remark that the case
"most probably would have to be referred to Washington for a decision."
And then the waiting began. Leaden silence from Antwerp. Not that I was
in a great hurry. This was still the fall of 1937, I had found interesting
work, and I was under no pressure to leave Europe. I was working on my
book on Eastern Europe and spent a good deal of time in London as

correspondent for the German-language Social Democratic papers in Czechoslovakia. The London Labour paper *Daily Herald* offered me its hospitality and its news service. From time to time I went to Belgium to find out the status of my visa application, but otherwise I spent a delightful fall in London. Every morning the sun was shining, and although the British climate is rarely regarded as one of the main assets of the country, fate gave the British the last beautiful fling before sending them into the hell of World War II. I would buy a number of newspapers and rent a deck chair in Hyde Park in the morning, and there read them in the mild September sun.

Prospects for the U.S. visa seemed to grow bleaker every day. Apparently the consul in Antwerp had carried out his threat to forward the "case" of the dubious foreigner to the State Department. Then some unforeseeable incidents occurred that were once again to change my prospects, indeed possibly save my life.

One of the consul's conditions for even considering my request was for me to get a passport valid for at least six months. He refused to accept my Austrian passport; my Swiss passport was destroyed and, of course, I would not have dared in any case to submit it to him. How was I to get a valid passport of any kind that would meet the consul's requirements? While living in Brussels, I had belonged to a car pool that included Louis de Brouckère, Belgium's representative in various League of Nations organizations and in the Bureau of the Labor and Socialist International. I knew him well from many meetings. When he learned that I was staying first in a pension, later in a small apartment near Brussels's famous tree-lined Avenue Louise, he suggested that I join a car pool that went into the center of the city every morning. Since my working hours at night were quite irregular I could not use the return service, but in the morning the car proved very useful. One of the members of the pool was Paul-Henri Spaak, then one of the most vocal left-wing leaders of the party and a member of the government. De Brouckère told Spaak about my manifold problems, and Spaak came up with a solution for one of them.

There existed a document called a *passeport* for foreigners valid for six months, i.e., permitting the foreigner to return from abroad to Belgium within a period of six months. This document, unknown to me until then, satisfied the requirements of the U.S. consul. But still, he did his best to persuade me to withdraw my visa application so that he could escape the awful dilemma of having to accept or reject my application.

A minor but bothersome problem was obtaining the so-called "certificate of good behavior" covering my entire life. This was a document, or rather a series of documents, to be issued by the police department of every city in which I had ever lived, testifying to the fact that I had not committed any serious offense while I resided in that particular city. The greater part of my life had been spent in Vienna. How could I get a certificate of good behavior from the Viennese police after having been deprived of my Austrian citizenship? A friend who worked in the U.S. embassy in Brussels knew the Austrian ambassador in that city and was on friendly terms with him. He volunteered to ask the ambassador whether he would be willing to issue such a certificate for me, or arrange to have one sent to me from the Vienna police. I listened in on another phone to the conversation and heard the Austrian dignitary say: "All I can promise is that I won't look up the name. If I don't know him, I'll give him the certificate." My friend turned to me and asked me whether he should tell my name to the Austrian dignitary. Since I had nothing to lose and everything to gain, I assented.

The response, if not surprising, was immediate and clear-cut, "That name," he said, "I need not look up. The best thing I can do for your friend is to forget this entire conversation. I am under orders to report his whereabouts to Vienna. Let us agree that we never talked about him."

Crestfallen, I started to look for alternative ways to obtain this apparently indispensable document. Nothing occurred to me until I remembered a joke that an Austrian friend had told me a few days before. A Viennese Social Democrat, who was in prison for political reasons, was taken before a court by three guards. He was dying to get some cigarettes and when they passed a *Tabak-Trafik,* as the tobacco stores are called in Vienna, he begged one of the guards to permit him to buy some. "You are asking the wrong guard," was the answer. "I am a Nazi, and that fellow behind us is an Austro-fascist. But the other guy, he is a *Sozi* [the Viennese nickname for members of the Social Democratic Party]; you'd better ask him."

What mattered was to find a Social Democrat in the Vienna police department who might be willing to issue the required document despite my earlier conflict with Dollfuss. Indeed, for many of my fellow Social Democrats, who equally had despised the murdered chancellor, this conflict might be a recommendation for me. In any case, they might just "fail" to look up the ill-named file of involuntary "expatriates." If everything failed, I could probably rely on locating a lawyer in Vienna who knew somebody, who in turn knew somebody who would do the necessary for a modest compensation. After all, Austria in the midst of the continuing depression was a very poor country, and a small amount of money would go a long way.

I did not know anyone who might help me, but I still had some friends left in Vienna who probably did. One letter was sufficient: a lawyer was found who for a remarkably modest fee produced an official "certificate of good behavior" covering my entire life span. This not only solved my political problem, but also relieved me of the tremendous burden of soliciting similar certificates from the authorities of all the numerous cities in which I had lived since I left Vienna. This proved to be a simple solution which seemed to satisfy the requirements of the U.S. consul and absolved me from all further worries on this score.

What remained now was the most difficult issue of all, namely, how to convince the U.S. consul in Antwerp of my "innocence," or at least of my innocuousness. For him, the fact that I had been deprived of my Austrian citizenship was convincing evidence that I was at least a suspicious character. How could I prove to his satisfaction that I was not and never had been a Communist, an anarchist, or other subversive character?

I was pondering this question one day in Brussels when I encountered an old friend, Henry K. Erlich. He was the foremost spokesman of the Jewish-socialist *Bund,* an anti-Zionist organization whose main base was Poland. In contrast to the other Jewish-socialist party, *Poale-Zion,* the *Bund* opposed the establishment of a Jewish state but favored instead the civic equality of Jews wherever they lived. While the *Bund* and *Poale-Zion* were both socialist organizations and both members of the Socialist International, their attitudes toward Theodor Herzl's advocacy of a Jewish return to Israel divided them. It is perhaps also not unfair to describe the *Bund* as slightly more leftist than *Poale-Zion,* but that difference mattered less than that of their attitude toward a Jewish "homeland."

I knew Erlich from numerous meetings of the Executive Committee of the Socialist International, of which he was a respected member. The respect was directed more at him personally than at the small organization which he represented. Erlich was a great admirer of my ability to interpret speeches given in French and English into German, and once told me jokingly how much he regretted speaking in German since that did not allow him to use my services. In any case, he was a good friend and proved of tremendous help to me in my quest to get an American visa.

"What are your plans?" he asked—a standard question then going around among socialists, and especially Jewish socialists. "Honestly," I said, "I don't know. I should like to go to the United States, but the consul in Antwerp does not seem to think too well of that idea." "Why not?" Thus encouraged, I told Erlich the sad story of my trials and tribulations in getting the immigration visa to the United States. Erlich listened quietly and then said rather authoritatively, "I have just come back from one of my frequent trips to the United States. We have some pretty influential friends there. Let me see what they can do for you."

I confess that I was not unduly impressed by this promise, but I had little or nothing to lose. Besides, I am rather optimistic by nature and thus hoped that, with or without the assistance of Erlich's friends, I would somehow manage to get the desired permission to emigrate to the United States. Still, I was more than pleasantly surprised when a few weeks later I received a copy of the letter that was to change the situation dramatically. It was a letter from Charney Vladeck, then leader of the majority in the New York City Council, addressed to the consul in Antwerp. It told the consul in no uncertain terms how much Vladeck was looking forward to my coming to the United States, how much I could contribute to the intellectual life of the country, and that my democratic convictions fitted me very well for life in America. A day or two later a copy of another letter arrived. This one was written by Mayor Fiorello LaGuardia, the most powerful elected official of the city of New York and immensely popular. In essence, though in different words, he told the consul the same things that Vladeck had written; a letter from such a source was bound to have influence on the lowly consul, just as Vladeck's letter written on the official stationery of the majority leader of the New York City Council must have too. Indeed, I suspect the consul may have expected the next letter in my behalf to come from a high official in the State Department or even the White House. All that of course was Erlich's doing, not my own. I doubt that either of these two eminent American officials had ever heard of me or read any of my books or articles. Erlich's word obviously carried a good deal of weight in New York.

In any case, a day or two later I received a telephone call from the consul asking me to "come and get your visa." I still had to pass a physical examination by a doctor designated by the consulate, which I did without a hitch and then, at long last, I got my immigration visa stamped into the Belgian *passeport* for foreigners. It was valid for four months; since I received it late in January 1938, this meant that I had to enter the United States before the end of May.

I was in no particular hurry to leave Europe, now that I knew I could go to the United States before long. A few months before I had been appointed London correspondent of the German-language Social Democratic newspapers in Czechoslovakia. This job pleased me a good deal and gave me an outlet for what I had to say about British and international politics. The job did not pay very much, but my needs were modest and so I managed quite well. I was thus under no financial pressure to leave Europe immediately. On the other hand, the Nazi threat against Austria made it clear that the hour of decision was rapidly approaching. Though I did not believe that Austria could still be saved, I hoped that Czechoslovakia, clearly marked as Hitler's next objective, would resist and get the support of the Western democracies.

In Austria matters were rapidly coming to a head. After Chancellor Dollfuss had been assassinated by the Nazis in 1934, his successor Kurt von Schuschnigg had continued the war on the two fronts that his predecessor had started, though with highly unequal vigor. The sharpest measures were taken against the Social Democrats who could have been his natural allies against the Nazis. Concentration camps, torture, and arbitrary arrests drove the supporters of that unhappy mass party into the "underground"—creating what must have been one of the largest underground political movements of all time. Considerably gentler methods were used against the Nazis, even though they were the deadliest enemy of the small Alpine republic.

As if this were not enough, Schuschnigg also got rid of any potential rivals in his own ranks. The Austro-fascist regime relied substantially upon the so-called *Heimwehr,* armed guards whose equipment and finances were provided largely by Mussolini. The main leaders of the *Heimwehr* were Prince Starhemberg and Major Fey. Everyone—Schuschnigg, Starhemberg, and Fey—suspected the others of being willing or even eager to betray one another to the Nazis, whose rapidly rising power they all felt and feared. Schuschnigg, by far the most intelligent of the three, emerged as the victor in this struggle. He successively got rid of Fey and Starhemberg, but only to submit in the end to the overwhelming power of Hitler.

The crucial signal for the destruction of Austria as an independent nation occurred on February 12, 1938, when Schuschnigg secretly crossed the border to visit Hitler on his estate in Obersalzberg in Bavaria. By chance or arrangement, this was the fourth anniversary of the day when Dollfuss had bombarded the workers' houses in Vienna. Schuschnigg must have felt how ominous his trip was, because he made arrangements for the defense of Austria's borders against Germany in case he was prevented from returning to Austria. He had been informed in no uncertain terms by the British and French governments—both deeply involved in their policy of appeasement toward Hitler—that he could not count on any help from them if Hitler were to take military measures against the little Austrian republic.

While neither Fey nor Starhemberg deserves more than passing attention because of their relatively modest roles in the destruction of the Austrian democratic republic, a few remarks may be directed deservedly to the far more interesting figure of Schuschnigg, the last chancellor of Austria prior to World War II. Incidentally, he was the man who as minister of justice in the Dollfuss cabinet in March 1934 signed the decree depriving me of my Austrian citizenship.

Like so many other Austrians, Schuschnigg was of Slavic origin. Both his grandfather, Major General Schuschnigg, and his father were officers in the army of the old Hapsburg empire. The semiaristocratic title *von* was awarded to the family only toward the end of the nineteenth century. His father had been stationed most of the time in the non-German parts of the empire, a fact that was not without impact upon the growing youngster. For these were the areas in which German nationalism was most pronounced and where lower-class people, even when of non-German origin, sought social advancement by becoming super-Germans.

In Schuschnigg's case, German nationalism was combined in a somewhat contradictory fashion with a second factor: a nostalgic loyalty to the pre-World War I Hapsburgs and to the old Imperial and Royal (*k. und k.*, in the traditional Austrian abbreviation) regime to which his father and grandfather had sworn allegiance. After all, until 1866 when Prussia defeated Austria, it was the latter that was held to be the leading German state in Europe, "destined to bring German civilization to the backward Slavic parts of the empire" just as the German knights had done in Prussia.

The third element that formed Schuschnigg's character was his education by the Jesuits. While he had little love for the Nazis with their old-Germanic, heathenish leanings and their desire to absorb Austria into a half-Protestant country, he had even less sympathy for the godless socialists. True, by no means were all socialists antireligious or even merely irreligious. In intensely Roman Catholic Austria, no political party could obtain two-fifths of the popular votes if it presented itself as an enemy of religion. The Socialist Party harbored not only an organization of "Freethinkers," but was also led by a group that consisted largely of either "Freethinkers" or Jews. Bauer was Jewish, as was the editor-in-chief of the main party newspaper. Indeed, for Schuschnigg the whole intellectual basis of the party, its invocation of Karl Marx and his teachings smacked of the Antichrist.

It is probably idle to speculate on what prospects Austria might have had in resisting the Nazis if Schuschnigg had been willing to come to terms with the labor movement rather than to seek a desperate refuge in negotiating with Hitler. The military factors were hardly promising. Mussolini, barely free of the burden that the war in Ethiopia had placed on the Italian people, deeply involved in the Spanish Civil War, and allied to Nazi Germany, had made clear to his satellites in Austria that he was in no position to oppose any German move into Austria. France and Britain had been unwilling to resist Nazi Germany even before its rearmament was half completed; they had shown this in 1936 when German troops were ordered into the demilitarized zone of the Rhineland at a time when Hitler was so unsure of himself that his commanding officers had secret orders to withdraw if they were to meet any resistance. What hope was there that the Western powers would risk a large-scale conflagration for the sake of an Austria whose people showed considerable sympathy for the German Führer, himself of Austrian origin? The only immediate military assistance could come from Czechoslovakia, and it required a good deal of optimism to expect open military action on the part of the Prague government. It required even greater trust in the intelligence and foresight of France and Britain to believe that they, having no doubt dissuaded Czechoslovakia from acting, would come to the rescue of their ally if it disregarded their warnings.

Still, even though resistance was a slender reed indeed, it was the only hope there was. The labor movement, emerging from its underground, was willing to take this chance and support the very same government that had so brutally suppressed it. Some workers, it is true, mainly those most directly involved in the civil war of February 1934, had gone over to the Nazis, not so much out of sympathy for their ideas and programs as in hopes of finding in them an instrument of revenge. The great majority of organized labor was willing, and to some degree prepared, to fight on the side of the government. Semisecret meetings of the underground organization took place in an atmosphere mixed with hope and desperation. The leaders recommended an understanding with the Schuschnigg government and its forces. Bauer and Deutsch, who had fled to Czechoslovakia and set up a party office there, counseled resistance against a Nazi invasion even at the price of an alliance with Schuschnigg. All to no avail. To the extent to which I was still in contact both with the leaders of the underground movement and with Bauer, I too urged resistance, only to be told that the government preferred to rely on Mussolini's ability to restrain Hitler rather than on an alliance with "Reds." In any case, my messages, though they reached the addresses, came too late.

Clearly, the fate of Austria was sealed when the chancellor visited the Führer and undertook to negotiate with him. Then, the only question was: When would the Third Reich take delivery? In weeks, months, or even right away? I was quite certain of the inevitability of the outcome. I wrote to my brother in Vienna urging him to take his wife and daughter abroad immediately. Apart from this, there was nothing else left for me to do but to await the catastrophe.

I was skiing in Mégéve, France, then just at the beginning of its greatness as a winter sports center for the well-to-do, when the news of Hitler's annexation of Austria reached me. On the same day, by a tragic coincidence, I also received news from my family in Vienna. They had been given assurance that my brother's very remunerative job was secure, and he felt too old to start a new life elsewhere. Apparently, the thought had not occurred to them that the guarantors of his job themselves might be in danger from the Third Reich. This took them only a few months to find out, and then mobilize heaven and hell in order to get out of Austria. So certain was I of this outcome that before leaving Europe, I established a small trust fund in Switzerland for my family to enable them to wait out the period necessary to arrange for their entry into the United States.

Anyhow, here I was in the French mountains when Austria fell. I rushed to Paris that same night, arriving the next morning, to see whether there was anything I could do to help the refugees who were bound to try to leave the new German province. There was indeed a lot to do, as I soon found out.

One of the first arrivals I met in Paris was an old friend, Albert Lauterbach, who later would successfully teach the dismal science of economics to young ladies at Sarah Lawrence College near New York City. Although married to a lovely lady of unquestionable "Aryan" extraction, he was doubly "suspect" in the eyes of the new regime: he was Jewish and a member of the socialist movement. Having closely followed the denouement of the Austrian republic, he was well prepared for a sudden departure. This was made easier for him by the fact that his wife, not sharing the most unreedemable of his defects, i.e., not being Jewish, could stay on in Vienna and liquidate their modest affairs. At that she was lucky. Others who followed this procedure under similar though not always identical circumstances missed the last "exit" from Vienna. She left unharmed a few weeks later.

Lauterbach contacted me almost immediately upon his arrival to Paris, to bring me bad news. Just after he entered France by way of Switzerland—the only relatively easy western exit from Austria—the French immigration officials had closed the frontier to Austrian travelers. This in fact meant that the border was closed to Austrian refugees. When the French decision became known to the Swiss authorities, they in turn refused admission to Austrians, on the theory that since none would be permitted residence—even temporary—in Switzerland, transit was the only purpose of entry. Since passage to France had become impossible, all traffic stopped for the unfortunate and desperate, eager to escape from Austria.

Fortunately, we were not completely without hope. Léon Blum was again the French prime minister, though his power was modest and his term of office, as was the custom in the Third Republic, would prove exceedingly brief. I reached Blum's *chef de cabinet,* a former Socialist Party official, on the phone, and reported to him what I had just learned. He was astonished since no orders had been issued from Paris, and according to him, either my report was incorrect or some subordinate official had acted on his own. In any case, he assured me that the necessary instructions would be issued to permit the entry into France of anyone who could plausibly claim to be a potential target of Nazi persecution. Also, the Swiss authorities would be informed of the French action.

A few hours later I learned that Blum had been true to his word. An unknown number of Austrians may owe their lives, or at least their freedom, to his action. Unfortunately, Blum was compelled to resign as prime minister soon afterward, and subsequent French regimes were far less hospitable to those who attempted to flee the dangers of Nazi concentration camps. Indeed, the government established by Marshal Pétain and Premier Laval after the defeat of France in 1940 did not hesitate to hand over refugees to the Nazi authorities. In this way Rudolf Hilferding, the former German minister of finance whose dedication to balanced budgets at any price had contributed so much to the downfall of the Weimar Republic, met his tragic end. He was about to board a ship in Marseilles to leave France, when at the last moment he changed his mind—why, no one knows. The French authorities soon afterward handed him over to the Nazis. Eventually he was found dead in his cell. His close friend Rudolf Breitscheid, foreign affairs spokesman for the Social Democratic Party in the Reichstag, shared this fate up to a point. He, too, refused to board the ship that was to take both of them to North Africa and was eventually transferred to Buchenwald concentration camp. However, perhaps because he was not Jewish, the Nazis assigned him to a special section in the camp. There, by a tragic irony of history, he was killed in an Allied bombing attack.

There was not much more for me to do in Europe. Most of my remaining duties concerned my family, more exactly my brother in Vienna. Apart from that, I concentrated on obtaining introductions to use in the United States in order to find my way about in that strange country.

My trip across the ocean preceded the Czechoslovak crisis of September 1938. Barely having absorbed Austria and transformed it into *Ostmark,* the Third Reich turned against the last remaining democracy in Central Europe and severed the Sudetenland from Czechoslovakia—a harbinger of things to come. In March 1939 Hitler's troops seized the rest of the country.

The New World

I went the way of most Central European refugees at the time. A modest room on Manhattan's upper West Side housed my belongings and myself. I searched out the few acquaintances I had in New York to get advice on what to do and what to avoid. I became acquainted with that—at the time—uniquely American institution, the cafeteria (which offered both cheap food and a modicum of sociability), and I made some new friends. Most of the social life I enjoyed was confined to a limited circle of other Central European refugees, although my better knowledge of English and greater willingness to accept alien mores made it easier for me to broaden my social contacts. The large number of new arrivals who rejected everything that was different only made life more difficult for themselves, and sometimes even for those who were identified erroneously with these recalcitrants.

The great majority of refugees shared two main concerns: getting jobs for themselves and visas for those who were still overseas and in danger. Jobs, of course, were hard to find. The United States was still in the throes of the Great Depression, with mass unemployment numbering in the millions. The newcomers, a large proportion of whom were professionals, were severely handicapped in the competition for the few available jobs. Their knowledge of English was limited or nonexistent. Notions of professional dignity prevented many from accepting "lower-class" jobs that occasionally came their way. How could a former lawyer, a pillar of society in his German city, be expected to work as a simple bookkeeper or, worse still, as a manual laborer? American law required that some professionals go through a new learning period and pass an examination before they could even begin to reestablish themselves in their old calling.

Journalists and writers, though free of legal restrictions, had lost the main instrument of their work; they not only had to learn English, they had to master it.

For the large number of professors who came from Germany and for those who were now arriving from Austria (with many others still to follow), special arrangements had to be made. The New School for Social Research in New York City added a Graduate School to its program and manned it predominantly with German and one or two Austrian scholars. This, however, took care of only a small proportion of the candidates. Younger men and a few women obtained financial assistance for a year or two of graduate study at first-rate universities. Combining the advantages of European and American education, and with the assistance of their graduate professors, they frequently succeeded in finding promising openings. A number of them became leading members of their profession in the United States and ended up in top universities to which they lent a cosmopolitan flavor. A select few—the physicists Albert Einstein and Wolfgang Pauli among them—were received with honor and distinction at the Institute for Advanced Studies in Princeton, New Jersey.

For the largest number, none of these arrangements applied. A committee collected some money for this group and made an interesting offer to American institutions of higher learning. The committee provided a monthly salary of $200 for a year for any newly appointed refugee faculty member, provided that the academic institution would retain the person in question beyond the first year at the institution's expense. Since the committee's means were limited, and few colleges or universities were making substantial additions to their staffs, the number of refugees thus placed was quite small in proportion to the supply.

My own problem was both more complicated and more simple than most. The complication arose from the fact that I was engaged in changing not only my country and language, but also my profession. Almost fifteen years had passed since I had completed my dissertation in economics, and in the meantime fundamental changes in economic theory and practice had occurred; I had followed these only inadequately. My experience in international affairs and especially international labor might come in handy, but first I had to catch up with at least the most fundamental advances that economists had made in the preceding fifteen years, and in addition I had to learn and adopt some of the more empirical, less speculative approaches of American economics. A few journalistic assignments from Switzerland kept me alive during this transition period.

In the meantime, problem area number two—visas—kept me busy, as did the duty of welcoming and offering what modest advice I had to newcomers. The latter assignment consisted mainly in inviting new arrivals to lunch, partly to make sure they would have at least one hot meal that day and partly to put them in touch with people who could be helpful in their search for a new beginning. I remember a surprising twist in this series of welcoming lunches.

The man in question had been one of the leaders of the underground movement in Austria; he had taken over after the first leadership team had been "caught" by Schuschnigg's police. Joseph Buttinger was an unusual person whose entire life had been shaped by his connection with the Austrian labor movement. Born in a rural, extremely poor environment, early in his life he entered the trade union movement where he drew the attention of local and later provincial labor leaders. He was sent to various Social Democratic Party schools, where once again he excelled. When, after the arrest of the first team of underground leaders, the search for their successors began, he soon emerged as a most promising candidate. Within a short time he acquired a dominant role in the movement.

One of the basic, yet eternal, problems of an underground movement is to find a safe place for meetings. In the years between February 1934 and Hitler's march into Austria, the apartments of U.S. citizens in Austria offered a secure refuge. The police did not yet dare enter these apartments; nor did they interfere with speeches of American journalists at underground meetings. Thus John Gunther, one of the outstanding American journalists who admired the Austrian labor movement, and other Western correspondents of distinction, spoke repeatedly at such meetings.

An American student of medicine, a woman from a very well-to-do family, Muriel Gardiner, volunteered her services to the underground organization. Her apartment was made available for meetings of the "illegal" organization. In this way the new underground leader became acquainted with the American woman, met her repeatedly, and the inevitable happened: they fell in love. In 1938 they left Austria and came to the United States. None of this was known to me, except the fact of a new arrival. As usual, I invited the newcomer to luncheon and talked about the problems facing a newcomer. When I inquired what his plans were, I was not a little surprised about his answer: "I guess," he said, "I am going to write a book about the recent events in Austria."

"I doubt that you can earn a living that way," I responded. "Few publishers, if any, would give you a large enough advance to ensure your livelihood while you prepare the manuscript. After all, and with due respect for your role in recent Austrian history, you are not known in this country. You will need a job to keep you going until the manuscript is ready." "No problem," was the surprising response. "My livelihood is assured." This was splendid, though surprising news for me. One problem less to worry about. Yet, I could not help but wonder what the explanation for this apparent miracle was. A few weeks later, in talking to another refugee, I got the explanation. I learned that my luncheon guest, who had permitted me to pay for his luncheon out of my meager savings, had married the American heiress of the Swift family. There was indeed no problem about where his livelihood would come from. Under the circumstances the reader may understand that I never quite forgave my comrade for having let me pay for his meal. In all fairness he still owes me a return engagement.

My quest for personal employment fairly soon found a satisfactory and somewhat surprising solution—or rather a series of solutions. The first was perhaps the most surprising. While in Washington on my job search, I was introduced to a professor of international relations at American University who wanted to be relieved of his teaching duties for at least one semester. The reason was his wish to move to New York in order to play the stock market, something which, he thought, could not be done as efficiently from distant Washington. The compensation he offered was ridiculously small, but, nevertheless, I was delighted to accept. Now I had my first academic appointment. I "belonged." Though it was obviously not a standard job and of necessity lacked permanence, I had made the great and difficult transition from nowhere into the American academic world.

For quite some time this was my one and only professional success. All my visits and interviews at Columbia and at Harvard—where I got good but fruitless advice from the famous Austrian-born economist Joseph

Schumpeter—led nowhere. Then, quite unexpectedly, I had my second successful introduction into what was possible in the country of "unlimited possibilities." Walking along New York's Fifth Avenue, I noticed a door sign: "Carnegie Corporation." Even though I had failed in my attempt to revive the Rockefeller Foundation fellowship which I had scorned ages ago, I decided to try my luck with another U.S. foundation.

Without any introduction whatsoever, not even knowing the names of any of the dignitaries of the Carnegie Corporation, I just entered the office. The receptionist asked me whom I wanted to see. Without hesitation, I replied: "I should like to talk to someone about a possible research grant." Though obviously bewildered by my unorthodox approach, but perhaps because she recognized my foreign origin, the young lady asked me to wait and disappeared into one of the rooms along the corridor behind her desk.

A few minutes later a young man appeared and introduced himself as assistant to the president of the corporation. I told him about myself and my plans. I intended to write, I said, the story of the tragic defeat of the European labor movement, partly to clarify my own thinking about the catastrophe that had destroyed the movement, and with it democracy, over a large part of the European continent, and partly to see whether the experience carried with it any lessons from which the United States might draw useful consequences.

The young man, John Gardner, later a leading figure in public life, listened patiently, took some notes, and asked a few questions about my training in the social sciences and the work I had done in Europe. I, in turn, asked him to find out whether an application for research support would be in order. "I would not want to go to the trouble of preparing an application, nor put the corporation to the trouble of having to examine it, if my project did not come within the province of the corporation's interests." Gardner promised to investigate and to let me know whether an application was in order. With this, we ended our conversation.

Several weeks passed, and I had given up hope of any kind of response, when I received a letter from the Carnegie people indicating that my application—which I had never submitted—had been favorably acted upon. The only question the letter raised was where the funds were to be sent. The amount was quite impressive for prewar days. Moreover, the corporation later added a subsidy to facilitate publication of my manuscript, which was published in 1943 by Columbia University Press under the title *The Tragedy of European Labor, 1918–1939.* This book went through two American and five foreign editions. The *New York Times,* then far more conservative than in later years, was critical of the book, but elsewhere the reception was quite friendly. Adoption by a book club in England even provided some monetary reward for my effort. Unfortunately, Columbia University Press let the book go out of print after its second edition—an error on their part as the editor himself later admitted.

Clearly, in light of my experience with the Carnegie Corporation, the United States was indeed the "land of unlimited opportunities." The funds I received were sufficient to tide me over the difficult period of adjusting to a strange land, a new profession, and a foreign tongue—all this in the wake of the worst economic depression and mass unemployment of the century. The grant also enabled me to devote a large portion of my time to research and writing, and not merely to the tedious and frustrating task of job-hunting—in a place and a time when jobs were practically nonexistent.

I have little doubt that no American scholar could have gotten away with the highly unorthodox procedure I followed in approaching the Carnegie Corporation. It is also likely that, unbeknownst to me, Gardner had made some inquiries and obtained reasonably favorable information about me. I had met, a few weeks before, Professor Leo Wolman of Columbia University, a specialist in labor problems, and, although I have no information about this, I would not be surprised if he had been asked for advice about my project and my person. In any case, this was an excellent introduction to the academic world which was to be my new home.

There were two curious incidents relating to the publication of my book. The English book club edition, published in London during the war, dropped the last chapter at the request of the Foreign Office. This chapter set out my perspective on the postwar world: there would be friction and conflict between the wartime allies, especially between the West and the Soviet Union. Apparently, in the view of the British Foreign Office, this should not be said so long as the war required cooperation with the Soviet Union in the struggle against the Third Reich. My publisher and I capitulated to the wartime considerations. Were we right?

Another incident had to do less with my book than with the commercial talent of my publisher. I was surprised by the high price of the volume. It is true that it was well prepared, had a hard cover, good paper, and so on. But I was interested in having students buy the book and asked whether a cheaper edition could be prepared. The answer was categorically negative: the hard cover alone made for a high price. "In France," I said, "most books are published in soft covers and are very cheap. A Frenchman might buy three or four books at the beginning of a railroad trip and discard perhaps half of them if he did not like them." "That is impossible in the United States," was the answer, "no American will ever buy a paper-covered book." That was said in 1943. I am not sure when paperback books came out, but surely it was soon afterward and, needless to say, they have been a huge success. So much for the commercial talent of my publisher. None of my later books was even offered to Columbia University Press. In fact, one of them, dealing with white-collar workers, was published by the University of Illinois Press in Urbana in both a hardcover and a paperback edition. I understand that both sold well. But that was quite a bit later.

One more incident deserves at least passing mention. Among the introductions I had brought along were some to the League for Industrial Democracy (LID), to its director Harry W. Laidler, the author of an excellent text on socioeconomic reform movements, and to its chairman, the well-known and widely respected socialist leader, Norman Thomas. The League held an annual spring conference, and in June 1938—shortly after my arrival—I was invited to engage in a debate on collective security with no less a person than Thomas, a leader of the so-called "isolationists." He was a master of the English language and the art of debate. The topic was such that we held exactly opposite views and thus were well chosen for a debate, except that my English was barely adequate. For me to take him on was, to put it mildly, foolhardy in the extreme.

But my cause was good and my heart was pure, or so I thought. I accepted. I carefully prepared my presentation in writing (something I never did when speaking in German or French), dictated it to the pretty woman who was secretary at the LID, and, thanks to a good memory, managed to give the speech without looking at the manuscript in my hand. The good-looking secretary, Hattie Ross, was impressed by my performance—so much so that she became my wife.

Although the year of my "rebirth," 1938, was quite positive in regard to my future, the following year was completely unproductive. I wrote a few articles for European magazines and gave two or three poorly paid lectures, but nothing emerged which pointed to a steady livelihood.

While I continued to look for a permanent occupation, I worked with Friedrich (Fritz) Adler, who had come to New York to organize an Austrian relief organization, Friends of Austrian Labor. The chairman, of course, was Fritz, but I was not a little shocked when he told me quite openly and, so to speak, in passing, "You cannot expect much more from me." In spite of this he accomplished much, but at heart he was clearly a broken man. During his lifetime the Socialist International, to which he had devoted so much effort, had collapsed twice. The work of his lifetime was destroyed; the task to which he had entirely dedicated himself was unfulfilled. His role as a leader was over; what he could do now was help others.

The consciousness of his tragic failure now became completely and shockingly clear to me. In the course of a discussion concerning prior events in Austria, without any introduction or preliminary remark, Adler, a hero to me and many others, pronounced the shocking words: "When I committed my great blunder . . . ." It was the murder of Stürgkh that he could now, in the light of all of his disappointments, only regard as his "great blunder." I had no answer. Clearly, Fritz did not speak of the moral question of political murder; he had only the political consequences in mind. His difficulties in coping with the moral significance of his action had been clear to me for quite a long time. Now, however, there was the political doubt as well. The greatest event of his life, that which had determined its whole course, had now become a "great blunder." This was the end of more than a legend, and for many years I hesitated to make his comment public, but eventually I decided that I owe this truth to history.

After 1945 Fritz had no close connection with the Austrian Socialist Party. To be sure, no Austrian Socialist leader dared to oppose Fritz openly. Yet, to everyone with even the remotest sense of Austrian politics after World War II, it was completely clear that the new leadership of Adolf Schärf, Heinrich Schneidmadl, and their friends attempted to distance itself as much as possible from the old party. It was precisely the enemies of Bauer and Adler within the party, kept in check by Bauer before 1934, who had now taken over the leadership of the Austrian Socialists.

For Adler, and, I may add, for me, a return to Austria was out of the question. Fritz, unable to make a positive contribution, would have been a heavy burden on the new party leadership. I was quite happy in my new country, I had lost confidence in my political judgment after the terrible defeat of the socialists in Europe, and I had an American family. Thus what Austria had to offer seemed small and unimportant to me, and I felt a kind of moral obligation toward the country that had offered me asylum in my plight caused by the turmoil in Europe. I have never regretted this decision, although I love Austria and like to visit it. Besides, the Austrian government has shown much kindness toward me: in 1975 I was awarded a decoration, the Grand Golden Badge of Honor for Merits, by the Republic of Austria; in 1980 I was the guest of the Austrian government at the twenty-fifth anniversary of the evacuation of the occupation forces; I was invited to the University of Vienna as a guest professor in 1982–83, and so on.

As I have already mentioned, we had established a new organization under the leadership of Adler and other friends of the party during the war, which we called Friends of Austrian Labor. At first, the activity of the organization was directed toward a negative goal: we wanted to prevent at the time any decisions by foreign governments or by émigrés concerning the postwar fate of Austria. A war fought in defense of democracy should grant Austrians the right to decide their own fate democratically as soon as circumstances would permit. For all practical purposes this meant preventing the establishment of an Austrian government in exile. In such a government the Christian Social Party would necessarily be represented along with the Social Democrats. The Christian Social Party had destroyed democracy in Austria, dissolved the trade unions and the Social Democratic Party, and introduced fascist methods of government which were moderated only by the weakness of the party. Moreover, there were persons and circles, especially in Washington, who had a certain influence in the White House, and were considering a return of the Hapsburgs to the throne in Vienna.

In our activities Friends of Austrian Labor ran across two persons who gave us a lot of trouble. One, Hans Rott, was a former member of the Schuschnigg government who now presented himself as successor to the last "legal" government of Austria. Since he had played only a subordinate role in the government and had shown a certain degree of liberalism, he could count on sympathy from a few Austrians.

More important to us, and more difficult, was the case of Julius Deutsch. He had always been in a hopeless rivalry with Otto Bauer. Frankly, his personal vanity was such that he met with resistance everywhere. I remember a small but characteristic scene during a meeting of the disarmament commission of the International, of which the Dutchman J. Albarda was the chairman. Deutsch presented an amendment to a resolution; I do not remember its content, but that is insignificant here. He handed the paper to Albarda, remarking, "Amendment Deutsch/Bauer." Albarda took the paper and said, "Amendment Bauer/Deutsch." Deutsch replied, "Deutsch/Bauer." Albarda said, unaffectedly, "That's correct, Bauer/Deutsch."

I am quite aware of the fact that a political leader is almost always vain or at least self-confident. Someone not convinced of the significance of what he has to say will hardly find the courage to stand before a crowd and give a speech. Yet, even if we take this into account, Deutsch, who also had many outstanding qualities, was an unusually vain man. The fact that he could not play an important part in emigration, and that, moreover, his poor English prevented him from giving impressive speeches, was unbearable to him. Therefore, the idea of establishing an Austrian government in exile, which was conceivable only with the collaboration of the former Christian Social Party, seemed to him at least worth considering. He, no doubt, would have occupied at least the second position in such a government; he would have had access to the most important political leaders of the Atlantic Alliance; and he would have been an interesting character for the press. All this made him amenable to the suggestions of Rott, a member of the Schuschnigg government—that is, of the last Austro-fascist government. In this Rott was aided by the fact that in England, where there were nonsocialist democrats among the émigrés, a kind of "foreign representation" had been founded. In the United States, on the other hand, there was a promonarchist "movement" which tried to establish an Austrian batallion to fight side by side with the American forces. "Unfortunately" it raised only twenty-nine recruits, and when Otto Hapsburg tried to enlist as the thirtieth, the American secretary of war turned him down. Deutsch apparently had nothing to do with these goings-on. Yet his connections with the "left" wing of Austro-fascism were very unpleasant; and his efforts to find support, or at least toleration, in the foreign committee of the Friends of Austrian Labor, failed. After 1945 the former leaders of the Austrian labor movement who had stayed in Austria reorganized the movement themselves without any help from abroad. Deutsch was accepted as a party employee without influence on the leadership, in an occupation which did not correspond to his abilities at all.

In the postwar United States, Friends of Austrian Labor had hardly any political tasks to fulfill. Austria had her own government, even if its power was greatly limited by the Allied occupation forces. Our organization had neither the right nor the intention to approach this government, nor its successor after the first free elections, as anything but supporters— if our support was needed. New York was the center of Friends of Austrian Labor. I became the chairman—which, for all practical purposes, I had been already. Fritz Adler returned via Brussels to his beloved Zürich where he remained, together with Kathia, until his death in 1960. For a few years the organization lingered on as a charitable and sociable society for the remaining émigrés, but it played no significant role. It may be interesting to point out that the percentage of émigrés returning to Austria from England was greater than that of émigrés from the United States. England is not a good host to migrants from the continent; it is not easy to adapt to life there. America, despite the many immigration restrictions, is far better prepared to absorb new people, especially intellectuals—such as Einstein, Pauli, Fermi, Schumpeter, and many others—who have contributed so much.

My professional development was accelerated by a striking coincidence. In New York I had met one of the leaders in the Austrian socialist student movement, my old friend Paul Lazarsfeld. He was extraordinarily active in the United States and was beginning an extremely successful academic career. Even in Austria, Lazarsfeld, originally a mathematician, had received attention for his empirical analysis of the social fate of the unemployed in Marienthal. The idea that sociology could be grounded in measurable facts rather than in semiphilosophical speculation was quite new in Austria. No wonder, then, that Lazarsfeld received a Rockefeller Fellowship for study in the United States—the same fellowship that I could have obtained if I had not, as it turned out, hesitated too long. He met with an extremely cordial reception in the United States. Social scientists in America were familiar with empirical methods and had little sympathy for the European inclination to speculate and philosophize. The leading thinker in empirical sociology was Professor Robert Lynd of Columbia University. Lynd became Lazarsfeld's protector and helped him obtain research material to continue his work. Lazarsfeld led a research group with Frank Stanton, before Stanton obtained a leading position at the Columbia Broadcasting System (CBS). Thus Paul became the sole director of the research group. He also accepted commercial commissions, but his main interest was the academic world. There he encountered a peculiar obstacle.

The two leading professors of sociology at Columbia University were Lynd and Robert MacIver, the latter more inclined toward European sociology. Each proposed a candidate for an appointment at the university. Paul was Lynd's candidate; MacIver wanted to appoint Robert Merton. For a long time, each turned out to be a match for the other, and Paul had to content himself with a modest occupation in Newark, New Jersey. I do not remember how the agreement came about, but one day Lynd and MacIver had the simple idea of appointing both candidates. Both senior professors probably expected that the newly appointed candidates would, so to speak, paralyze each other.

To everyone's surprise, the two became good friends and found it easy to work together. I met Paul in New York shortly after my arrival, and every once in a while we got together. Through him I met Lynd, on whom I seemed to make a favorable impression. Presumably this tipped the scales during the next decisive step in my academic career.

Bard College had a new dean, Harold Grey, who completely reorganized the college. Among other things, Grey was looking for an economist. The dean asked Lynd for advice, and he suggested me. As I later found out, the Belgian economist Robert Triffin was also a candidate. Somehow, I got the appointment. The first year was not easy. I had much to catch up on, since I had had little opportunity during my years in Zürich and Brussels to keep up to date with the progress of economics. Despite this, I survived the most difficult year. I even managed to get a research commission from the Sloan Foundation, for which Lazarsfeld, once again, was very helpful. The task was to study the effectiveness of film as a medium in presenting economic problems. What I discovered was simply that the taste of students did not differ from that of the general public in any significant manner, and that students have no more appreciation or understanding of artistic values than a randomly selected group. This was no extraordinary research discovery.

In 1942, two years after my appointment at Bard College, I was promoted to full professor without having ever reached the level of associate professor. Bard, which later under president Leon Botstein achieved considerable success, was during Grey's tenure an extraordinarily dynamic college. Grey had an interesting circle of friends and brought outstanding talents to the college. The English literature department was equal to if not better than that in the leading universities; Mary McCarthy, Saul Bellow, Fred Dupee, Ted Weiss, Bill Humphrey (*Home from the Hill*), and Irma Brandeis were stars in the literary firmament. Hannah Arendt and Heinz Blücher taught sociology and political science. The art department was first-rate. Despite a gifted science faculty, the college's equipment was, for monetary reasons, not up to the latest standards. At any rate, it was a joy for me to teach at this institution. I succeeded in enlisting excellent assistants in economics: the most notable was probably Franco Modigliani, later a Nobel prizewinner in economics, but also George Rosen, presently professor at the Chicago branch of the University of Illinois, William Cooper, and others. The fact that we could teach macroeconomics to undergraduates was at that time considered remarkable; we were probably one of the first colleges to do this.

Gradually World War II became noticeable in college life as students were drafted into the armed services. Since Bard was an all-male college, it was affected more and more by the military draft. For some time we helped prepare a few hundred young soldiers for their future tasks as occupation troops in France and Germany. We offered, therefore, instruction in both foreign languages, as well as in the history, geography, and sociology of both countries. Not only were we all at work, but we had to employ, especially for language instruction, additional teachers who, however, were not considered Bard faculty members. For me, this was a very interesting and instructive period.

In 1944, the year of the Allied landing on the continent, the special instruction suddenly came to an end. The young soldiers were just at the

age which the army high command regarded as particularly suited for
military service and for the heavy fighting anticipated in the landing on the
continent. They were, therefore, dispatched within a few days, and presumably transported to England, where the troops which had been selected
for the landing were gathered. There remained barely thirty students and a
faculty of approximately the same size. For the limited budget of the
college, this was not a feasible situation. Whoever could find employment
elsewhere went on leave.

Unexpectedly, I found a new appointment which seemed extraordinarily interesting. A telephone call from a professor at the University of
Michigan, who had accepted a high position in Washington, opened up a
new occupation for me. I was not told very much over the telephone, since
it concerned a job in intelligence, but it was enough to induce my wife and
me to move to Washington. Bard was only too happy to give me leave.

My stay in Washington was short but exciting. During this time the
Allied troops landed in Normandy, battled for firm ground where the
troops could assemble, and finally broke through to the Rhine. My task, or
rather the task of about 120 persons whom I directed at the Office of War
Information, was to collect information that might be of value either for
warfare or for propaganda in Nazi-occupied territory.

I could not determine whether our work was of any value. At any
rate, it gave me satisfaction to contribute something to the defeat of the
Hitler regime. I was told quite emphatically during a session of a committee in which the intelligence section of the army was represented that we,
the émigrés, were particularly useful in this task. At the end of this session
the colonel who represented the army took me aside and inquired as to my
origin; my accent made it obvious that I had grown up abroad. When I told
him that I was from Vienna, the officer asked me which language was used
in Vienna. I admit that the intelligence officer's question disturbed me; it
reminded me of a story by the satirist Gustav Meyrink, in which the
Austrian army mistakenly captured the city of Agram, which belonged to
Austria, taking it to be the enemy's capital. My consolation was that
presumably there were also officers of the same quality on the opposite
side.

I heard rumors about a secret weapon of a completely new kind, but I
placed little credence in such rumors. Fritz Adler had talked to me about

this once or twice; he probably knew more than most people outside of the Manhattan Project because he had contact with many physicists. I was therefore somewhat less surprised at the news of the atom bomb and its use against Japan than were most of my contemporaries; I also underestimated the meaning of the event. When the German émigré Fritz Baade came to me after the war—he had returned to Germany from Turkey—and expressed his horror about the new weapon, I reassured him in the honest but mistaken conviction that the difference in quality between traditional bombs and the atom bomb was greatly overestimated. How wrong I was . . . .

I returned to Bard in the fall of 1944. The college began to accept women, which led to its exclusion from its earlier association with Columbia University. Barnard College, which taught only women, insisted on a monopoly on instruction for women within the university.

Some time later I received an interesting offer: in the course of establishing new relations with the former enemy states (symbolized by the Marshall Plan), the development of new relations of confidence with German trade unions was contemplated. Trade union delegations were to come to the United States in order to become acquainted with the new superpower and, above all, to get to know the American system of labor relations.

I was invited to be chairman of this new program. By lucky coincidence Bard had just received as a donation the Zabriskie Estate, located in a rustic neighboring area. A large building resembling a castle provided room for our offices and sleeping facilities for the overseas delegations. New personnel were employed. Both of the American trade union federations (AFL and CIO) sent a representative. The trade unionists from overseas spent a few days at the college, where they heard lectures about American institutions and history; afterward they toured carefully selected industrial plants. The program limited the visitors to tours of unionized plants, presumably to convey the impression that this was the typical American factory. In other words, it was a large and very expensive propaganda maneuver, not quite untrue, but very one-sided. The intentions were, or so I assumed, to dissuade the Europeans from their politically tinted trade unionism, and to convert them into supporting socially neutral, purely practical, American-style trade unions.

I personally took part in only one or two of these tours because at bottom I did not like the job. I remember one German trade union official—he was from Munich, I believe—who was aware of the propagandistic nature of the whole operation. The tour ended with a declaration from the guests, in which they were to relate their impressions. He refused to give a general declaration. I was very happy about this and suggested a wording in complete accordance with the truth. "In the factories which we have seen," the declaration said, "the trade union organizations play a decisive role." This corresponded exactly to what he had seen and did not force him to go beyond what he had experienced. He was content with this, and I was glad to agree.

My employment as a "tour guide" for European trade unionists was interrupted by a call in 1952 to teach at Cornell University, which was well known in the study of labor movements and labor relations. Although I regarded my work at Bard College, especially my study of trade unions, as extraordinarily interesting, I could not resist the Cornell offer. At Cornell the Institute for Labor Relations was about to establish a Department of International and Comparative Labor Relations, and they selected a younger colleague and me as pioneers of this experiment. I suggested that we begin with a study of Mexico, and the institute agreed. We spent almost a year in Mexico, and published two studies concerning the connections between labor relations and economic development.

The most interesting conclusion, strangely enough, I put into a footnote, probably because it did not quite fit with the main theme of the study. I bluntly predicted that industrialization would not solve Mexico's main problem, mass unemployment.

My research in Mexico led to a strange coincidence associated with my former work in Zürich. In Zürich I had met a young lawyer, Kurt Düby, at a meeting of socialist students. We had become good friends. He lived with his wife, Gertrude, a lovely blonde woman, in Bern, and whenever my business led me to Bern, I usually stayed at the Dübys'.

The last time I had seen Gertrude was at the Congress of the Labor and Socialist International in Brussels in 1928; Gertrude was a delegate to the Swiss socialist women's organization, which was then still quite weak because women did not have the right to vote in Switzerland—the model country of democracy! After Brussels, Gertrude vanished from my sight; I heard rumors that she had gone to Moscow and become a Communist. Whether that was true, I do not know to this day. She and Kurt were divorced, and Kurt married a wonderful woman, today his widow.

During my stay in Mexico I had contact with several foreign journalists, among them the correspondent for the *Christian Science Monitor*. One day she told me that she had just returned from a journey to Chiapas, the southernmost province of Mexico. She told me to be sure not to miss the trip; the province of Chiapas was among the most beautiful regions that Mexico had to offer. And if I went there, of course I had to go to the Cristobal de las Casas, and that would mean staying at Gertrude Düby's. I was thunderstruck. I had not heard that name for many, many years. "Is she Swiss?" was my first question. "Yes, I think so; she is from Bern." She showed me a photograph of Gertrude. No doubt, it was her, somewhat older, but still very good-looking. Then I heard, at least in fragments, her story. At some point she had moved from Moscow to Mexico, where she attached herself to a well-known anthropologist, who unfortunately was too inclined toward alcohol. They moved to Chiapas, which was at that time barely explored. She learned the language of the natives, their customs, and also their bad habits; such as, for example, their inclination to kill strangers. Of course, whoever was under Gertrude's protection was safe. She led expeditions into the jungle and took strangers into her house. Many years later the value of her knowledge about the natives of southern Mexico was finally acknowledged by the government; she received medals and awards, well deserved, albeit belated. Unfortunately, I did not manage to go to Chiapas and renew our acquaintance.

A Visit to Europe

Following the war I visited Austria for the first time since my emigration. I had traveled to Germany earlier, on behalf of the State Department, to study the job market. Now I went to Austria at my own initiative and expense, not only to see the reborn Austria, but also, in my capacity as chairman of Friends of Austrian Labor, to negotiate the return of those émigrés who wished to spend their last years in the old country. Among these were Wilhelm Ellenbogen, a comrade of Viktor Adler and a minister in the First Republic, former Constitutional Court member Arnold Eisler, and a few others—all told, they numbered hardly more than a dozen. The journey provided, all in all, a number of astonishing experiences.

Austria was still occupied by foreign troops, and I needed a special entry permit. As a professor, I was referred to the educational agency of the American occupation army. Their head official was, I soon found out, a colonel who had been on General Douglas MacArthur's staff. He told me he once had been a professor of geology somewhere in Pennsylvania. His official duty was to teach the Austrians the principles of democracy. This he did, though in a peculiar manner.

He was very friendly and offered me the support of his agency, of course without telling me what this support would entail if I ever planned to take him up on the offer. Then came a strange part of the conversation. What he said was approximately this: "I quite understand that people like Oskar Morgenstern and Gottfried Haberler want to return to Austria, but from our point of view it would be much better if they did not." I tried to comprehend the underlying meaning of this remark. Did he perhaps take me for a Gentile, while taking Morgenstern and Haberler for Jews whose visit he would not welcome? The name of Morgenstern is frequently Jewish, but Haberler certainly is not. He presumably did not know that Morgenstern may have been descended from an illegitimate relationship involving a Hohenzollern prince. Haberler, on the other hand, who came from Liechtenstein and belonged to an old family of high officials, could hardly be "suspected" as being of Jewish descent. As far as I am concerned, I do not look the way *Der Stürmer* (*The Storm Trooper*), the Nazi paper in Germany, pictured a Jew; but the fact is that I am primarily of Jewish descent, even if I am not completely Jewish. However, this complaint from the colonel who was to teach the Austrians democratic equality seemed odd. Maybe my explanation was wrong, but I could not imagine any other. Since I hoped not to see the "Herr Oberst" again, I left his office without much thought about the peculiar role of this prophet of democracy.

My host in Vienna was Karl Hans Seiler, who was important in both the underground movement and in emigration, and who had resumed his old function as editor of the *Arbeiter Zeitung*. I do not remember whether I told him about my strange conversation with the "Herr Oberst," but that is not particularly important.

As I had expected, the party, trade unions, and other groups invited me to give lectures about America. These were unpaid lectures, of course. They were announced in the newspapers, and the *Arbeiter Zeitung* and other papers published reports about my presentations. This had surprising consequences.

One day I received a telephone call from the WAC sergeant (a female noncommissioned officer) who worked in the colonel's antechamber: "The colonel would like to see you immediately. Can you come to his office?" Surprised and curious, I accepted at once: "I can be at the colonel's office within half an hour."

When I appeared at his office in the Hotel Regina, I was immediately conducted from the antechamber to the colonel's office. Without any greeting he said in a strong voice, "I hear that you are giving lectures here." "Certainly, Colonel," was my answer (I almost said "confession," because I found myself unexpectedly in the role of the accused). "Who gave you the permission to do so?" was the next question. "Permission?" I said with honest astonishment. "Why do I need permission?" "Without my permission," my accuser said—for that is what it sounded like at this point—"you cannot give public speeches here." In a few seconds I grasped what was going on. "May I ask why, sir?" "You are here due to my forbearance. You cannot give public lectures without my permission." I began to compose myself. "Sir," I said, "as you know, I am a naturalized American citizen. That means that I have read the Constitution. And I am quite certain I found something there about freedom of speech." Without hesitation, my inquisitor gave me his answer: "To hell with the Constitution; you are here under orders of the United States Army." "You see," he continued, "I have here the manuscript of a speech which another ex-Austrian wants to give. I will read it. If I agree, he can give his lecture. If I demand changes, he has to make them. Without my permission, you simply cannot give a speech."

I had finally composed myself. "Sir," I answered, "I have never in my life given a censored speech. I will not do it now. I do not have to speak. I am not getting paid for my lectures. I will simply stop speaking in public. My next lecture has already been announced in the newspaper. I guess we will also have to publish the cancellation." With that I took my leave.

While still in the antechamber, I overheard the colonel: "Sergeant, if Professor Sturmthal gives even one more speech without my permission, put him on the next train leaving Austria."

Confused, I started on my way to the Seilers' apartment. What was I supposed to do now? I was not willing to surrender and simply accept the colonel's prohibition. It would not have been difficult for me to make the matter public and to embarrass the American military government considerably. That would have been a very nice gift to the Soviet authorities in Vienna, who would have been able to ridicule the so-called democrats in the American military agency. But to accept the prohibition silently was equally intolerable. So I turned the matter over and over in my mind.

First of all, I indeed had to cancel the lecture which was announced the following day. I called Oscar Pollak at the *Arbeiter Zeitung* and requested a notice to that effect. I added that I could not give him any further explanation on the telephone, which was no doubt tapped, but that I would make up for this as soon as possible. I ended the call. Then the telephone rang; the Harvard Summer School at Schloss Leopoldskron was on the line. "We have just found out that you are in Austria. Would you like to pay us a visit and give a lecture?" I was then given a list of names of the people present, among them a number of Harvard professors, a few of whom I knew. I gave an evasive reply and promised to get back to them a few days later. Actually, this invitation made the problem worse. Harvard had a bad reputation with the American military.

Then the second—the relieving—phone call came. Jack Afros, an American acquaintance, was on the phone; he could best be described as a social democrat. I knew him from the Rand School, which was connected with the moderate wing of the American socialists. He was head of the social welfare division of the American military government and held the same rank as my colonel. "I just heard that you are in the country. How nice! Would you be so kind as to give a lecture for us about Austrian affairs?" "Nothing would please me more," was my honest answer, "but first of all you have to come to an understanding with the colonel of the educational agency." "What does he have to do with it?" "Well, I think you'd better find that out from him." "What did the idiot do? Doesn't he know who you are?" I did not know an answer to that. "Please stay around the phone! I'll call you back in a few minutes."

A few minutes later—it was getting close to noon—the call came: not from Afros, but from my colonel. "Well, that was a bad misunderstanding," he said. "We should clear that up right now. May I send you my car and ask you to come to my office?" I was ready. Apparently my friend Afros had soundly intimidated the colonel.

The car appeared and took me to the colonel. The WAC sergeant was not there, and the colonel conducted me into his office personally. "That was a strange misunderstanding," he said. "What I explained to you were the normal rules for visitors from the United States. Of course, they do not apply to you. We have all the confidence in the world in you. You know yourself under what difficult conditions we are working here. Of course, you are at liberty to give lectures whenever and wherever you think fit." "So I don't have to show you the text first?" "Of course not." "That holds also for a lecture at the Harvard Summer School?" "Oh, you don't want to speak there. They are all Communists," was the surprising answer. I kept my calm. "Incidentally, I know a few of the Harvard people there, and I am quite sure that they are not Communists," I replied. With obvious reluctance the colonel agreed.

I left his office and went immediately to the inner court of the office building where the social welfare officials of the American military government had assembled. The chairman of the assembly was, to my surprise, a female colonel. She introduced me to the audience, and without any preparation I gave my speech straight from the shoulder. The topic was Austrian trade unions. Although I was, of course, familiar with the subject, conditions had changed considerably since the 1934 prohibition of trade unions by Chancellor Dollfuss. There were now unified trade unions instead of the former politically divided organizations, and the influence of the trade unions had become extraordinarily strong. In addition, there was the new policy of social partnership of employer and employee, which presented a drastic contrast to the management-labor struggles of the time before 1934. The lecture was not one of my best, but the most important thing for me was that I could speak without censorship.

My triumph was all the greater because I could see the sergeant who had been in the colonel's antechamber, and who had been charged to put me on the next train leaving Austria, in the audience. The poor woman got up from her chair in amazement when I entered; she clearly did not know what to do. After all, I was accompanied by a colonel and introduced to the assembly. She could not very well arrest and convey out of the country someone who was being treated with such distinction.

This episode, so agreeable to me, was not quite over. After my lecture the female colonel asked the audience to put questions to me or to make critical comments. Leaden silence ensued. In order to overcome this obstacle, the chairman asked a question herself, directing it, however, to the audience: "Why are we discussing the topic of this lecture?" Again silence, until finally "my" WAC sergeant got up and gave the only appropriate answer: "Because the officer in command put the topic on the agenda."

Luckily, the discussion at the Harvard Summer School in Schloss Leopoldskron went better, and my lectures in Austria were not disturbed by further "military" interference.

As much as I enjoyed giving the lectures, they were not the main purpose of my journey. Reestablishing contact with friends with whom I had not been in touch for years was enjoyable as well, but this was also only a side benefit of my trip. Strangely enough, these contacts had already started during my trip to Vienna, in the sleeper of the train. A few hours before our arrival in Vienna I met Austrian trade union chairman Johann Böhm and his assistant Emil Stark, who years earlier had been one of my "opponents" in the discussions among socialist students. But the main task was still ahead. I had to meet Adolf Schärf, vice-chancellor of the Austrian government and chairman of the Socialist Party, to renew my acquaintance with him and to discuss the return of Austrian émigrés from the United States.

I knew Schärf only very slightly. In the old days he had been secretary of the socialist faction in the National Council; his immediate superior, therefore, had been Otto Bauer, the chairman of the faction. Among the many and outstanding qualities that Bauer had possessed, one was clearly missing: the art of approaching people, especially those whose intellectual capacity he was not impressed with. This pertained to Schärf. Otto took him to be a loyal and reliable person, but thought of him as capable of only very unoriginal ideas. To Bauer, Schärf was too much of a bureaucrat. Since Schärf had nothing to do with the International, I did not know him well enough to form my own judgment. In any case, I now showed him the respect which his post and his standing in the party required. Furthermore, he received me in his office at the *Ballhausplatz,* a historic spot endowed with all the splendor with which the empire had furnished the office buildings of the highest officials. I think that this was the first time in my life that I had gone there to be received by a high functionary. Of course, my position was quite strong. In the United States, shortly after Adler left, I had become chairman of the Friends of Austrian Labor, which collected money and materials, especially medications, for Austrian friends. I had no demands or wishes in my own interest. But I came shortly after the Otto Leichter incident.

Leichter had been editor of the *Arbeiter Zeitung,* and he had been very close to Bauer. He was a very good journalist and was loyally devoted to the party, connected to its left wing. His wife, Käthe, had also played a considerable part in the movement. Unfortunately, she had not left Austria with her husband and two sons but had stayed behind to settle personal affairs. She died in a concentration camp. The name of Leichter had a particular meaning in the party, even though Otto, in contrast to his wife, appeared rather too self-confident.

When travel to Austria became possible, Otto Leichter returned from the United States. To his surprise, the party leadership greeted him with little enthusiasm. He had to find employment not with the party but with the trade unions. Rumor had it that Schärf, the new party chairman, and Heinrich Schneidmadl, an important party functionary from Lower Austria, had greeted his return with studied coldness. Heinrich Schneidmadl always had a reputation for treating Jewish party members with little sympathy. He was considered the leading anti-Semite in the party leadership. Leichter returned to the United States after a relatively short stay in Austria. This happened just before my departure for Vienna, and I had not yet had an opportunity to talk to Leichter about his experiences in Vienna. Moreover, I have to confess that I was not particularly close to Leichter. It seemed to me that Leichter—in contrast to Pollak, who clearly restricted himself to the tasks of chief editor of the *Arbeiter Zeitung*—made considerably greater demands on the party. As someone not associated with the party leadership intimated to me, Leichter somehow arrived in Vienna with the idea that he was the successor to Bauer. I doubt that he made this too obvious to the party leadership; but it did not seem impossible to me that the people around Schärf and Schneidmadl had expected something like that from Leichter.

Although Leichter had not embarrassed us during emigration in New York—he had even given a few lectures for our organization—he had not been particularly interested in our activities either. His relationship with Fritz Adler was not cordial. For example, when Fritz discussed the question of selecting a chairman for our organization—I seemed unsuitable because I did not live in New York—he mentioned Lazarsfeld, but not Leichter.

Schärf obviously had a great interest in relating to me his version of Leichter's visit. This is the only way I can understand why the vice-chancellor of Austria spent almost two whole days with me and openly spoke his mind. I had little interest in being informed about the Leichter affair in detail, on the one hand because it was already over, and it seemed to me irreparable, and on the other hand because I had a completely different task. I therefore listened calmly to the vice-chancellor without uttering my own opinion; in reality I did not have an opinion since I had not even heard the other side, that of Leichter.

Finally I succeeded in turning the extremely friendly conversation with Schärf to the question of the return of those émigrés who were still in America. At this point, the conversation took a very interesting turn. At first Schärf told me that my return, which was not even being discussed, would be very welcome. "We need theorists," Schärf said. "People like Benedikt Kautsky or you would be very welcome to us." When I did not react to this, Schärf added: "You know, there is not a single party board meeting without Schneidmadl asking why Sturmthal does not return."

With all respect to the vice-chancellor, this story seemed odd to me. Of all people, Schneidmadl, who hardly knew me personally, and was considered the leading anti-Semite of the party, was supposed to be interested in my return? To this day I consider this account by Schärf hardly credible. Even Schärf, who knew me as an admirer of Bauer, had made no real effort to further my return. Admittedly, Schärf was not an anti-Semite, but he would probably have regarded a flood of returning Jewish émigrés as a problem for the party in a country with a long anti-Semitic tradition. Out of curiosity I asked him: "What do you want to do with me? Am I supposed to accept a chair at the University of Vienna?" I did not ask this without purpose, since a question of this kind had indeed been addressed to me by the state secretary of the nationalization board, Franz Rauscher. Schärf answered that appointments to universities were not within the authority of the Socialists. "You know," he said, "the coalition means that the parties do not interfere with each other's responsibilities. But we will surely find something else for you." I contented myself with this answer, since I did not want to negotiate my own return anyway.

"How about Ellenbogen, Eisler, and Robinson from Graz?" I asked. Schärf's answer was surprising. He divided the émigrés into three groups. The largest was those of whom Schärf said: "I cannot think of anyone who would have anything against them." If I had not been convinced of Schärf's pure "Aryan" descent, I would have spoken of a Jewish trick. Two negations in one sentence . . . . I only remember one name for sure which Schärf put into this group: this was Ernst Papanek, a former municipal councillor and head of the Socialist youth organization and a very pleasant and distinguished child psychologist. (He did not return.) At any rate, it was quite a large group.

The second group consisted of people whose return was undesirable.

There were very few names. The editor, Moritz Robinson from Graz, was one. Of him, Schärf said: "We cannot use him. He starts crying whenever something goes wrong. Someone like him does not suit our situation." Wilhelm Ellenbogen and a few others were flatly rejected. I admit, I was prepared for all kinds of things, but not for the possibility that people like Ellenbogen, a comrade of Viktor Adler and a historic figure whose merit in the Austrian labor movement nobody could deny, could be rejected. I thought that possibly in the past there had been conflicts between Schärf and Ellenbogen—who also had been close to Bauer—so that this only reflected Schärf's personal opinion. It was a dubious proposition because Eisler, who had little to do with Bauer, was also rejected. I could not find a better explanation.

And then there was the last group, consisting of two names. Those were the people whose return would be desirable. One of them was Benedikt Kautsky, known as "Bendel" to his friends; the other was me. These were the "theorists" of whom Schärf had spoken. Bendel, the son of the famous Marxist theorist Karl Kautsky, returned and was extraordinarily useful to the movement. Strangely enough, however, the "theorist" became the president of one of the nationalized banks. As far as I know, there is still a group of "friends" in Austria which gave itself a name that still connects it with Kautsky, and if I am not mistaken, I myself once gave a lecture in Vienna under the auspices of this association. As I said, my return was out of the question, and I did not even pursue the possibility. Whether Schärf was serious about it or just mentioned it out of deference to me, I of course do not know. The remark about Schneidmadl's alleged interest in my return leaves me somewhat doubtful to this day.

I made a second effort, particularly in the matter of Ellenbogen. I was ashamed to return to New York with a negative answer. I went to Pollak in the editor's office of the *Arbeiter Zeitung* and related to him the part of my conversation with Schärf which concerned Ellenbogen. Much to my dismay, Pollak was in complete agreement with Schärf's answer. "What are we supposed to do here with the old man?" he said. I called his attention to the fact that there would not be any financial obligation for the Austrian party. Without having talked to Buttinger, I was certain that he and the group in New York could come up with the modest sum of money which would ensure Ellenbogen's livelihood. It was only a matter of finding an apartment for him, which admittedly was very difficult in Vienna because of the massive destruction. That was precisely why the support of the party and of the officials was necessary. "Well," Pollak said, "all he wants to do is return with his old sisters. Who is supposed to take care of all these old people?" I was speechless and broke off the conversation. I had always admired Pollak as a first-rate journalist and as a wonderful editor of the *Arbeiter Zeitung*. I also knew that he was not exactly a sentimental person—quite in contrast to his wife, Marianne. But I still had not expected this rejection of Ellenbogen. I came to realize that I was helpless in the matter.

One little incident which is factually irrelevant, but symbolically important, deserves mention. In our efforts to obtain financial donations in the United States, above all donations of medications which were still not available in sufficient amounts, we met with the counterargument that the Austrian embassy in Washington had an excess of financial means. I could not verify this statement, but I related it to Schärf. To my surprise, he admitted this and explained it as follows: Karl Gruber, the minister of foreign affairs, who was in the People's Party (and still is), had reserved the Washington ambassadorship for himself in the future, and therefore had begun supplying it somewhat more plentifully than other embassies. Moreover, Schärf said, it was not clear what standard was properly applicable concerning the allocation of funds of an embassy.

I suggested that war-ravaged Austria should not have greater expenditures of this kind than Switzerland. Switzerland, I said, did not have to go begging, and what was sufficient for her ambassador should be enough for an Austrian diplomat. Schärf answered somewhat impatiently: "Look, the Foreign Ministry is controlled by the People's Party. We cannot interfere with that." Here, too, I met with no success.

Of course, I was constantly asked by all kinds of acquaintances whom I met during my stay in Vienna whether I would come back. Although I have no proof whatsoever for this, I do not want to conceal my impression that my negative answer was not exactly received with sorrow. As I said at that time: "The Austrian cake is not very large, and some of those who asked me that question may have calculated secretly how much of their part of the cake they would have to share with me if I returned." But maybe that was just my imagination. Of course, I do not have any evidence for this. On the contrary, many years later I was told by one of the highest functionaries of the party, "what we have here in terms of intellectuals is not worth much. The really valuable ones did not come back. I guess they had better luck abroad."

That, too, is hardly conclusive. Austrians have always esteemed success abroad much higher than a good reputation at home. Of course I have to admit that when I spent a semester at the University of Vienna as a guest professor many years later, I had the impression that, apart from a few exceptions, the critical judgment I just mentioned cannot be considered entirely unjustified.

In Germany I fared completely differently. I flew directly from Vienna to Berlin, where I met two old friends: Paul Hertz, chairman of the senate of the city of Berlin, and his colleague Hans Hirschfeld, press secretary of the magistrate of Berlin. I knew Paul Hertz from the old days in Weimar, when he had been close to Hilferding and a good friend of Fritz Adler. I had met him frequently, and despite our twenty-year age difference, regarded him as my friend. I was less well acquainted with Hirschfeld, whom I met only after he had fled to Switzerland in 1933, but I was on friendly terms with him, friendly enough, at any rate, to be able to speak openly.

First I went to see Paul Hertz in the mayor's office. It was the old city hall in Schönberg, which had been converted into the city hall of the three Western occupation sectors after the division of the city into Communist East Berlin and Western-oriented West Berlin. Paul Hertz's office was located between that of the chief mayor Ernst Reuter and that of the city council chairman, Otto Suhr. The spacing had a political character; Reuter and Suhr were not always on good terms and Hertz had to play mediator. He was quite successful at this. His character as well as his connections made him a first-rate go-between, who could easily bridge opposites—if he wanted to. In emigration he had shown his teeth to the old party leadership, and he had had closer connections with the "New Beginning" oppositional group than the party leadership wished. Somehow the connection with "New Beginning" was viewed as disloyal in the circle around SPD leaders Otto Wels and Siegmund Crummenerl.

After a short conversation we went to see Reuter, whom I knew only by name. Ernst Reuter had been a Communist for a long time during the days of Weimar; he had emigrated with the economist Fritz Baade and some others to Turkey. After his return, he asserted himself quickly in the party in Berlin and became its leader, unopposed (with the possible exception of Suhr). We knew each other by name, but this was our first personal meeting; it was extraordinarily warm and, in some ways, astonishing.

Reuter was sitting at his desk in his large study. When Hertz and I entered, he got up and came toward me, crossing the entire room with open arms, and embraced me. It was truly a cordial welcome, quite different from that which I had experienced in Vienna.

After a few words Reuter surprised me by asking: "What were you thinking of?" My blank face made it obvious that he had to express himself more clearly. "You are coming back, aren't you? Which position would you like to take over?" I looked at him, perplexed. "In my case you cannot talk of coming back," I said. "I am an Austrian by birth." "Yes, but that doesn't matter at all. We need people like you, and apart from the three posts filled by Suhr, Hertz and me, everything is open and at your disposal."

I was honestly at a loss for an answer to this exceedingly cordial invitation from a man whom I admired so much. I tried delaying tactics. "I would like to think about it thoroughly and give you an answer as soon as possible. In the meantime, please let me know if I can do anything for you. I would like to do whatever is in my power."

After we left the study, I turned to Hertz and asked, "Did he mean that? Did you know of this?" Paul answered, "Of course he means it. We have talked about you a few times since we heard that you are in Europe." "I have to admit that I am completely unprepared for this," I said. "I am glad that Reuter received me so cordially. But I am at a loss, since I had no idea that something like this would come my way." I then told him how different this reception was from the one I had just experienced in Vienna. He was surprised, although he knew the internal affairs of the Austrian party quite well. "They are afraid of the competition," he said. "They would rather remain an undisputed minority than win a majority if that puts them into danger of losing their leadership posts." I assured Hertz that even if I had the power I certainly had no intention of expelling anyone, in Austria or Germany, from his leadership position. After all, I had been away from Austria for many years, and I was completely unknown to the public. My circle of acquaintances was mainly limited to readers of the *Arbeiter Zeitung* and of the theoretical organ of the party, *Der Kampf.* My chances in a conflict with the party leadership were surely worse than Otto Leichter's had been. But this reasoning was to no purpose, since I did not even consider returning to Austria. The Germans, on the other hand, did not make it easy for me.

After my conversation with Ernst Reuter I had another, much more serious discussion of the same kind with Kurt Schumacher, the undisputed leader of the German Social Democrats. Schumacher, wounded severely in World War I, had spent the Hitler years in a concentration camp. In the Weimar Republic he had been one of the "rising" young men of the party, comparable to Carlo Mierendorff, who had perished so miserably during the Third Reich. I knew Schumacher only by name; his position in the party before 1933 had not been high enough for him to take part in international conventions. However, after his liberation from the camp, his apartment in Hanover had become a headquarters for the reestablishment of the Social Democratic Party, and when the party was officially reconstituted, Schumacher became its undisputed leader.

Erich Ollenhauer, formerly a youth leader, had returned from exile and became vice-chairman. I was well acquainted with Ollenhauer; we had met occasionally before 1933 and during the years away from Europe. He had originally been the chairman of the German socialist youth movement and had naturally played a leading role in the Youth International. Ollenhauer had advanced to the party leadership while in exile. He then worked for the SPD exile leadership in Prague, Paris, and London, and had returned to West Germany from London as soon as circumstances permitted. With Fritz Heine and Alfred Nau, who later also filled important functions in the party, Erich formed a kind of triumvirate, with which I kept in contact until the deaths of Ollenhauer and Nau. I still have close contact with Fritz Heine.

Ollenhauer told me several things about the party and its internal affairs, two of which I remember most clearly: the leaders utterly refused to collaborate with the Communists, and wished to emphasize the turning away of the German people from National Socialism. This involved, for instance, sending a comrade to Paris to induce an old Jewish comrade who lived there to return to Germany. They insisted that a Jewish party comrade had to appear on the list of candidates for the German parliamentary election. The German party wished to demonstrate clearly that it had nothing to do with the anti-Semitic crimes committed by the Nazis—which was completely true. I cannot recall ever having heard so much as an anti-Semitic joke from any of the German comrades I knew.

After a few friendly remarks, Schumacher quickly brought up the main topic of our meeting. He wanted not only to get to know me—he already knew a few things about me from the literature—but also to induce me to "return" to Germany. He soon made quite clear what he had in mind for me. At first I would be appointed secretary to the SPD group in the newly elected German Parliament and soon thereafter become a member of Parliament myself. The position, he said, was not yet taken and offered considerable possibilities for development. Everything was still in flux; someone with new ideas who had not been incriminated by the dark German past could exert a decisive influence. Of course, the party was now in the opposition; but that would not last forever, Schumacher thought, and a young man like me could afford to wait until things took a decisive turn.

When I hesitated to answer this flattering offer—not because I was in doubt about the answer but because I did not want to hurt Schumacher's feelings—he added a few thoughts. It was understood that, coming from the United States, I was used to a high standard of living (this factor was somewhat exaggerated), and of course it would be considered in my conditions of employment. I made it clear that this question was not the main one in my mind. Finally, I said that I would consider this generous offer at length and discuss it with my wife. I also made it clear that I had not come to Germany to look for a position but to acquaint myself with the situation and with the new generation of party leadership.

Schumacher took notice of this but did not give up. He called in Erwin Schoettle, one of the deputy chairmen of the parliamentary faction of the party, to introduce us. Schoettle did not seem very interested, stayed for only a few minutes, and asked only a few harmless questions—maybe because he assumed that Schumacher's decision would be final anyway. At any rate, he showed less interest than Schumacher, although he would have been my immediate superior if I had accepted Schumacher's offer. I do not remember exactly how I finally ended the matter. In any case, no further conversation about the possibility of my employment ever took place.

A few years later I was again offered a post in the German labor movement, this time in the Economic Research Institute of the Trade Unions, the WWI (*Wirtschaftswissenschaftliches Forschungs-Institut der Gewerkschaften*). The impetus for this was the dismissal in 1955 of Viktor Agartz as director of the WWI; he was much too radical for the mainstream of the German trade unions. On the other hand, his co-director and successor, Bruno Gleitze, was regarded as too weak, maybe unfairly so, and another director was sought who would be on a par with Gleitze and who would be capable of working with him. (Erich Potthoff became the co-director.)

My being considered for this position was due, I assume, to a coincidence. As soon as the United States permitted visits from German citizens, Fritz Baade, one of the three partners of the WTB plan, was one of the first to arrive. He had not been to the United States and had no personal contacts there. He was also only very slightly acquainted with me, but he knew of me and came to see me shortly after his arrival.

In any case, his seeing me may have led to my being invited to Düsseldorf to a board meeting of the DGB, the German Trade Union Federation (*Deutscher Gewerkschaftsbund*), where I was introduced to many people. Among them was the representative of the Christian faction of the DGB, who had held the post of vice-president of the DGB since the establishment of the unified trade unions. He was apparently interested in finding out how far I was willing to occupy myself as a propagandist for the socialists. I do not know whether I was able to dissipate his worries. I was quite uncomfortable during the whole affair, for on the one hand I wanted to refuse, while on the other hand I was looking for a way to make it easy for myself, and, of course, not to hurt the feelings of the German trade unionists.

My search for a "friendly" way out—as Paul Hertz termed it—was greatly facilitated by a private conversation with Ludwig Rosenberg, one of the DGB leaders and later chairman of the DGB. Rosenberg, a Jewish trade unionist, had fled the Nazi regime and returned from England after the defeat of the Nazis. In Germany he was quickly offered high positions in the trade union movement. His opinion was very interesting. He briefly said to me, "If I were you, I would not accept the position." He did not give me a reason, but I did not ask for one. Here I had the easy way out: I did not have to say no. Indirectly the others did it for me.

Politics in America

As mentioned earlier, Fritz Baade was known to me from the WTB debate. While in the United States on a visit, he wanted to establish contact with Americans who would understand the problems of the German labor movement. Walter Reuther, the president of the United Automobile Workers, was the obvious choice.

I do not remember how I became acquainted with Walter. But I remember very clearly that we became good friends. Of all the Americans I have met, he was probably the one most comparable to a European social democrat. I visited him at his Detroit apartment, and later, after the attempt on his life, at his well-guarded house in the country. Walter's singing deserves special mention. His father was from southern Germany, and Walter knew German well, which he pronounced with a good Swabian accent. To other German speakers this soft dialect is somewhat comical, and I had to keep my facial expression under strict control whenever I heard Walter talk or sing in German. That did not prevent us from singing German folk songs, with me at the piano and him in a full voice, in his most beautiful Swabian dialect. His wife, of Jewish descent, knew German quite well and liked to listen. They and their amateur bodyguard perished in an airplane crash in May 1970 on a stormy flight to the UAW education and vacation center in Michigan.

Baade met Reuther and established a contact valuable to both sides. Every once in a while I met Baade during visits to Germany. He had become director of the World Economic Institute in Kiel in 1948, where later, upon his invitation, I once gave a lecture.

Another European labor functionary I introduced to Reuther was Konrad Ilg, president of both the Swiss Metal Workers' Trade Union (the largest in Switzerland) and the International Metal Workers' Federation, which is the international trade union secretariat with the largest membership. I had been friends with Ilg for a long time. Occasionally, I wrote articles from the United States for his union's newspaper and weekly journal. I met Ilg in New York and had a long conversation with him; I inquired about his plans and advised him to get in touch with Walter and Victor Reuther. Victor, Walter's younger brother, was in charge of international affairs for the United Automobile Workers. I wrote a short note to the Reuthers introducing Ilg as they had not met him before.

In these ways I succeeded in establishing or facilitating contact between American and European trade unions. The tremendous influence that the United States had after World War II in sharing the postwar world made such connections extremely important, especially since relations in the past between trade unions on both sides of the Atlantic had not always been smooth. What had been lacking was experience in international collaboration and tolerance of the very different conceptions that trade unions had, and still have, of their tasks. After World War II these differences were intensified by the great difference in financial means at the disposal of American trade unions compared to those in impoverished Europe.

Unfortunately, some American trade union leaders could not always refrain from reminding their European colleagues of their union's great wealth. At the founding congress of the International Confederation of Free Trade Unions (ICFTU) in London in 1949, for example, some American officials arrived at the congress building in luxurious chauffeur-driven limousines, while most of their colleagues from other countries used the excellent services of the London underground. Even more conspicuous was an interruption by David Dubinsky, president of the International Ladies Garment Workers Union, during the debate about the future location of the General Secretariat of the ICFTU. When Brussels was suggested (which the Americans liked because they wanted to weaken English influence in the organization), a continental delegate pointed to the high cost of living in Brussels at that time. "Don't worry," Dubinsky exclaimed, "we'll undertake it to come up with the difference." That was certainly well meant, and Dubinsky was indeed involved in the American trade unions' support for their European colleagues after the war. But from the point of view of the recipients of American generosity, the manner in which support was offered, and given, was at times not easy to bear.

Later, some American trade unions became the vehicles through which money, at times coming from undesignated sources, was channeled to trade unions and functionaries in order to further anti-Communist trends in the labor movement. This problem is too important to be treated superficially. I would like to point out one aspect of this question, because I played a certain role in connection with it.

A subcommittee of the U.S. Senate Committee on Foreign Relations, which was concerned with the American hemisphere, commissioned the Research Center in Economic Development and Cultural Change at the University of Chicago to study relations between American business and the labor movement in Latin America. The report was printed as an official document on January 22, 1960, by the Senate Committee on Foreign Relations. (The chairman at that time was Senator J. W. Fulbright.) The Research Center commissioned David Felix and me to write the report. Felix primarily examined the business part, while I investigated the problems of the labor movement. We had two assistants and a few legal advisors.

Presumably, my appointment was largely due to the studies of Mexican economic development which I had conducted in the fifties for Cornell University. One of these studies, published in the *Journal of Political Economy,* was, to my knowledge, one of the first to point out that industrialization would not eliminate the high rate of unemployment in Mexico, nor in most countries of the Third World. A few years later this study served as a guide for a series of studies about developing countries done by the International Labor Organization in Geneva. No less important, I assume, in my being selected to take part in the Senate's study was the fact that although I was very sympathetic toward the labor movement, I certainly was not uncritical. Above all, I was wary of the unrestrained anti-Communist policies of the leadership of the American trade unions, which often aligned them with the most reactionary trends in the country. In spite of my rejection of Communist thought, it seemed to me an inadmissible simplification of world politics to attribute all difficulties to Communist machinations, or even to support dubious political figures as long as they presented themselves as enemies of communism. Some in the trade unions disliked my attitude; however, to many in the academic world and to statesmen like Senator Fulbright, my cooler perspective made sense.

For a long time rumors had been circulating that some American trade union officials were serving as financial channels for the American government, but no clear evidence was available. However, the lack of clarity about the situation damaged the reputation of American trade unions and hurt their effectiveness within the international trade union movement. Well-justified actions were criticized or even rejected simply because they were initiated by American trade unions, and because it was supposed the actions were financed or initiated and controlled by the CIA. I was supposed to contribute to the task of lifting the veil from these dark secrets and to bring to light the truth, as far as I had access to it.

I suggested the following basic policies for dealing with Latin American colleagues:

Policies in the labor field should be based on an outright recognition of the diversity of labor movements. While U.S. interests require the strengthening of those labor organizations which aim at the development of democratic institutions, it should not be assumed that such organizations will be patterned after the model of U.S. trade unions. Cooperation with democratic unions, rather than teaching—and surely not with the intention of imposing particular patterns of union action—should be the spirit of U.S.–Latin American labor relations. In order to be effective, democratic cooperation between U.S. and Latin American labor should observe the following principles: (a) Both sides must recognize and wholeheartedly accept the diversity of the labor movements in the various parts of the Western Hemisphere. They must understand that this diversity corresponds to basic differences of historic background, of present conditions, tasks, and experiences. Any conscious or unconscious attempt to shape the other movements after the pattern of one's own would not only be futile, but also disastrous for real democratic cooperation. Democratic labor movements must distinguish themselves from the Communist-dominated movements by the recognition of international diversity and by an absolute rejection of the idea that there is one and only one effective method of operation for all labor movements.

(b) This does not mean, of course, that there is nothing one movement can learn from the other. Learning, however, is not identical with imitating; nor can learning be imposed by authority or bought by offers of material assistance.

(c) Given the tremendous differences in power, prestige, and wealth of the different movements, tact in the relationships is a first imperative if fruitful and lasting cooperation is to be achieved.

(d) In order to accentuate democratic cooperation it would seem advisable for the movements to make deliberate efforts to find common activities in which cooperation on a footing of reasonable equality is feasible. Practical union activities and educational enterprises with a minimum of ideological content would seem to offer the best prospects for democratic cooperation.[1]

Subsequently, I discussed the acute problem of providing financial support to Latin American trade unions from their U.S. colleagues. Such support, I said, should be granted, but under a series of conditions. It should only be temporary.

No workers' organization can be autonomous which is permanently based on outside financial assistance. Aid is to be rendered publicly. Secret assistance by U.S. unions to Latin American unions may be warranted in a particular emergency, but as soon as the emergency is over the facts are to be revealed to the public.[2]

The source of financial aid would have to be the labor movement itself. There should be no doubt as to the source of financial means.

I suggested that the study program that brought Latin American trade unionists to the United States should be examined. In general, I said, those trade unionists who are invited are sympathetic to the ideas and methods employed in the United States. "We are preaching to the converted." On the other hand, it would probably be much cheaper to send American experts to Latin American countries for a longer period of time, where they could teach and administer technical aid—for example, collecting statistics and monitoring labor protection laws, etc.

Unfortunately, the main organ of the AFL-CIO in Latin America was the American Institute for Free Labor Development, or AIFLD. Its public reports from 1962 to 1967 show that during this period the contributions of

1. U.S. Senate, Committee on Foreign Relations, *United States-Latin American Relations* (Washington, D.C.: U.S. Government Printing Office, 1960), p. xvi.
2. Ibid., p. xvii.

the U.S. government increased from $397,000 to $5,112,000, while the total sources of income of the institute increased from $640,000 to $5,475,000. This means that by 1967 U.S. government contributions amounted to more than 90 percent of its total income. In other words, the institute was practically a government agency and completely dependent on contributions from the government. In addition, the institute was managed by a corporation in which not only U.S. trade unions but also employers and government were represented. In most, if not all, Latin American countries, such collaboration would be unthinkable, and if it came about, most union members would consider it a betrayal of the labor movement.

The consequence was that the Latin American trade unionists who worked with the institute, or were invited to its center of instruction in Front Royal, Virginia, were regarded as agents of a foreign, almost hostile, government by many, if not most, of the workers of the particular country. To a certain extent the work of the institute was thus self-defeating. Having been selected as potential coworkers, the foreign participants at the institute were disqualified from holding leading positions in the trade unions of their own country because of their involvement in its work.

In July 1968 another study conducted for the Senate, this time by the staff and advisors of the Senate Committee on Foreign Relations, vindicated me. This report was published. I was pleased to find the following words in this report:

> Greater consideration should be given to the guidelines and observations offered in the study of United States–Latin American labor relations made for the Subcommittee on American Republics Affairs in 1960 by the University of Chicago. In large measure, these guidelines (which are reprinted in an appendix to this study) continue to provide valid basic ground rules for the conduct of United States– Latin American labor relations. There is reason to believe that had these guidelines been followed, many of the problems now troubling United States–Latin American labor relations could have been avoided.[3]

3. U.S. Senate, Committee on Foreign Relations, *Survey of the Alliance for Progress: Labor, Politics, and Programs* (Washington, D.C.: U.S. Government Printing Office, 1969), p. 20.

Of course I do not know whether the repetition of good advice contributes to its being observed. I rather tend to assume that it was not taken very seriously at high levels. The United States and its labor movement are still involved in a process of learning how to establish, improve, and maintain international relations.

This is a serious problem not only for the United States but for the whole world, since whatever the United States does is of importance even at the other end of the globe. Is this country, so deeply focused upon itself, ready to assume its responsibility? The ignorance of world affairs among large parts of the population makes it more difficult to reach democratic decisions concerning international questions. The business world also tends to judge the effects of all events in the light of future decisions, often of the next elections. I am willing to admit that this also happens in many other countries. However, in those countries this does not have the world-wide consequences that American decisions have. For some time, I am afraid, the world will have to put up with this state of affairs.

I considered it one of my unofficial tasks to do my share in establishing relations between progressive Americans—who are oddly enough referred to as liberals in the United States—and European social democrats. I maintained connections to the latter, since I visited Europe frequently and for long periods of time.

I was on a European trip when the idea of acting as a middleman between American and European "left of center" groups occurred to me. I discussed it first with Erich Ollenhauer, then chairman of the SPD. He liked the idea very much and encouraged me to go ahead. I could count on his moral and, if necessary, financial support. For the time being the latter did not mean very much since I did not yet have a clear idea of the form such international cooperation could take. The French Socialist Party was in the midst of one of its eternal crises, and its electoral support had sharply declined. I decided to bypass it for the time being, and I proceeded to England.

My first step was to get together with Anthony Crosland. I had met this young but rapidly rising star of the British Labour Party for the first time in the early fifties in Vienna at a conference arranged by the Congress for Cultural Freedom. Crosland, author of a number of books dealing with problems facing British Labour, was an original mind, and I found great satisfaction in discussions with him. He moved in an interesting milieu, which included his brother-in-law, the famous historian A. J. P. Taylor. Tony Crosland, who was not easily pleased with someone else's ideas—he had plenty of his own—thought the plan was worth submitting to Hugh Gaitskell and proceeded to arrange a meeting with Gaitskell for the following day.

I had made Hugh Gaitskell's acquaintance during the Vienna International Socialist Congress in 1962. That evening in Vienna, a whole group of his former Viennese friends—as well as Philip Kaiser, later the U.S. ambassador to Vienna—accompanied him on an endless stroll through the places he remembered so well from his student days in Vienna. He was due to deliver a major address at the International Congress the next morning, but this did not keep him from walking into the early hours. I dropped out by about 2:00 A.M., but Hugh appeared to have boundless energy. I do not know when he finally gave up.

Hugh Gaitskell was one of the many Hugh Dalton disciples who contributed greatly to the British labor movement. He had studied economics for some time as a young man in Vienna, at first as a student of ultraliberals such as Ludwig von Mises; but later had become an admirer of "red Vienna." Gaitskell loved Vienna, had many friends there, and visited the city whenever he could. At British party meetings, he ostentatiously wore in his buttonhole a red carnation, the symbol of the Austrian Social Democrats. He was one of the most important players in my effort to establish international cooperation between progressives. By this time he was the leader of the British Labour Party, the chief spokesman of the opposition, and the designated prime minister should Labour return to power. But this was not to happen, since Gaitskell died an early death.

At the meeting Crosland had arranged, Gaitskell sat reclining in his chair and listened without interruption while I outlined my ideas. He had only one comment: "As leader of the Labour Party, I am the designated future prime minister of Great Britain. You must be sure that the partners to future meetings will be of similar status." I undertook to provide for this, and not to proceed with the project if I could not guarantee such representation.

John F. Kennedy had been elected president of the United States, and it appeared to me that this was the best chance to establish closer contact between U.S. progressive Democrats and European socialists. Since there was no socialist party of any significance in the United States, progressive Democrats—in American language, "liberals"—would have to do. The only organization representing them was Americans for Democratic Action (ADA), a small group consisting mostly of intellectuals, among them the well-known historian Arthur Schlesinger, Jr. He was personally close to the president. Indeed, upon learning of his election, Kennedy had paid his first visit as president-elect to Schlesinger. Now the historian had moved into the White House as one of Kennedy's closest advisors. This could be the moment when the traditional American tendency to deal only with European conservatives could be reversed and the non-Communist left be established as a partner for progressive American forces. In fact, when Kennedy met the conservative German chancellor Konrad Adenauer on an official visit to Europe, their personal relationship proved quite hostile, while Kennedy and the mayor of Berlin, the Social Democrat Willy Brandt, got along very well.

Equipped with Ollenhauer's and Gaitskell's acceptance, I returned to the United States and got in touch with the ADA. Schlesinger was one of its leaders, Professor Samuel Beer of Harvard its chairman, and G. Mennen Williams its secretary. I submitted my ideas to Beer and Schlesinger in a brief outline. A short while later—I do not remember how much time passed—I received an invitation to visit Schlesinger in his office at the White House. It was a rather difficult meeting as it took place in the midst of the Cuban missile crisis and Arthur was interrupted by numerous telephone calls.

Still, we settled on the next step—a meeting with a number of "interested parties" in the White House, to be organized by the ADA. This took place a short while later in one of the large meeting halls of the White House Annex. I had not received any instructions for the meeting and was quite surprised when I—having passed the scrutiny of a guard at the entrance who was equipped with a list of names—entered the room. There were perhaps one hundred persons present, instead of the eight or ten I had, in my naïveté, expected. I remember only a few names: Ambassador Chester Bowles, one of the high dignitaries of the Kennedy administration;

"Pepe" Figueres, president of Costa Rica; and various other U.S. ambassadors, with Arthur Schlesinger in the chair. I sat in the middle of the room, waiting for developments.

Arthur opened the meeting, and then I was asked to present my plan. Since I had not been warned of the size of the meeting or the procedures to be followed, I had neither a prepared speech nor notes. So I simply summarized my idea, stressing that the Kennedy administration had created the conditions necessary for an exploration of the possibilities of cooperation with European socialists and social democrats on a high level. I reported briefly on my conversation with Ollenhauer and Gaitskell and their willingness to participate in at least an exploratory meeting. I could not refrain from pointing out that in the past, American official or semi-official organizations had cooperated almost exclusively with European conservatives and that now an opening to democratic left-of-center forces in Europe seemed both possible and desirable. John Kennedy fascinated people not only in this country, but in Europe and elsewhere, and his person almost guaranteed the success of the enterprise I was proposing.

There followed a brief discussion with only one dissenting voice. One man pointed out that in his profound conviction the non-Communist left in Europe was doomed to perish. No one bothered to respond; no vote was taken, and I was asked to act as general secretary with the assistance of a professor at the Johns Hopkins School of International Affairs in Washington, whom I did not know. The meeting ended in this informal consensus, except that a number of people, including Chester Bowles, assured me of their support in whatever I would need, money being probably foremost on their minds.

In a mood of great satisfaction I left Washington on a shuttle plane to New York. Sitting next to me was a Columbia University professor who had been present at the meeting. Later he was an assistant secretary of state. (His life ended in a senseless murder.) Of course, we talked about what had happened. "You know, of course," he said, "that the Johns Hopkins professor, who is to be your assistant, is a CIA agent." I was flabbergasted. Not even in my wildest dreams had I imagined that the CIA would be permitted in the White House at all; and even less that, apparently, I was to serve merely as a *conduit* to channel a CIA man into the international group I was to organize. Not being used to the peculiar mores that the Cold War had introduced into politics and other fields, I was frankly horrified.

Whether what I did in response to this information was wise or not, I shall never know. I informed the ADA that I would have nothing more to do with the project. They could go ahead on their own, but I would not deceive my friends overseas. I recognized that there had to be a CIA in the dangerous world in which we lived, but I did not think that I should be a CIA agent, especially by way of trickery: trickery committed by me on my friends who trusted me, and trickery committed against me by smuggling a CIA agent into what I envisaged as a means of friendly cooperation. Still, instead of withdrawing, I could have checked on the information I had received regarding the Johns Hopkins professor. If it was confirmed, I could have insisted that he withdraw and I select a new assistant. Even an unspoken threat of revealing what had happened might have swayed my partners. Obviously, they attached a good deal of importance to my participation, since an intermediary—a personal friend of mine from Washington—appeared in Champaign and made a valiant effort to persuade me to participate in the project. I still refused—in a state of shock. I was not yet used to the ubiquity of the CIA.

I shall of course never know whether I was right or wrong, although I now lean to the view that instead of quitting I should have fought—even if my chances of success were rather small.

More important, my plan was at least partly realized—without me. Tage Erlander, the Swedish Social Democrat prime minister, arranged for annual gatherings of a number of socialist leaders on a small island property off Stockholm. At the first meeting the United States was represented by Hubert Humphrey and Walter Reuther—I could not think of better representation for the non-Communist left of the United States. I understand that similar meetings took place annually for some time thereafter.

Epilogue

T he biblical age that I very unexpectedly reached permits me, perhaps even obliges me, to draw up a kind of balance sheet of my life. It is probably unavoidable that I, like most people who reach old age, am much more critical of the present than I am of the past. But this evaluation is thrust far into the background in the face of my amazement at the rate of changes taking place in our world; in its institutions, its technology, its ideology, and, above all, its customs.

If my father, who died before his fiftieth birthday in the year 1909, came back in 1986, he would be a stranger. His birth coincided approximately with the American Civil War. The old Austria-Hungary in which he lived has shriveled to the status of a small state: a state which, after a series of catastrophes, seeks intellectual connections to the Western world. A series of calamities that he did not witness seriously hampered the artistic and scientific life of Vienna and seriously weakened the consciousness of ethical responsibility in public life. Austria, full of hatred, deeply divided, and impoverished, began to decline after 1918 and drove many of its most talented citizens abroad: Hans Kelsen, Karl Popper, Wolfgang Pauli, Viktor Weisskopf, Rudolf Hilferding, Paul Lazarsfeld, and so many others for whom there was no room in the First Republic. There followed the calamity of 1934; then came the mass migration (and not only of the Jews who had contributed so much to the intellectual and artistic life of Austria) after the "annexation" of 1938; later came the not-very-radical "purging" after 1945 and the severe failures concerning the return of the émigrés, a dismaying list of the stages in Austria's decline. Granted, efforts to repair these severe losses have not been entirely in vain. A socialist leader, Hertha Firnberg, took great pains to rebuild Austrian culture—not without success—but now the overwhelming competition of West Germany must also be taken into account. The German neighbor offers research possibilities and incomes to talented Austrians which Austria can offer only with great effort and in rare instances. For a while, foreign institutions, especially the Ford Foundation, provided valuable support, but all in all, the intellectual contribution of the Second Republic is far less impressive than its artistic or musical achievement.

For me personally, one special aspect bears a tragic meaning—the fundamental change in the character of the Austrian labor movement. This happened because of the radical change of the Western non-Communist labor movement in general, and the specific processes which have altered the character of Austrian social democracy and the trade unions in comparison with the movement between the wars.

Slowly and reluctantly, I realized through the experiences of my own life—my first life in Europe and my second life in the United States—how inadequate Marx's teachings are. However, I find it impossible and intolerable to join the chorus of Marx-despisers, and I find it even harder to let myself be paid off with a shallow pragmatism that does not want to look beyond the next few months or election dates.

When I was employed as a guest professor at the University of Vienna for one semester, I was shocked at the inclination of so many students to find the solution to social or economic problems in a more or less fitting quotation from Marx. But equally frightening to me is the widespread habit of rejecting an idea on the grounds that it is referred to as "Marxist."

For someone like me, who received his basic political education during World War I, the teachings of Karl Marx came as a revelation. They offered an insight into the social and economic processes of my time. I had the special misfortune to encounter a professor at my academic middle school, Ferdinand Bronner, who could be described as the downright paragon of undignified conformity. At the beginning of World War I he was an old-Austrian patriot; in the course of the war he changed more and more clearly to a German nationalist, and soon afterward warmed up to the democratic republic. My distrust toward academic opportunists—confirmed again during the Reagan administration—has its basis in my early youth, a time when unconditional loyalty to one's conscience and a refusal to compromise were greatly esteemed.

This does not mean that I automatically rejected any theoretical system opposed to Marxism. For example, even before my enrollment at the University of Vienna, I read Eugen Böhm-Bawerk, Friedrich von Wieser, and even Ludwig von Mises, and thus developed an understanding of marginal utility theory. My first contribution to *Der Kampf,* the esteemed theoretical organ of the Austrian social democrats, was a review of a book by the Bolshevik theorist Nikolai Bukharin—in which my approach to the ideas of the Austrian school of economics was clearly evident. However, I could not find any perspectives on the problems of social development there. And these seemed to me the most important ones that the social sciences would have to solve.

So I plunged into the study of these questions, and Marx, especially as he was interpreted by Austro-Marxists, was my teacher. In Marx's writings I found reference to forces that influence or determine social development and to the stages of social change. History was subject to social laws; consequently, it was meaningful, and the future was predictable. It was equally important to me that this development corresponded to my ethical ideas. Not only could I predict the future, I could also look forward to it. The working class was the power that would create the great future. Of course, the economy and technology would have to create conditions that would enable the working class to obtain power by democratic means and to use it democratically, except where the bourgeoisie threatened the democratic process. In that case the workers, against their will, would have to resort to force in order to defend democracy. Added to this was the idea of internationalism, which was familiar to the working class from the basic idea of worker solidarity or, in any case, could be made familiar and intelligible. Only through international collaboration could workers of different countries defend their interests effectively against internationally mobile capital and combat the permanent danger of war inherent in capitalism.

Socialists and social scientists have for a long time found it difficult to explain why, of all countries, it is in the United States—the classical country of capitalism—that the socialist movement is extremely weak and the trade unions a rather conservative element of society. This is in contrast to everything that Marx's theory predicted. To me, in my youth, the United States was an unknown country on the margin of social development. To me and to many others at that time, only Europe was at the center of world history. It was not until the 1930s that, on Otto Bauer's advice, I began to study American literature, economics, and history. My old dogmas were shaken by the experience of the tremendous economic power of the United States during World War II.

Even before the war I had my doubts about basic elements of Marxist theory. Was the working class really revolutionary? In the revolutionary movements of 1917 and 1945 it had not been capitalist exploitation but military defeat that led to the overthrow of the political order. It was the landless peasants in Russia, defeated armies elsewhere, and occupation by hostile troops that led the revolution to victory. The role of the industrial workers was subsidiary, although important.

As became evident again and again, internationalism was not a necessary part of the class consciousness of the proletariat. Far more frequently it was scientists who were members of the international brotherhood. Even managers of the economy, especially in times of rapid technological change, are more open toward the world than are their workers. (The central educational agency of the AFL-CIO in the suburbs of Washington does not list a single course concerned with international questions in its catalog.) Repeatedly, when difficult decisions had to be made, the workers' patriotism—or even their chauvinism—proved much stronger than their internationalism.

Marx's predictions proved deceptive. World capitalism was not declining rapidly; the proletarianization of the population did not increase—at least there was no disproportionately large increase in the industrial working class. Movements that professed socialism won, not, as Marx predicted, in the economically most advanced countries, but in those where capitalism and industrialization were only beginning. It is shocking to compare "real" development with Lenin's expectations as they were expressed in his 1917 farewell letter to the Swiss workers:

> To the Russian proletariat has fallen the great honour of *initiating* the series of revolutions which are arising from the imperialist war with objective inevitability. But the idea that the Russian proletariat is a chosen revolutionary proletariat among the workers of the world is absolutely alien to us. We know full well that the proletariat of Russia is *less* organised, less prepared, and less class conscious than the

proletariat of other countries. It is not any particular virtues it possessed, but rather the specific historical circumstances, that have made the proletariat of Russia for a certain, *perhaps very brief,* period the skirmishers of the world revolutionary proletariat.

Russia is a peasant country, one of the most backward of European countries. Socialism *cannot triumph there directly at once.* But the peasant character of the country, coupled with the vast land possessions of the noble landlords, *may,* to judge by the experience of 1905, give tremendous scope to the bourgeois-democratic revolution in Russia, and make our revolution a *prelude* to and a *step* towards the world socialist revolution.[1]

Lenin's revolution, then, was based on the certain expectation of the European revolution. The more developed and skilled workers of Germany and Western Europe would soon stage their own revolution; they would aid and teach the Russian proletariat and enable it to complete its revolutionary task successfully. The revolution of November 1917 was based on this expectation, and it was only in 1921, when the bourgeois-capitalist and democratic character of the German revolution itself was not in doubt, that Lenin gave up his hope.

What was Lenin supposed to do now? Excuse himself, saying that everything, the bloodshed, the destruction of millions of lives and other millions of livelihoods, was due to an error and return to the chaotic situation of 1917? Obviously, this would have been suicidal and impossible. So Stalin, after an interval of confusion and internal struggle, made the attempt to "stand Marx on his head," as Marx had stood Hegel on his head. Instead of adapting the social and political institutions of the country to its economic foundations, as Marx's teachings prescribed, Stalin undertook the opposite: the economic and social institutions in Russia had to adapt to political conditions, meaning the dictatorship of the proletariat, or rather the dictatorship of the Bolsheviks. The terrorism, the destruction of agriculture, the bloodbath of the opponents, the establishment of a totalitarian dictatorship—all these were the result of the decision to employ Marx's theories where, according to Marx himself, they were not applicable.

1. V. I. Lenin, *Collected Works* (Moscow: Progress Publishers, 1964), vol. 23, p. 371.

Ever since that time the world has lived under a great illusion: that what is happening in Russia is socialism because it is done in its name. Naturally, this illusion is facilitated by the fact that in the West, where socialism according to Marx should have been victorious, the development of socialism got stuck halfway.

Because of this, Marxist socialism is in a deep crisis. Neither the totalitarian systems of Eastern Europe nor the "mixed" systems of the West correspond to the laws of economic development that Marx preached. Of course, that does not mean that the social order we see in the West today is the final point of social development. On the contrary, the speed of social change has increased more and more during the last decades. What we are lacking, and what made Marx's theory so captivating and convincing, is a broad outline of long-term laws of development, notwithstanding everything that the philosopher Karl Popper had to say on the subject.

Above all, we should not forget how much idealism, altruism, and dedication to a great task, even if it was Utopian, socialism called forth in so many of its followers. The ethical level of labor politics since 1945, or rather of politics pursued in the name of the workers, unfortunately can bear no comparison to that of the time before the war. Corruption once was a rare and shocking event. Since then it has become almost an everyday occurrence.

I remember a so-called case of corruption at the time of the First Republic of Austria. A Social Democratic delegate of little importance had speculated on the stock exchange. That was regarded as unforgivable corruption. The party took proceedings against the accused. An investigative committee dealt with the case. In a somewhat whiny tone the accused gave the excuse that he had lost money speculating. "You are not only a corruptionist," Otto Bauer bellowed at him, "you are an idiot besides." Since that time there has been more corruption and perhaps fewer idiots.

The basic ideas behind what I have written remind me of Eduard Bernstein's famous slogan: "the movement means everything, the final goal means nothing." The ethical power of democratic, nontotalitarian socialism has enriched the world as few things have since the rise of Christianity. But the goal has remained Utopia, inspiring and unattainable.

Index

Adolf Sturmthal (1903–1986) was a distinguished Austrian socialist and scholar of international labor. Among his books are *The Tragedy of European Labor, 1918–1939; Unity and Diversity in European Labor; Workers' Councils: A Study of Workplace Organization on Both Sides of the Iron Curtain;* and *Left of Center: European Labor Since World War II.*

Library of Congress Cataloging-in-Publication Data
Sturmthal, Adolf Fox.
Democracy under fire : memoirs of a European socialist / Adolf
Sturmthal.
p. cm.
Includes index.
ISBN 0-8223-0840-1 : $29.95
1. Sturmthal, Adolf Fox. 2. Socialists—Austria—Biography.
I. Title.
HX254.7.S78A3 1989
335'.0092'4—dc19
[B]   88-21131 CIP